# SERIAL KILLERS

## OF THE '80s

**Other books in the Profiles in Crime Series**

*How to Catch a Killer*–Katherine Ramsland, PhD

*Killer Cults*–Stephen Singular

*Extreme Killers*–Michael Newton

*Serial Killers of the '70s*–Jane Fritsch

# SERIAL KILLERS OF THE '80s

## STORIES BEHIND A DECADENT DECADE OF DEATH

### JANE FRITSCH

UNION
SQUARE
& CO.

NEW YORK

**UNION
SQUARE
& CO.**

**NEW YORK**

UNION SQUARE & CO. and the distinctive Union Square & Co. logo are trademarks of Sterling Publishing Co., Inc.

Union Square & Co., LLC. is a subsidiary of Sterling Publishing Co., Inc.

ISBN 978-1-4549-4168-2

For information about custom editions, special sales, and premium purchases, please contact specialsales@unionsquareandco.com.

Printed in Canada

2 4 6 8 10 9 7 5 3 1

unionsquareandco.com

Cover design by Jo Obarowski
Interior design by Gavin Motnyk

# INTRODUCTION

By the end of the 1970s, it was clear why the second half of the twentieth century was becoming known as the "Golden Age of Serial Killers." The unimaginable had happened—more than once, and often in full view of television news crews. Perhaps the most astounding case began with the drama that played out over the Christmas holidays in 1978, when investigators began unearthing bodies buried under a small house in a Chicago suburb. The owner, John Wayne Gacy, was a local building contractor and small-time politician. Day after day, the news was full of videos and photographs showing yet more bodies and body parts being driven off for examination. In the end, Gacy was charged with murdering thirty-three young men and boys from 1975 through 1978. Most of their bodies were found in the crawl space. Some of the victims remain unidentified.

Gacy was convicted of all thirty-three murders, putting him ahead of Juan Corona, who had been convicted in 1973 of killing twenty-five men, mostly itinerant farm workers in northern California. Dean Corll, a candy shop owner known as The Candyman, was connected to the murders of as many as twenty-seven young men and boys in the Houston, Texas area in the early 1970s. Corll was never charged, because he was shot and killed by an accomplice, who later led officials to the burial sites. And there were others. Rodney Alcala, dubbed "The Dating Game Killer," was convicted of killing four women and a twelve-year-old girl in the 1970s, and was still under investigation by authorities across the country looking to solve cold cases when he

died of natural causes in prison on July 24, 2021. Ted Bundy confessed to killing dozens of women across the country before he was executed in 1989 for the rape and murder of a twelve-year-old girl, whose body had been found in 1978 under a collapsed hogshed in Lake City, Florida.

David Berkowitz terrorized New York City in 1976 and 1977 with a series of murders and highly publicized threats. He called himself "Son of Sam," perhaps a reference to a brutal—and imaginary—father figure. The assigning of nicknames to serial killers dates back to London in the 1880s, when newspapers carried huge headlines about "Jack the Ripper," the mysterious man assumed to be responsible for the murders of at least five women in the city's Whitechapel area. He was never caught. But the use of nicknames lived on.

Vaughn Greenwood, known as the "Skid Row Slasher," was convicted in 1979 of nine murders in the Los Angeles area—one in 1964 and the others in 1974 and 1975. The "Hillside Strangler" turned out to be two men, Angelo Buono, Jr. and Kenneth A. Bianchi. Buono was convicted of killing nine young women in California in the late 1970s, and Bianchi pleaded guilty to five murders in California and two in the state of Washington. Southern California was also the hunting ground for the "Trashbag Killer," Patrick Wayne Kearney, who murdered young men and boys and dumped their bodies in plastic bags along highways in the mid-1970s. The youngest victim was five, and the oldest was twenty-eight. Coral Eugene Watts, known as the "Sunday Morning Slasher," did most of his killing in the early 1970s in Michigan and Texas, where he confessed to twelve murders in a plea deal. He was a suspect in dozens of other murders in the 1970s.

It was a time when police departments across the country had great difficulty sharing information. They used desktop telephones and fax machines. The Gacy case sparked the creation of a computer database in Chicago to track missing persons, and by the end of the 1980s there

was nationwide cooperation. The term "serial killer" came into common use in the 1980s, replacing "mass murderer." The Justice Department defines serial killings as incidents separated by days or weeks, as opposed to mass killings, like the shooting at Sandy Hook Elementary School in Newtown, Connecticut, where twenty-six people were killed one day in 2012, or the incident at Marjory Stoneman Douglas High School in Parkland, Florida, where seventeen people were shot to death one day in 2018.

The FBI's Behavioral Analysis Unit, created in part as a reaction to the surge of murders in the 1970s, would be confronted by even more incomprehensible crimes in the 1980s. DNA comparisons were still years away, as were cell phones and other kinds of electronic tracking. Security cameras were not yet in broad use, and still relied on cumbersome videotape that was not easily searched; nor were scans of license plates at tollbooths and red-light cameras.

Perhaps the most surprising news about murder in the 1980s was the emergence of female serial killers. Nearly all known serial killers at the end of the 1970s were white men in their thirties. Dorothea Montalvo Puente was fifty-three years old in 1982 when she committed her first murder. She had turned fifty-nine by the time investigators began digging up bodies in 1988 in the yard of her Victorian boardinghouse not far from the California state capitol building in Sacramento.

But Puente was soon upstaged by Aileen Wuornos, who was thirty-three years old when she killed a middle-aged man who had picked her up as she was hitchhiking in Florida. Soon she would become known nationwide and beyond as the "Damsel of Death." She was convicted of one murder and pleaded no contest to five others before she was executed—at her own request. Both Puente and Wuornos quickly became the subjects of FBI analysts and academic researchers nationwide. The Wuornos story, perhaps like no other, set off intense competition and interest by publishers, Hollywood producers, and

television networks. In a 2003 documentary, *Aileen: Life and Death of a Serial Killer,* Wuornos was interviewed on the day before her execution. Staring into the camera, she said "You sabotaged my ass, society. And the cops. And the system. A raped woman got executed and was used for books and movies and shit." She was executed by lethal injection on October 9, 2002.

# CHAPTER 1
# DOROTHEA PUENTE

The stench wafting up from the backyard of the Victorian house not far from the California state capitol building was more than the neighbors could bear. "We couldn't stand it," one man said. "It definitely was something dead. It had a sweet sickly smell." They complained about it in 1987, but little was done. They were told that fish emulsion had been used there as a fertilizer. It wasn't until November 11, 1988, that the first body was unearthed in the yard on the tree-shaded street in Sacramento. The owner of the house, fifty-nine-year-old Dorothea Montalvo Puente, told the police she had no idea how it had gotten there.

Investigators had first gone to the house on Monday, November 7, looking into a report by a social worker that one of her clients was

missing. She had placed him at Puente's boardinghouse, and his checks were being cashed regularly, but she had not seen him since August. The police had some suspicions, but they didn't have a search warrant. So they politely asked Puente if she would allow them to dig in her yard, and told her that she could refuse. "Dig in the yard," she said. "I don't know what's out there."

By Sunday, November 13, investigators had found five bodies buried in the yard, and they thought there might be as many as eight. It was a guess based on the number of people who had lived at the boarding-house and were now missing. The fifth body was found at about noon on Sunday, wrapped in a sheet in a shallow grave. They were proceeding cautiously with their digging. They had come to realize that they had a new—and possibly more serious—problem: they hadn't seen Puente since Saturday morning.

Puente had told the police that she was going to run an errand, and she walked off casually in the rain with a pink umbrella. She was wearing a red coat, a pink dress, and purple high heels, and—unknown to the police—carrying about $3,000 in cash. Once out of sight, she took a taxi to a bar in a suburb across the Sacramento River. She drank there for a while, then took another cab to Stockton, about fifty miles away. There, she got on a Greyhound bus headed to Los Angeles, about 340 miles to the south. On Sunday she was in Los Angeles. She got off the bus and checked into a motel near the Civic Center downtown. By then, the police back in Sacramento were embarrassed. They had no idea where she might have gone. They continued their careful excavation and sent out an all-points bulletin as they, along with the FBI, began a nationwide search.

The scene outside the boardinghouse at 1426 F Street was chaotic on that Sunday afternoon. At times, there appeared to be as many as 300 onlookers gathered in the street. It was chillingly reminiscent of an astounding episode that had occurred nearly a decade earlier on a quiet

suburban street near Chicago. Just before Christmas in 1978, investigators began finding bodies buried in the crawl space of a house owned by John Wayne Gacy, a building contractor. Word leaked out one night, and by morning a swarm of news reporters and camera crews had descended. The digging went on for weeks as the death toll mounted. Gacy was eventually convicted of the murders of thirty-three young men and teenage boys. Most of their bodies were found under the house. When he ran out of space there, he buried some in the small backyard and under the garage. Eventually, he began tossing bodies in a nearby river. But Gacy was in police custody when the digging started.

In Sacramento, a beleaguered police lieutenant repeatedly told the news media that there hadn't been enough evidence to arrest Puente, or even a reason to follow her when she walked off to run her errand. She

POLICE AND CORONERS REMOVE A SIXTH BODY FROM THE YARD OF A ROOMING HOUSE IN SACRAMENTO, CALIFORNIA OWNED BY DOROTHEA PUENTE ON NOVEMBER 14, 1988.

had said she would be right back. The police had a secondary suspect in custody. John McCauley, a fifty-nine-year-old resident of the boarding-house, was being held on suspicion of being an accessory to homicide. They believed he had helped Puente bury some of the bodies.

Peggy Nickerson, the social worker who called the police, said she had sent nineteen clients to Puente's boardinghouse over the previous two years, but stopped about three months earlier after she heard Puente verbally abuse a boarder. Until then, Puente had seemed to be giving loving care to the transients, mentally disabled, and elderly people who were sent her way. Investigators suspected that Puente was collecting their welfare and disability benefits. Nickerson began providing names of other missing clients, and Social Security Administration officials began researching records to see whether benefits had been signed over to Puente.

On the subject of Puente's disappearance, there was more embar-rassment to come. It turned out that, unbeknownst to the tenants and the people in the neighborhood, Puente had been on probation in 1985 when she took over the eight-room boardinghouse on F Street. She had rented a room in the converted single-family home, and managed it for the owners. The seemingly thoughtful and pleasant older woman had been convicted in 1982 of charges of robbery and administering stupefy-ing drugs to commit robbery while she was working as an in-home care-giver. After meeting three elderly people in local bars, she drugged them and stole their possessions. She was sentenced to five years in prison, but was paroled in 1985, after earning two years' credit for good behav-ior. A probation report noted that she had "concentrated her criminal efforts on a segment of the community that is the most vulnerable, the ill and the elderly." A psychiatric report described Puente's condition as "chronic undifferentiated schizophrenia."

And there was another revelation. Puente had been convicted in 1978 of federal charges of check forgery and was sentenced to eight

years' probation. After she was released from state custody, her federal probation was revoked and she had to serve another eight months in federal custody. She was ordered to remain on federal parole until 1990. Under the terms of her release in late 1985, she was not allowed to handle U.S. Treasury checks, care for the elderly, run a boardinghouse, or handle other peoples' government support checks.

Almost immediately, she began renting rooms to the elderly, the mentally disabled, and people on the fringes. In many cases, she persuaded the tenants to let her handle their Social Security and disability checks. And she persuaded two social workers to place clients in the house. Desperate to find homes for their clients, the social workers did not have the time or resources to check Puente's background, and there were, of course, no online databases to use for research at the time. Technically, the boardinghouse was not a nursing home, so it did not require a license. For Puente, it was all a bold violation of her terms of release. But no one seemed to notice.

On Tuesday, November 15, 1988, three days after Puente strolled away from the house, the chaos outside seemed to reach a peak. Investigators had finally gotten a search warrant so they could take a look inside. By then, they suspected that Puente had been cashing welfare and Social Security checks that belonged to former residents—at least some of whose bodies had been unearthed on the property. Police officers and news reporters began tracking down people who had once lived there.

John Gerard Corrigan, a sixty-three-year-old retired aerospace worker who had lived there for a time in 1986, said Puente once gave him a drugged Bloody Mary. "After I drank it, everything went fuzzy on me," he told a reporter for the *San Francisco Examiner.* "All I knew after I woke up was that two hundred bucks was missing." He assumed that another resident had drugged the drink, so he moved out a few weeks later. But he learned eventually that Puente had forged some checks of his that were missing. "I asked around, and that's when I started hearing

the tales about her," he said. "That's when I figured it out that she had slipped me a Mickey." He felt "lucky to be alive."

Puente made a crucial error on Wednesday, November 16, four days after she walked away to "run an errand." Still staying at the Royal Viking Motel near downtown Los Angeles, she went to a local bar and struck up a conversation with Charles Willgues, a sixty-seven-year-old man who lived in an apartment nearby. The friendly, gray-haired woman, who said her name was Donna Johansen, seemed pleasant enough. She said she was from San Francisco, and her husband had died recently. The cab driver who dropped her at the motel had stolen her luggage, she said, and she needed to get her shoes repaired. She even suggested that they live together. He thought that was odd. He became suspicious when she showed a little too much interest in his Social Security and disability checks. Even so, he agreed to meet her again the following day to go shopping. Meanwhile, he took her shoes across the street to a repair shop. Later that day, after he returned to his apartment, he realized that he had seen her face on a television newscast that morning. He called the local CBS station and told a producer about the incident, and the motel where she was staying. The producer met Willgues at his apartment, and together they called the police. Puente was arrested a short time later in her motel room.

Puente's extraordinary return to Sacramento made national news and became the subject of legal arguments for years to come. The CBS station had scored a major scoop by having a camera crew waiting outside the motel to capture Puente's arrest. But the NBC station in Sacramento ultimately won the day. Unable to book a commercial flight quickly enough, the station chartered a jet to get its crew to Los Angeles. Once there, they worked out a deal with Sacramento police to fly Puente and the Sacramento officers back home on the jet. On the return trip, the station recorded an exclusive interview with Puente, who appeared remarkably calm. The station had agreed not to ask her any specific

questions about the bodies or the Social Security checks she was accused of stealing. But as the camera was rolling, she volunteered her thoughts: "Thanks for believing me. I have not killed anyone," Puente said. "The checks I cashed, yes." Later, she added "I used to be a very good person at one time."

Things had calmed down by the time Puente was brought into court in Sacramento later that day. She was wearing an orange jumpsuit and had little to say. She listened quietly as the charge of one murder was read. The victim was Alvaro Gonzales Montoya, a fifty-one-year-old mentally disabled tenant of the boardinghouse who had disappeared about three months earlier. Investigators were still working on identifying the bodies, and the prosecutor said more murder charges would be filed. If convicted, he said, Puente could face the death penalty. Asked if she wanted a public defender to represent her, Puente nodded her head.

Outside the courtroom, Peter Vlautin and Kevin Clymo, the assistant public defenders assigned to the case, expressed outrage at the situation. "It's unheard of that a law-enforcement agency would team up with a news organization to transport a person to jail," Vlautin said. "The Sacramento Police Department have enlisted the aid of the media to create a circus atmosphere." Clymo complained that Puente had been put on the plane with "no opportunity to talk to anybody who had her interests in mind," and had not had a chance to talk to a lawyer before the flight.

It was a difficult time for the Sacramento Police Department. John Kearns, the police chief, had already acknowledged some missteps. He said the department "blew" a golden opportunity when they let their only suspect walk away while body parts were being unearthed on her property. "She should have been followed. She should have been tailed very closely." Puente was "the prime suspect in a homicide investigation, and there isn't any excuse, as far as I'm concerned." Police believed that she had killed the mostly elderly and disabled tenants so that she could

collect their benefit checks, but had not had enough evidence when she walked off from her house the previous Saturday. Since then, officials had dropped the charges against John McCauley, the boardinghouse tenant suspected of helping Puente bury the bodies. Kearns also acknowledged that the department had gotten a tip about the bodies in the garden the previous January. It came from an informant in another case, he said, and was not followed up.

Inevitably, the media began comparing the Puente boardinghouse to the Bates Motel in *Psycho*, the 1960 Alfred Hitchcock movie starring Anthony Perkins and Janet Leigh. A headline in *The San Diego Union-Tribune* read "In the death garden of Sacramento boardinghome, roses flourished." Puente had been a regular at Harry's Lounge, a block from the capitol, where elderly men went to drink. She listened to their troubled stories, bought them drinks, and frequently urged them to move into her boardinghouse. John Terry, a sixty-seven-year-old regular, told a reporter that Puente had often pushed him to move in. "About every time she would see me, she'd hit me up about it," he said. "She asked me where I got my money from, where I was working." He never accepted her offers, but others did. Midge Harper, a bartender, said Puente was popular, often bought drinks for the house, and talked some of Harry's best customers into moving into the boardinghouse. "I haven't seen three of them since," Harper said.

Over the years, the social workers who had placed some of their clients in Puente's house realized that they seemed to be missing. Puente said they had moved out or gone to live with relatives. In the weeks after Puente was arrested, the coroner's office was hard at work trying to identify bodies, and prosecutors began to work out how this all could have happened. Complaints about Puente possibly poisoning patients as early as 1980 began to surface. Doctors at University Medical Center in Sacramento had done toxicology tests early that year on a seventy-nine-year-old emergency room patient, Esther Busby.

Her physician, Dr. Jerome Lackner, suspected that Puente, her live-in companion, was feeding her overdoses of a heart medication he had prescribed. He notified Adult Protective Services "that Puente was poisoning or making Busby sick by overmedicating her." He also suspected that Puente was "ripping off Mrs. Busby." Officials looked into it and found that her Social Security check had been cashed with a forged signature. "I told Esther what was going on, and she got rid of Puente," Lackner said. Investigators found a second, similar incident and sent out a warning to all the Sacramento hospitals. The investigation led to Puente's 1982 arrest on charges of forgery, grand theft, and "administering stupefying drugs."

As 1988 was coming to an end, there was one happy note in the midst of the horror and sadness. Charles Willgues, the man who had met Puente in the bar in Los Angeles and eventually helped alert the police, was reunited with a son and two daughters he hadn't seen since he left their Detroit home thirty years earlier. The nationwide publicity about the case had helped them locate him. After embracing his son at the Detroit Metropolitan Airport, Willgues said "This is the moment I've been waiting for for the last thirty-two years. I'd always hoped, but I was about to give it up. You know the record by Frank Sinatra 'For Once In My Life'? That's what I'm experiencing right now."

Puente, too, had an estranged daughter, Linda Bloom, who was given up for adoption when she was three months old. Bloom was in her thirties when she learned in 1982 that Puente was her mother. She described Puente as "shy, withdrawn, and reserved" with "no real personality." Documents that gave details of Puente's murky and troubled past were beginning to emerge. Her record went back to 1948, when she had been convicted of forging checks.

After her 1982 conviction, Puente wrote letters to the judge who was preparing to sentence her, claiming that her life had been plagued by hardship. She said she had had four failed marriages, and was the

youngest of eighteen children in a Mexican family. "When I was 3 years old, I had to start picking cotton, potatoes, cucumbers and chilies, then fruits," she wrote. She claimed that she had married when she was thirteen years old, and her husband died a few days later. She married again, but "much to my shock, he was a homosexual. I stuck it out for seven years to not let my family in Mexico know I'd made another mistake." In 1976, she married "a Mr. Montalvo." On their wedding night, she wrote, he "killed a mother cat I'd had for 17 years." Over the years, he beat her, and she left him several times, but kept returning. After one reconciliation, she wrote, "he stabbed me between the eyes." It was then, she said, that she started writing checks. "I just wanted you to know I'm not a street bum. All my problems started when I married Mr. Montalvo."

But her story conflicted with her birth certificate. It had been issued in San Bernardino County and said that she was born Dorothea Helen Gray on January 19, 1929, in Redlands. Her parents were listed as Jessie Gray, an ex-serviceman, and Trudy Yates, a housewife.

Attempts to identify the bodies and determine the causes of death went on over the months following Puente's arrest. Traces of benzodiazepine, used in tranquilizers and sleeping pills, had been found in all seven of the bodies unearthed in the yard.

With Puente securely in jail in 1989, investigators continued their work and the courtroom drama got underway. Prosecutors got a search warrant for the office of Puente's psychiatrist, Thomas E. Doody. Records showed that he had prescribed the tranquilizer Dalmane to Puente at least eighteen times from 1985 to 1988. On one occasion, both Doody and a general practitioner gave Puente thirty-day supplies of the drug on the same day. Traces of Dalmane had been found in all seven bodies buried in the boardinghouse yard. The prosecutor, Tim Frawley, contended that Puente had used the pills to "stupefy and kill" the seven residents.

In April, Puente was charged with eight more murders, bringing the total to nine. As in other high-profile legal cases in California, the legal proceedings ground on at a snail's pace. The preliminary hearing to decide whether she should be held for trial didn't begin until April of 1990, a year and a half after her arrest. Prosecutors argued that she had administered stupefying drugs to her intended victims, and killed them for their Social Security and other benefit checks. Flurazepam—a prescription tranquilizer also called Dalmane—was detected in all seven of the bodies buried in the boardinghouse yard. Puente's lawyers, from the Public Defender's Office, said there was little evidence to back up the charge of murder, and that the alleged victims were mostly poor and alcoholic. They had died either by suicide or natural causes, and their ailments, the lawyers said, included a brain tumor, lung disease, heart disease, and diabetes.

In June 1990, a judge ruled that there was sufficient evidence for the case to go to trial. Legal wrangling about the trial went on for more than a year, and in February 1992 the judge granted the defense request for a change of venue. A defense survey suggested that nearly all the residents of Sacramento County were aware of the case, and most people thought Puente was guilty. "The news coverage was and is inflammatory and prejudicial," he wrote. The trial would be moved to San Jose, about 120 miles to the southeast in Monterey County, and begin on November 2.

As the trial began, the white-haired Puente, by then 63 years old, sat quietly at the defense table wearing a lavender dress with a floral print. A pool of 900 prospective jurors had been arranged. It was the end of December 1992 by the time a jury of eight men and four women was chosen, but opening statements were put off until February because of a problem with the selection of alternate jurors. Three hundred more possible jurors would be called to court in January.

When the trial finally got underway in February, the jurors had the unusual task of imagining the quiet, bespectacled, gray-haired woman

seated before them as a calculating serial killer. One reporter wrote that Puente "looks for all the world like the grandmother from central casting."

The chief prosecutor, John O'Mara, argued that Puente had preyed on "shadow people" whose disappearances would go unnoticed for months or years. Puente's lawyer said the deaths were the result of natural causes, and there was no conclusive evidence that any of the dead had been murdered. Kevin Clymo, Puente's public defender, said his client may have been a thief, but she was no murderer. "My God, how little progress we've made since the Salem witch trials," he said.

More than one hundred witnesses were called to the stand over the following five months to tell the story of Puente's deeds and misdeeds over her lifetime. Puente did not take the witness stand to testify in her own defense. The case went to the jury in mid-July, but after seven days of deliberation the jurors said they were deadlocked. The judge ordered them to go back and keep trying. On August 26, they reached a verdict: they found her guilty of two counts of first-degree murder for the deaths of sixty-four-year-old Dorothy Miller and fifty-five-year-old Benjamin Fink, and one count of second-degree murder for the death of seventy-eight-year-old Leona Carpenter. The first-degree murder conviction made Puente eligible for the death penalty. They were deadlocked on the other six murder charges.

It had taken them twenty-four days. Puente sat still and showed no emotion as the verdicts were read, but her lawyers said later that she was shaken. "She was crying, it's a tough day. We're prepared to stand by her, and that's what we're going to do," co-counsel Peter Vlautin said.

The jury spent another six weeks deliberating on whether to recommend the death penalty, but they were unable to reach an agreement. In the end, she was sentenced to life in prison without parole.

Puente died of natural causes on March 27, 2011, at the Central California Women's Facility in Chowchilla. She was eighty-two years old.

## THE VICTIMS

- **Ruth Munroe.** Sixty-one years old. She died at 1426 F Street in 1982 before Puente ran the boardinghouse. Her death was ruled a suicide, but her family suspected that Puente, who had tended to her there, was to blame.

- **Everson Gillmouth.** Seventy-seven years old. He was Puente's boyfriend while she was in prison, and her fiancé when he died. His body was found in January 1986, in a box on the bank of the Sacramento River.

- **Leona Carpenter.** Seventy-eight years old. She was a tenant of the boardinghouse. Her body was found in the yard.

- **Alvaro "Bert/Alberto" Gonzales Montoya.** Fifty-one years old. He was a tenant of the boardinghouse. His body was found in the yard.

- **Dorothy Miller.** Sixty-four years old. She was a tenant of the boardinghouse. Her body was found in the yard.

- **Benjamin Fink.** Fifty-five years old. He was a tenant of the boardinghouse. His body was found in the yard.

- **James Gallop.** Sixty-two years old. He was a tenant of the boardinghouse. His body was found in the yard.

- **Vera Faye Martin.** Sixty-four years old. She was a tenant of the boardinghouse. Her body was found in the yard.

- **Betty Palmer.** Seventy-eight years old. She was a tenant of the boardinghouse. Her body was found in the yard.

# CHAPTER 2

# GERALD AND CHARLENE GALLEGO

Charlene Gallego was twenty-four years old and pregnant when investigators began hunting for her in late 1980. They were also trying to find her husband, Gerald Gallego, a thirty-four-year-old who had served three years in prison for armed robbery. The problem was a new one for the Gallegos—they had left a live witness. The body of Craig Miller, a student at California State University in Sacramento, was discovered just before noon on November 2 near Bass Lake in El Dorado County, about

180 miles southeast of Sacramento. Miller had last been seen about twelve hours earlier, wearing a tuxedo as he left a restaurant after a fraternity dinner-dance with his fiancé, Mary Beth Sowers, also a student at California State.

A fraternity brother, Andy Beal, left the restaurant a few minutes after Miller and Sowers. Oddly, they were in the back seat of an Oldsmobile Cutlass, a car that Beal, a close friend, had never seen before. Not particularly suspicious, Beal approached the car and jumped into the empty driver's seat. Then he saw an older man, a stranger, in the front passenger seat. Beal looked back at Miller, and saw that his face was serious and drawn. "You don't belong in this car, Andy," Miller said. The man in the front passenger seat told Beal to "take a hike." Just as Beal got out of the car, a young blonde-haired woman walked up and slapped him in the face. "What the fuck are you doing in my car!" she shouted. Then she got into the driver's seat and the car sped away.

Now Beal was worried. He wrote down the license plate number. "There's something awfully wrong here," Beal told his date. In the morning, he returned to the parking lot and saw that Sowers's car—the one the couple had taken to the dance—was still there, unlocked. Her coat was on the front seat. Beal flagged down a passing police car and asked for help. The officer listened, and pointed out that Miller and Sowers were adults. The normal waiting time to file a missing person report was twenty-four hours. But there were exceptions, the officer said, such as a person's failure to show up at a place and time where he or she was expected.

Beal went home and called Mary Beth's roommates. She had not returned home that night. Craig lived at his parents' house, and his mother said he had not come home either. At 10 A.M., Beal called the hardware store where Miller worked, and learned that he had not turned up for his 9 A.M. shift, which was quite unusual. His concern growing, Beal gathered some fraternity brothers and a roommate of Mary Beth's.

They returned to the parking lot and found that the keys to her car were underneath it, as if they had been thrown there. None of this made sense. They weren't going to wait for twenty-four hours. They went to the Sacramento police headquarters and made their case, quite persuasively. Two homicide officers were assigned to look into it, and Beal repeated the story of what had happened that night with the strange car in the parking lot. He pulled a piece of paper out of his pocket and showed them the license plate number.

For law-enforcement agencies, it was still a time of limited communication. The use of computers was spotty, leaving many departments to depend on their fax machines, radio channels, and land-line telephones. Investigators in El Dorado County had quickly identified Miller's body on that Sunday, but it wasn't until nearly 6:30 P.M., about six hours later, that they notified the police in Sacramento.

Unaware that Miller's body had been found with three bullets in the back of the head—and that there was no sign of Sowers—the Sacramento homicide detectives went to the address listed for the license plate that Andy Beal had given them. It was the home of Charles and Mercedes Williams in an upscale area of Sacramento. "Charlene Williams" was the registered owner. Charlene wasn't there when the police arrived. She and Gerald had spent much of the morning deep-cleaning his apartment. They wanted to remove anything that might link them to the murders, including any spent shells that might be around. They had already dumped the gun into the Sacramento River.

Hauling a load of clothes they wanted to wash, Charlene and Gerald were about to walk into her parents' house through a door on the back porch when her mother appeared. She told them that the police were in the living room. Gerald told Charlene to say nothing, then left. Charlene—wearing a T-shirt that said "I am the Veribest"—walked into the living room nonchalantly. The police began to question her, but she told them she had no idea what they were talking about. She had gone

to a movie the night before with her boyfriend, Stephen Feil. She gave the detectives permission to search her car. It was parked in the driveway. They found that it was quite clean—maybe too clean. They said they would be back later to take a photograph of Charlene. She said she would be happy to cooperate.

Outside, the officers noticed a car parked in front of the house and wrote down the license plate number. After the detectives were gone, Gerald called Charlene and told her to meet him at a nearby ice cream shop. She drove there in her car, and he told her they needed to go back to the lake area to move Miller's body.

Meanwhile, the detectives were busy tracing the license plate of the car in front of the house, as well as the driver's license of its owner: Steven Feil. They showed the photograph on the license to Andy Beal. It was the man who had been next to him in the passenger seat of the car outside the fraternity dance. He was sure. The officers returned to the Gallego home later that afternoon, but Charlene was gone. While they were talking to her parents, the phone rang. It was headquarters calling to tell the officers that Miller's body had been found near Bass Lake earlier in the day. The detectives kept that news to themselves. They told the Gallegos that they would return later, and asked when Charlene would be home. Unwittingly, Charlene's mother provided a relevant clue. Charlene had called to say that she and Gerald would be late for Sunday dinner because they were at a restaurant in El Dorado County, not far from Bass Lake.

Gerald and Charlene had spent much of the afternoon searching for Miller's body, but they finally gave up. They were sure they had found the place where Gerald had fired three shots into the back of Miller's head, but there was no body there. They did find cigarette butts and trampled grass. Eventually, they gave up and headed back to Sacramento to make sure they had left no evidence at Gerald's apartment. When they got close to the building, they saw police cars everywhere. Panicked, they decided to drive back toward Bass Lake to keep looking for the

body. They stopped on the way to buy a blanket to wrap the body in. Eventually, they gave up and telephoned Charlene's parents, who agreed to meet them at a diner near Sacramento. They talked for a while. Gerald and Charlene said the police had it all wrong. They had nothing to do with the body near the lake. They all agreed that Gerald and Charlene would leave town for a while and wait for things to settle down.

The following day, Charlene's father admitted to the police that Stephen Feil was really Gerald Gallego, and that he had once been charged with incest. That arrest warrant was still pending. Meanwhile, Charlene and Gerald drove to Reno, Nevada, in her car, then took a bus to Salt Lake City, Utah. From there, she called her mother to tell her where she could find the car, and urged her to have the tires changed. The tracks might match some that the police had found, but Charlene didn't mention that. Then Charlene dyed her hair and stole someone's purse so that she could change her identity.

They took a bus to Colorado, where they got false birth certificates for themselves, then boarded another a bus and headed east to Omaha, Nebraska. On November 17, after two weeks on the run, Charlene called her parents and asked them to wire $500. Her parents drove to a Western Union office in Sparks, Nevada, but this time they notified the FBI. They had seen the news stories about the missing college students, and were afraid that Charlene might become Gerald's next victim. When Charlene walked into the Western Union office in Omaha and stepped up to the counter, agents who had been waiting inside arrested her. Outside, they had been watching Gerald, and they quickly grabbed him, too.

Four days later, on November 21, the Gallegos were brought into a courtroom in El Dorado County, where Craig Miller's body had been found. The chaotic scene offered a hint of what was to come in the long and fraught legal journey of Gerald and Charlene Gallego. Seated in the jury box, they appeared before a judge to enter their pleas to the charges

against them: kidnapping and first-degree murder. If convicted, they could be sentenced to death. "We're not animals! What happened to a fair trial?" Gerald shouted. "Why are you doing this to us?" Charlene, seven months pregnant and handcuffed, shouted "You're treating my husband like an animal, chains on his legs and everything." Charlene's parents had hired a lawyer to represent her. She pleaded not guilty. Gerald, who had not yet been assigned a public defender, did not enter a plea.

There was still no sign of Mary Beth Sowers. Her parents had begged the public for help in finding her. On the following day, November 22, her body, still in the pale blue gown she had worn to the dance, was found in a shallow trench in a pasture in Placer County, northeast of Sacramento. She, too, had been shot in the back of the head. Four days later, her body was buried beside Miller's grave at Calvary Cemetery in a private ceremony attended by several hundred friends and relatives.

CHARLENE AND GERALD GALLEGO AT BAIL REQUEST HEARING JANUARY 15, 1981.

Nine weeks later, Charlene gave birth by Caesarean section to a five-pound, eleven-ounce boy. She named him Gerald Jr., and gave custody to her parents. Given the gravity of her situation, her next legal move was unexpected. She began a lengthy battle to be allowed to hold her son during visits at the jail, where she was only allowed to see him through a glass partition in a jail visiting area. "The baby has a right to be held by his mother," her lawyer argued. Litigation on the matter went on for more than a year, and eventually reached the California Supreme Court. Her request was turned down.

By then, Gerald and Charlene Gallego had become the prime suspects in a series of baffling and seemingly unrelated murders of young women that had happened in the Northwest over the two years before their arrest. And there was much more legal drama to come. Charlene ultimately turned on Gerald.

Things came to a head in July 1982, when Charlene and her lawyers finalized a deal with prosecutors in three states—California, Nevada, and Oregon. She would tell them the stories of eight more murders committed by Gerald, and she would acknowledge that she had played a part. More importantly, she would testify against Gerald in court. In return, the prosecution would take the death penalty off the table for her, and agree to a prison sentence of no more than sixteen years and eight months, including the time she had already served. The *Sacramento Bee* newspaper reported at the time that she described the killings as a "sexual fantasy" in which Gerald was searching for a "perfect lover." Six of the victims were teenagers. One of the women was pregnant. Charlene told the investigators that she had not committed any of the murders herself, but had lured some of the victims for Gerald. In return, he had promised not to make her take part in the killings. Before the authorities agreed to the deal, Charlene agreed to take lie detector tests. She passed. They already knew what had happened on the night of the fraternity dance. Now the complete list of the ten murders became clear.

Craig Miller and Mary Beth Sowers, victims nine and ten, were college students kidnapped after a fraternity dinner-dance in Sacramento and shot to death on November 2, 1980.

Virginia Mochel, the eighth victim, was killed a few months before Miller and Sowers. Mochel was a thirty-four-year-old bartender and mother of two who encountered the Gallegos on July 17, 1980, in the bar at the Sail Inn in the Sacramento Delta. The Gallegos had spent the day fishing nearby. Gerald drank heavily that night and told Charlene he wanted to rob the bar. He saw Mochel, and said he wanted to "get her" too. When the bar closed, they waited outside in his van. Mochel locked up, then went outside and got into her car. Gerald jumped out of the van, pointed his gun at Mochel, and ordered her to get in the back of the van. Meanwhile, Charlene jumped out of the van, wiped the car's door handle to get rid of any fingerprints, and returned.

Gerald then drove to their home, and ordered Charlene to go inside. She watched television and waited. He stayed in the van. Later, he summoned her back into the van, and he drove to the area where they had been fishing earlier in the day. Gerald ordered Charlene to turn up the radio and look away. He went to the back of the van, where Mochel, on a mattress, was whimpering, and repeating "Why don't you just go ahead and kill me." He strangled her. They dumped her body, then drove back home and went to work on a thorough cleaning of the van.

Mochel's body was found about three months later. Her hands had been bound with fishing line. Her body was badly decomposed, and investigators were not able to determine whether she had been sexually molested. But there were clues for the police to follow. When Mochel failed to return home on July 17, her babysitter notified police. They talked to the people who had been at the bar that night, and one remembered that while he was in the parking lot outside, he'd seen Mochel lock up and leave. The Gallegos were still in the parking lot.

Linda Aguilar, the seventh victim, was five months pregnant on June 7, 1980, when the Gallegos saw her hitchhiking on a highway near the Pacific Coast in Oregon. Gerald offered her a ride to a nearby town, and when she accepted he pulled a gun and tied her hands behind her back. Then he forced her into the back of their van and drove to a nearby field and ordered Charlene to walk away. Later, he told Charlene to return and she noticed that Aguilar was putting her clothes back on. Gerald tied her hands behind her back again, then drove to a nearby beach. He assured Charlene that he would not do anything to Aguilar because she was pregnant. Then he knocked Aguilar unconscious, strangled her, and buried her body in the sand. He used a hubcap to dig the grave. She was reported missing, but it was nearly two weeks before her body was found, about ten miles from her home. The degree of decomposition made it impossible to determine whether she had been sexually assaulted.

Stacy Redican, seventeen years old, and Karen Chipman Twiggs, also seventeen, were the fifth and sixth victims. Charlene sized them up at the Sunrise Mall in Sacramento on April 24, 1980, then approached them and asked if they liked to smoke dope. The girls seemed happy to follow Charlene outside to the van. As they got into the back, Gerald approached and pointed a gun at them. He told them they were being kidnapped. Charlene climbed into the driver's seat and headed north. Sometimes she glanced at the rear-view mirror and saw their naked bodies as Gerald abused them. At one point, they pulled off the freeway and Gerald went into a store to buy a hammer. When they reached an area near Lovelock, Nevada, they stopped. One at a time, he took them out of the van, then beat them to death and buried their bodies. Investigators found the bodies on July 27, 1980.

Brenda Judd was thirteen years old, and her friend Sandra Colley was fourteen when they became the third and fourth victims. On June 24, 1979, Gerald, determined to find two more young girls, sent Charlene into the bustling Washoe County Fair in Reno, Nevada. The

plan was for Charlene to recruit the girls by offering them money to place fliers on the windshields of cars in the parking lot. Brenda and Sandra agreed, and followed her out toward the van. Gerald was waiting with a gun. He tied them up on a mattress in the back, and drove off toward the high desert, stopping on the way to buy a hammer and a shovel. Charlene drove the van for a while, to give Gerald time to sexually assault the girls. When he was done, he bludgeoned them to death and buried their bodies in the desert. It would be twenty years before their skeletal remains were found. A property owner discovered the remains on November 20, 1999, in a shallow grave off U.S. Highway 395, north of Reno. Investigators used DNA found on items at the site to confirm the girls' identities.

Kippi Vaught, sixteen years old, and Rhonda Scheffler, seventeen, were the first victims. Charlene, on orders from Gerald, went into the Country Club Plaza, a Sacramento shopping center, on September 11, 1978, to find him some "sex slaves." She spotted the pretty young girls and casually asked them if they wanted to smoke some pot. They followed her out to the parking lot, where Gerald was waiting in his van. They got in, and Gerald drove north, toward an agricultural area. After he stopped, he sexually abused them for hours. Finally, he ordered them out of the van along a dark, deserted road, then followed them and shot both to death. Their bodies were discovered on September 13, 1978.

Who were the Gallegos? And how, like so many serial killers, had they managed to appear normal much of the time, then veer into the commission of the unspeakable acts that investigators attributed to them? A look back at their childhoods offers some clues. Gerald Armond Gallego was born in 1946, while his nineteen-year-old father, Gerald Albert Gallego, was serving time at San Quentin State Prison for check-fraud and auto-theft convictions.

Young Gerald never really knew his father. Gerald Albert Gallego was executed in Mississippi's gas chamber in 1955 for the murders of two

men. He had killed a town marshal in Ocean Springs, Mississippi, and beaten a jail employee to death with a pipe after throwing cleaning acid into his eyes.

Gerald learned about his father's execution several years later, during his own troubled youth. He was arrested five times as a preteen on charges of vandalism, burglary, and other crimes. When he was twelve, things got quite serious. He was charged with committing lewd and las-civious acts with a six-year-old girl, and spent several years in the custody of the California Youth Authority. He escaped from a reform school, but turned himself in a few days later. Eventually he was paroled, and attended Sacramento High School, but was soon suspended. That was about the time that he learned the truth about his father.

Young Gerald married for the first time in 1963, when he was seventeen years old. His first child was born in 1964. He was divorced within a year, after he beat his wife with a hammer. He married three more times, and each marriage involved beatings. In 1974, he married for a fifth time, after spending three years in prison for a series of armed robberies in California, as well as an escape from prison.

Charlene Adele Williams had a vastly different upbringing. She was an only child, the center of attention for her parents and grandparents. She was considered a bright student in grade school. At Rio Americano High School in Sacramento, she was a member of the campus orchestra for a time. But she got into trouble at school and became involved with sex and drugs, despite her parents' attempts to keep her under control. She married twice, but neither marriage lasted long. Her parents helped her rent an apartment, and bought her a car. Then, in 1978, she met Gerald on a blind date.

The courtroom drama that would echo through years of litigation began in earnest in October 1982, when Gerald announced that he had fired his lawyers and would defend himself. He was about to stand trial for the murders of Mary Beth Sowers and Craig Miller. In January 1983, Charlene took the witness stand, and they confronted each other. She

told the jury that Gerald had forced her—against her will—to get an abortion in 1978. She wept when she was shown a photograph of Mary Beth Sowers. Charlene said her role had been to act as a lure by striking up a conversation with young girls who could fulfill Gerald's fantasies.

Gerald's questioning of Charlene dragged on for days and brought frequent warnings from the judge. On day six, Gerald demanded, in front of the jury, "Isn't it a fact . . . you are a murderess?" She replied "No, I am not, Jerry." Gerald raised his voice and said "Yes, you are!" Charlene replied "You liar!" In another confrontation, he asked whether she ever loved him, and, if so, when. Weeping, she replied "You kept telling me over and over how much you loved me and how much you would take care of me and never let anybody hurt me, which was just another lie." In the end, the jury convicted Gerald of both murders. Next, they had to decide whether to recommend that he be executed. Charlene, the prosecution's key witness, told the jurors about the other murders he had committed. By this point, Gerald had agreed to have a lawyer represent him. "Looking back now, there had to have been some way that I could have stopped all this," she said. The lawyer asked her whether she thought her own punishment of sixteen years and three months was sufficient. "My own feeling? I wish I was dead," she said.

The jury also heard the testimony of Gerald's nineteen-year-old daughter. She was not in court, but a transcript was read into the record. She said that her father had sexually assaulted her from the time she was six years old until she was about fourteen. It took the jury less than two hours to recommend the death penalty. In 1984, Gerald was tried in Nevada for the murders of Karen Chipman Twiggs and Stacey Ann Redican. Again, he was convicted and sentenced to death. Years of litigation followed. It all came to an end on July 18, 2002, when Gerald died of cancer in a Nevada prison hospital. He was fifty-six years old. His appeal was still pending.

"I've never seen anything equal to his pure depravity or lack of remorse," Richard Wagner, a Nevada judge, told a reporter after Gerald's

death. He had prosecuted Gerald in Nevada for the Twiggs and Redican murders. "This case points out the absurdity of the appeals process. God's justice beats the hell out of man's justice."

Charlene fared better. She was released from prison in 1997 after serving the sentence of sixteen years and eight months that she had negotiated. A few months later, she talked to a news reporter on the condition that no photographs would be taken and that her location would not be disclosed. She said she was afraid that Gerald might have taken out a contract on her for testifying against him. On the day she was released from the Nevada Women's Correctional Facility, a female deputy dressed as a decoy boarded a prison van to fool the news media waiting in the parking lot. Charlene had already left. "When I first went to prison, I truly believed I deserved the death penalty," she said. Looking back, she had come to see that anyone who is emotionally and physically manipulated by a man like Gerald is a victim, not a criminal.

Charlene surfaced again in 2013, when she was interviewed by a Sacramento television station. She had changed her name, she said, and was living quietly in the Sacramento area, doing charity work. She called Gerald "one sick bastard," and said "I put him on death row. Am I proud of that? Yes, I am."

## THE VICTIMS

- **Kippi Vaught.** Sixteen years old. She disappeared from a Sacramento shopping center on September 12, 1978.

- **Rhonda Scheffler.** Seventeen years old. She disappeared from a Sacramento shopping center on September 12, 1978.

- **Brenda Judd.** Fourteen years old. She was kidnapped from the Washoe County Fair in Reno, Nevada, on August 24, 1979.

- **Sandra Colley.** Thirteen years old. She was kidnapped from the Washoe County Fair in Reno, Nevada, on August 24, 1979.

- **Stacy Redican.** Seventeen years old. She was kidnapped from the Sunrise Mall in Sacramento on April 24, 1980.

- **Karen Chipman Twiggs.** Seventeen years old. She was kidnapped from the Sunrise Mall in Sacramento on April 24, 1980.

- **Linda Aguilar.** Twenty-one years old. She was five months pregnant on June 7, 1980, when the Gallegos saw her hitchhiking on a highway near the Pacific Coast in Oregon and offered her a ride. Her body was discovered in a shallow grave about two weeks later.

- **Virginia Mochel.** Thirty-one years old. She was kidnapped from the bar where she worked in Sacramento on July 7, 1980, and her decomposed body was found about three months later.

- **Mary Beth Sowers.** Twenty-one years old. She was kidnapped from a fraternity party in Sacramento on November 1, 1980.

- **Craig Miller.** Twenty-two years old. He was kidnapped from a fraternity party in Sacramento on November 1, 1980.

# CHAPTER 3
# ROBERT CHRISTIAN HANSEN

Authorities in Alaska finally began to have serious doubts about Robert Hansen in 1983, when—like Gerald and Charlene Gallego before him— he made the mistake of leaving a live witness. Hansen had intended to kill Cindy Paulson, a young woman he picked up on an Anchorage street one night in June. He offered her two hundred dollars to perform oral sex on him in his car, and she agreed. But then he pulled a gun and handcuffed her. "You're a professional," he said. "Don't get excited. If you do exactly what I tell you to do, you're not going to get hurt."

Hansen drove Paulson to his house in Anchorage, then took her down to the basement, where the heads of wild animals he had shot were mounted on the walls. He placed her on a rug made of the skin of a bear he had killed. Then he raped her, bit her nipples, and thrust a hammer into her vagina. When he was done, Hansen handcuffed her and chained her to a pole, then went to sleep. After about five hours in the basement, he told her he was going to take her to his cabin in the woods, where they would spend the weekend together. She was terrified, and told him "All I want to do is go home, 'cause I live with my mom and I won't never tell nobody."

But he insisted. He said he had a plane at Merrill Field, a nearby airport. They would fly to the cabin, and he would bring her back later. She went along with the plan, or pretended to. At the airfield, he left her momentarily to put a seat into the plane so he could tie her up inside. "I knew I wasn't going to live. I mean, the man, what he did to me. He had to kill me. I opened the back door and I ran." Hansen, carrying a gun, began to chase her, but she got far enough away that a truck driver saw her—handcuffed, running in her bare feet, and seemingly hysterical.

Anchorage police officer Gregg Baker was out on patrol in the early morning hours of June 13, 1983, when he and his partner, Wayne Vance, got an emergency dispatch call on their car radio: "White female running down Fifth Avenue naked and handcuffed." The truck driver had stopped to pick her up. He took her to a nearby motel, got her out of the handcuffs, and found her some clothes. Then he called the police. The officers found Paulson there, alone in a room. She was seventeen years old and "extremely distraught." She agreed to let the officers take her to the hospital for a sexual assault examination. On the way, they passed Merrill Field, and she pointed out the plane she had escaped from. Later, the officers traced it to its owner, Robert Hansen, and went to his house. Hansen let them in and was cooperative, but said he had no idea what they were talking about. There was no obvious physical evidence at the

house, and he had an alibi. He gave the police the names of two business associates, and said they had been at his home having dinner with him at the time in question. The men corroborated Hansen's story. DNA testing was not in general use at the time. Hansen was not charged.

Over the previous decade, dozens of young women had disappeared without a trace from the cities, towns, and vast wilderness of Alaska. At 665,384 square miles, Alaska is by far the largest American state. It outranks the next three states combined—Texas, California, and Montana. But Alaska's population is tiny. In 1980, it had 401,851 permanent residents. Only Vermont and Wyoming had fewer people. California, with 23,667,902 people, ranked first. But the 1970s had brought phenomenal growth to Alaska's population: about 100,000 people—nearly 33 percent of the 1970 population. California's population had grown by only 18.6 percent over the same time period.

The emergence of the Trans-Alaska Pipeline had made the difference. The largest oil strike in United States history was discovered in 1968 under Prudhoe Bay in the Arctic Ocean on the north coast of Alaska. The pipeline was to run 789 miles south to the small town of Valdez near the Gulf of Alaska. Workers, mostly men, were drawn to the thousands of high-paying jobs created by the pipeline venture. Other types of workers, including waitresses, prostitutes, exotic dancers, and drug dealers were also drawn to the area. Many ended up in Anchorage, Alaska's largest city, also in the south part of the state. It was not unusual for them to come for a time, then move on, disappearing without a trace. It was, of course, the age before cell phones, security cameras, and the broad use of credit cards. Cash and paper checks were the currency of the time.

The incident with Cindy Paulson in June 1983 was a turning point. Baker, Vance, and others in the Anchorage Police Department had had enough. They had been analyzing the unexplained disappearances of women and adolescent girls over the previous decade. Now they would

focus their attention on a possible suspect. But it would be eight more months before the world would hear about Robert Hansen, the pleasant owner of a local bakery. Abruptly, Bob the baker would become known as "The Butcher Baker."

It all happened very quickly on Monday, February 27, 1984. "Alaska Man Confesses Killings of 17 Women" was the headline the next day on a five-paragraph story on page 14 of the *New York Times*. "Killer of 17 Calls Deaths Summer Project" ran on page 2 of the *Los Angeles Times*. In the coming days, the news media would scramble to report the gravity and magnitude of Hansen's crimes, and explain why they had been hidden from the public.

Frank Rothschild, an assistant district attorney in Anchorage, had offered a succinct overview in his unexpected court appearance that Monday: "Before you sits a monster. An extreme aberration of a human being. A man who was among us for seventeen years serving us doughnuts, Danish, and coffee with a pleasant smile. His family was a prop. He hid behind decency. This hunter who kept trophies on the wall now has trophies scattered throughout south-central Alaska. And while he doesn't talk about or admit it, it's obvious from looking at where things started, and where women ended up. He hunted them down. He let them run a little bit and he enjoyed a hunt just like with his big-game animals."

Decades later, Rothschild talked about that morning in the courtroom: "I don't know how I delivered that," he said. "The system failed the public, which allowed him to prey on women for a long time." Rothschild and others touched by the case reflected on their involvement and the societal changes that have given them—and the world—a new perspective. In *The Butcher Baker: Mind of a Monster*, which premiered on the Investigation Discovery channel in the fall of 2020, Rothschild said "We spent two days with this guy looking right across from him . . . getting him to talk about what he did. It was

like cat and mouse. He wasn't going to admit to anything." Hansen was "like a moth drawn to light," he said. "It scared me." Ultimately, Hansen crumbled, and, as he did, the investigators were recording his words on reels of audiotape: "I need help. God, I've wanted help so damn much of my life."

Hansen was born in Estherville, Iowa, on February 15, 1939, and grew up in the small town of Pocahontas, about 120 miles northwest of Des Moines. His father, an immigrant from Denmark, ran a bakery in Pocahontas. Robert worked there, along with his mother, and spent most of his time there when he was not at school. He had an unhappy childhood. He was left-handed, but his parents insisted that he use his right hand while serving at the bakery. He thought his father was too demanding, and felt that he was never able to please him, no matter how hard he tried. He stuttered and developed a severe case of acne as a teenager. He had few friends and was prone to fits of rage. He also developed a fondness for shoplifting, which he continued into adulthood. In 1953, he entered high school, and began hunting with bows and arrows as well as guns. After graduation, he joined the Army Reserve and did his basic training at Fort Dix in New Jersey. Stationed at Fort Knox in Kentucky, he had his first sexual experience—with a prostitute.

In 1959, still in the Reserves, he returned to Iowa, where he moved back into his parents' house and worked in the bakery again. From time to time, he continued his Army Reserve training there, and volunteered as a drill instructor at a police academy. In 1960, he met a young woman, and they quickly married. On December 7, 1960, he persuaded a teenager to go with him to the county school-bus garage, and they set the building on fire. Hansen pleaded guilty to a charge of arson and was sentenced to five years in prison. His wife quickly divorced him. He was to be eligible for parole at the earliest date allowed by law, with the proviso that he get psychiatric counseling. He appealed the sentence, and was released in June 1962 after serving twenty-three months in a reformatory.

Hansen's parents promptly sold their bakery and moved to Minnesota, where they bought a resort. On a visit to the resort, Hansen met Darla Henrickson, a guest, and persuaded her to marry him. They moved to Anchorage in 1967 for a fresh start. She was a college graduate, and got a job as an elementary school teacher. He was a warehouse worker for a time. They had two children—a boy and a girl. Hansen began hunting big game in the wilds of Alaska, and found that he was quite good at it. He won some awards and brought many of the bodies home to preserve and keep as trophies. Some heads were mounted on the walls in the basement of their house. In 1981, he filed an insurance claim over the theft of some of the trophies from his house. He got a big payout, and used the money to open his bakery in Anchorage. In 1982, he bought a small plane—a Piper Super Cub—so that he could more easily reach hunting areas.

But there had been trouble along the way. In November 1971, he pointed a gun out the window of his car on an Anchorage street and ordered a young woman to get in. She ran away, and he followed her to her home. He was ultimately charged with assault with a deadly weapon and sentenced to five years in prison, with a recommendation that he receive psychiatric treatment. After three months in prison, he was sent to a halfway house and put on a work-release program. Six months later, he was paroled. He had been diagnosed with bipolar affective disorder and a variant of manic depression.

In late 1976, when Hansen was thirty-seven years old, he saw a chainsaw he liked at an Anchorage store. He found an old receipt for something else and placed it on top of the box that contained the saw. Then he casually walked outside with the package. Someone in the store had been watching him, and he was immediately arrested. The incident led to his third felony conviction. He pleaded guilty to larceny and was sentenced to five years in prison, with the provision that he be paroled at the earliest possible date. But the parole board took too long, in Hansen's

view. He appealed, and on August 11, 1978, the Supreme Court of Alaska reversed the sentence, noting that his previous offenses had been five and fifteen years earlier. He had generally conducted his life in a "normal and respectable manner," the court said. "He has been a good provider for his family, and has earned the reputation of a hard worker and a respectable member of his community." The court ordered that he be released for time served.

Hansen's ultimate fall from grace had its beginning on September 12, 1982. John Daily, an off-duty Anchorage police officer, was hunting moose with a friend near the Knik River northeast of Anchorage. They saw a depression in the ground that looked unnatural, then found some pieces of clothing. When they pulled up a flap, they saw what appeared to be human skin. They called in the state police, and ultimately found that it was the decomposing body of a white female. There was something that looked like an ACE bandage over her head and eyes, so whatever had happened to her was no accident. Within a week, they learned that the victim was Sherry Morrow, a twenty-three-year-old who worked as a topless dancer, and had disappeared from Anchorage on November 17, 1981.

Maxine Farrell, one of the first female officers in the Anchorage Police Department, had been keeping track of Alaska's missing girls and women as a kind of unofficial project. "When I read about this body that was found over in the Knik area, I knew that it matched what was going on with all the other girls," she recalled in an interview for the Investigation Discovery channel project. "I said, 'There's a serial killer,' but they wouldn't listen." At the time—forty years ago—female officers were frequently ignored, she said. "We had no locker rooms. We had no bathroom to change [in]. People would come up to us and say 'Why aren't you at home taking care of kids instead of working here?'"

Farrell had begun collecting the data after she was sent out on a case in July 1980. The body of a young female had been found in Eklutna,

about twenty-eight miles north of Anchorage near the Knik River. It was a remote location that served as an access point for electricians. Some of the workers had noticed an unusual—and suspicious—depression in the ground. "We started digging," Farrell recalled. "Immediately it struck me that this is a prostitute—the dress and the jewelry that was on her. There was no identification. We had no report of her. We thought, 'Is she somebody new and had just come into Anchorage?'" The cause of death was determined to be a knife wound to the body. "We had most of the skull there, so it wasn't difficult to reconstruct the face and come up with a picture of what they thought this person looked like. And I sent that everywhere. Everywhere I could think of, I sent it. I got no response. Never did find who she was. And I wondered who could have done this, because it doesn't seem like the usual crime." They called the victim "Eklutna Annie."

Soon, Farrell got a report of another missing woman, who was known to be a prostitute. "After that, almost every month I had two or three women missing," she said. "That's when I started asking questions." Farrell collected missing-person reports, got information about relatives, and learned details about the types of clothes the women and girls usually wore. "I was a psychology major, so I knew that a lot of these serial killers kept souvenirs," she recalled. Ultimately, she made a spreadsheet listing ten young females, and what was known about them. She took it to her supervisors. "I advised them that there's a serial killer because of the number of girls I was collecting as missing persons, and they laughed at me," she said. "And they said 'No, you're wrong.' They felt I was stupid. Stupid woman thinking there's a serial killer. I wasn't stupid."

Hansen was able to go on with his seemingly normal life. He went to church with his wife and was respected there. His children did well in school, and his wife was considered a model teacher. They seemed unaware of his extracurricular behavior and voracious appetite for women. At one point, he placed an ad in the *Anchorage Daily News* "Sunday Singles" section.

ADVENTUROUS M, 42, 5'11", 165. Looking for a lady proud to be a woman, to share sincere honest attachment. Must like to dance & enjoy social life, willing to put on jeans join me in finding what's around the next bend, over the next hill. Enjoy flying (own plane), beach combing, fishing, camping. Life is beautiful, much fuller if shared. Recent photo. D74.

When the incident with Cindy Paulson happened in June 1983, Hansen was living alone in his house. He had sent his wife and children to vacation in Europe for the summer. Despite his alibis, both the Anchorage police and the Alaska state police began to focus more intensely on him. On September 2, the body of Paula Goulding was found in a shallow grave near where the body of Sherry Morrow had been found by the off-duty police officer a year earlier. They were, indeed, dealing with a serial killer. It was time to seek help from the FBI's Investigative Support Unit in Quantico, Virginia. Special Agent John Douglas, a pioneer in criminal psychological profiling, got the assignment. He saw by the file that Hansen appeared to be Paulson's kidnapper. She had identified Hansen's house as the place he had taken her, and had pointed out his plane at the airport. The police needed a confession. The records showed that as a youth, Hansen had stuttered and had severe acne, so he was shunned and belittled by boys his age, as well as girls. Abusing prostitutes, Douglas noted, was a standard way of getting back at women, a "modus operandi" of sorts. Hansen viewed prostitutes as more worthless than himself. He was, as well, a proficient hunter. Douglas predicted that souvenirs and jewelry belonging to the victims would be hidden somewhere in the house, along with the weapon Hansen had used to kill them. This would be the first time criminal profiling was used to support a search warrant.

Then there was the matter of the alibis from Hansen's friends. The Anchorage police, working with the district attorney, got a grand jury formed to investigate Paulson's kidnapping. Hansen's friends were called

as witnesses, and were reminded that perjury was a crime. They admitted that they had not been with Hansen that night. So there was no alibi. The investigators decided it was time to search Hansen's house, so they asked him to come in to headquarters so that they could interview him. He agreed. On October 27, 1983, Hansen went in for questioning. The investigators, having won a search warrant, descended on his house and airplane. His rifle was found in the attic of the house, and the shell casings found at the scenes of the murders matched the weapon. Also in the attic was jewelry that had belonged to the victims, a driver's license, and some identification cards. More importantly, they also found an aviation map with more than twenty X marks drawn on it, clues, they believed, to the locations of bodies. One week later, Hansen was indicted on charges related to the incident with Cindy Paulson—first-degree assault on a person, second-degree theft, and misconduct with a deadly weapon. He was also charged with insurance fraud. The investigators had found items that Hansen had claimed were stolen years earlier, and had used to get the insurance payout that enabled him to open his bakery.

Now the authorities had him in custody. What they really needed was a confession. He requested a lawyer, and for the next four months he continued to deny any involvement in the murders. Things changed on Sunday, February 19, 1984. He arranged to have the pastor from his family's church—Wayne Coggins—visit him in jail. It was a brief conversation, Coggins recalled: "I got one question for you, preacher. What kind of sins does God forgive?" Hansen asked. "I said 'Well, the Bible says in Mark, Chapter 3, God will forgive all manner of sins, except for blasphemy against the Holy Spirit.' Hansen said 'Thank you. That's what I wanted to know.'" He ended the conversation and called for the guard to return him to his cell.

Three days later, Hansen began to confess. "My main purpose, of course, behind the whole thing is to minimize in any way possible the hurt and so forth that this is going to bring upon my family," Hansen

began, as Rothschild and other investigators sat with him in an interrogation room, recording the session on reels of tape. "His intention was to return them [his vicims] back to the world," Rothschild said. "If they didn't behave properly, or asked for money, they stayed." As Hansen explained, "Then she's no longer, I guess, what you would call a decent girl." In the lengthy and rambling session, Hansen described the killings that he knew the investigators could connect him with, based on some evidence, then said "That's it." But the investigators didn't budge. "If we would have," Rothschild said, "he knew he would have been able to live out his life thinking 'I won. I beat them.'" Ultimately, when they let Hansen know that they had the aviation map with all the X marks on it, Hansen folded. "At that moment, his face changed and I saw not Bob the Baker," Rothschild said. "I saw Bob the Serial Killer." In the end, he confessed to seventeen murders.

By the following week, when the case erupted publicly in court for the first time, a deal had been worked out. Hansen agreed to plead guilty to the murders of Sherry Morrow, Joanna Messina, Paula Goulding, and Eklutna Annie, as well as theft and weapons charges. He also agreed to assist the investigators in locating and identifying the bodies of the missing victims. And he pleaded guilty to kidnapping and raping Cindy Paulson, the teenager who had escaped in 1983 and led investigators to Hansen's airplane and home. In return for his cooperation, he would be sentenced to three hundred seventy-seven years in prison plus life without parole, and would not be tried for the additional murders. Paulson was in the courtroom on that morning in 1984. In the following months, Hansen, using the map that had been found in his attic, directed investigators to the sites where he had hastily buried the bodies of other women and girls. He couldn't remember most of their names. In the end, only twelve bodies were found. Investigators concluded that some of the remains had been eaten by bears or other wild animals.

IN THIS SEPTEMBER 3, 2014, PHOTO, WORKERS AND MEDICAL EXAMINER CREW MEMBERS WORK TO EXHUME THE BODY OF JANE DOE #3, A PRESUMED VICTIM OF ROBERT HANSEN, FROM A CEMETERY IN ANCHORAGE, ALASKA.

Hansen, afraid of running into relatives of his victims in Alaska prisons, spent several years in federal custody in Minnesota and Pennsylvania before returning to Alaska prisons in 1988. In 1990, while Hansen was working in a supply room at the prison in Juneau, officials there made what they called "the bust of the decade." They found an aeronautical chart, plastic explosives, and some correspondence with a boat broker. "We nabbed him before he could do any damage to anyone," Dan Corothers, a prison official, said. Also in 1990, Hansen's wife, Darla, filed for divorce and moved out of Alaska. Hansen gained new notoriety in 2013 with the release of the movie *The Frozen Ground*, a fictionalized version of his life. The actor John Cusack played Hansen, and Nicholas Cage played a dogged investigator.

Hansen died of natural causes in August 2014 at a hospital in Anchorage. Prison officials said that he had been in declining health for about a year, and had a do-not-resuscitate order. He was seventy-five years old. "As far as Hansen is concerned, this world is better without him," Glenn Flothe, a retired state trooper, told the *Anchorage Daily News* at the time. Flothe had been instrumental in the original investigation and arrest of Hansen thirty years earlier.

Of Hansen's known victims, the first three were tied to bullets from his rifle. The fourth, Eklutna Annie, was stabbed to death.

## THE VICTIMS

- **Sherry Morrow.** Twenty-three years old. Disappeared in November 1981. Her body was discovered along the Knik River in December 1982. She had been an exotic dancer in Anchorage, and agreed to pose nude for Hansen, who told her he was a photographer and would pay her $300. In his confession, Hansen described how he killed her. When she got into his car, he handcuffed her and wrapped a bandage around her eyes. At the Knik River, she began to struggle with him, kicking and screaming as she tried to escape. He shot her with his rifle, then buried her body in a shallow grave along with the shell casings from his rifle.

- **Joanna Messina.** Twenty-four years old. Disappeared in July 1980. She had a job at a cannery and also worked as a topless dancer. Hansen tried to pick her up, but she resisted, saying she did not want to be late for her shift at the cannery. Her body was found later that month in a gravel pit in the Eklutna area northeast of Anchorage. He admitted raping and killing her. When state troopers found her body, they had to contend with a large bear nearby, which had apparently gnawed at her body. The bear finally retreated.

- **Paula Goulding.** Thirty-one or thirty-two years old. Disappeared in April 1983. Her body was discovered in September 1983, in a shallow grave along the Knik River. She had worked as a secretary, but lost her job and began working as a topless dancer. Hansen confessed that he had forced her into his plane, then flown her to a cabin, where he raped and tortured her. Eventually he released her, and, as she ran away, he hunted her down and shot her in the back with his rifle. He re-dressed her before he buried her body.

- **"Eklutna Annie."** In her late teens or twenties. Was given the name after her body was found on July 21, 1980, near Eklutna Road about thirty miles north of Anchorage. Hansen said he picked her up in his truck, then took her into the woods. She eventually ran away from him, but he caught up, and she pulled a knife. He grabbed the knife and stabbed her to death.

- **Lisa Futrell.** Forty-one years old. Was a sex worker who disappeared on September 6, 1980. Her body was found on May 9, 1984, near the Old Knik Bridge, about forty miles northeast of Anchorage. Hansen had marked the spot on the map he shared with the police.

- **Malai Larsen.** Twenty-eight years old. Disappeared at an unknown date. Her body was found on April 24, 1984, near the Old Knik Bridge. Little is known about her. Hansen led authorities to the site and admitted that he had killed her.

- **Sue Luna.** Twenty-three years old. Was a topless dancer and prostitute who disappeared from Anchorage on May 26, 1982. Her body was found on April 24,1984, buried near the Knik River. She had been shot several times in the back.

- **Tamara Pederson.** Twenty years old. A stripper and prostitute who disappeared from Anchorage in August 1982. Hansen admitted killing her. Authorities found her body in a shallow grave near the Knik River on April 29, 1984.

- **Angela Feddern.** Twenty-four years old. The mother of a five-year-old girl, who disappeared in February 1983. She lived in Fairbanks and worked as a prostitute in Anchorage. Her remains were found on April 26, 1984, near Anchorage.

- **Teresa Watson.** Age unknown. A prostitute who was last seen alive on March 25, 1983. Hansen admitted raping and killing her. He threw her body out of his plane about sixty miles north of Anchorage, near the shore of a lake. Her remains, which had been attacked by wildlife, were found about a year later.

- **DeLynn "Sugar" Frey.** Twenty years old. A prostitute who moved to Alaska from New Mexico. She disappeared in April 1983. Hansen admitted that he shot her to death. Her body was found on August 25, 1985, buried in a shallow grave about sixty miles north of Anchorage.

- **Andrea "Fish" Altiery.**

- **"Horseshoe Harriet."** About twenty years old. Disappeared at an unknown date, and her identity was never determined. The skeletal remains of her body were found on April 25, 1984, near Horseshoe Lake. It appeared that she had been stabbed and shot in the back.

- **Roxanne Easland.** Twenty-four years old. Worked as a prostitute in Anchorage in 1980 and lived in a motel with her boyfriend. On

June 28, she left to meet a client in a hotel on 4th Avenue. She was never seen alive again. Hansen admitted that he had kidnapped and killed her, but her body was never found.

- **Celia "Beth" Van Zanten.** Seventeen or eighteen years old. Disappeared after leaving home on December 23, 1971 to walk to a convenience store. Her body was found on Christmas Day in a wilderness area of McHugh Creek State Park near Anchorage. She had been sexually molested, slashed with a knife, and, apparently, left to freeze to death.

- **Megan Emerick.** Seventeen years old. Disappeared on July 7, 1973. She came from Delta Junction, near Fairbanks, and was a student at a technical school in Seward, south of Anchorage. She was last seen leaving a laundry room in her dormitory. Her body was never found.

- **Mary K. Thill.** Twenty-two or twenty-three years old. Disappeared on July 5, 1975. She was a student at the Seward Skill Center on the Kenai Peninsula in southern Alaska. She was last seen when friends dropped her off at a store in downtown Seward. Her husband, who worked on Alaska's North Slope, reported her missing when she failed to return home. Her body was never found, but Hansen conceded that he had been in the area at the time.

# CHAPTER 4

# BOBBY JOE LONG

It was a Friday afternoon in November 1984. The matinée at the theater near Tampa, Florida, was *Missing in Action,* a rugged, violent tale starring Chuck Norris, the martial arts champion and military veteran who was becoming a serious Hollywood star. The movie told the story of a Marine who had escaped from a prisoner-of-war camp and returned to the jungles of Vietnam years later to free his colleagues who were still there. For Bobby Joe Long, the macho thrills of the film would pale in comparison to the shock that would come when the movie ended and he walked outside. Law-enforcement agents from two counties, the City of Tampa, and the FBI were waiting. They wrestled him to the ground and arrested

him on the spot. He was ultimately charged with murdering nine women over the previous six months. He was also charged with kidnapping and raping some of the victims. One teenage girl had survived, and Long was charged with raping her.

Like so many victims of serial killers, most had been living on the fringes of society, distanced from whatever family or friends might have taken notice of their disappearance. Security cameras, cellphone tracking, and DNA remained largely the work of science fiction. But communication among local law-enforcement agencies—still working with fax machines—was emerging as a critical tool. The local police departments in Florida had noticed similarities in the deaths of the women whose bodies had been turning up in ditches and fields over the previous six months, and they formed a task force to share their information. The break came in early November when Long—like other serial killers—made the crucial mistake of leaving a live victim.

Lisa McVey was seventeen years old in early November 1984. She was riding her bicycle home from her job at a donut shop when Long grabbed her, pressed the tip of a gun against her left temple, and threw her into his car. He took her to his apartment, blindfolded her, and raped her repeatedly over the next twenty-six hours. Then, oddly, in the early morning hours he put her—still blindfolded—back in his car and dropped her off near her home. She told the police everything she could remember about her attacker, and described the red car that had passed her just before she was grabbed and blindfolded. She also described the red carpet she was able to glimpse on the floor of the car while she was tied up in the back seat, and the word "Magnum" she had seen on the dashboard. Investigators had been looking for a maroon Magnum with wire spokes on the wheels.

Eight months earlier, on March 6, 1984, a young woman was drying her hair as she prepared to go to work not far from her home in a middle-class area of Port Richey, on Florida's Gulf Coast, about forty miles northwest

of Tampa. She heard a knock on the front door. She answered, and a man in a brown suit said he was looking to buy a home in the area. Uninvited, he walked into the living room and began looking around. He grabbed her, pushed the front door closed, and put a gun to her head. Then he took her to a bedroom, bound her hands, and put surgical tape across her eyes. He forced her to perform oral sex on him and raped her. They struggled, and eventually he left. She alerted neighbors, and when police arrived she told them that before the man knocked on her door, she had noticed a red car in the driveway with the word "Magnum" on it. And, she remembered, the rims of the wheels had spokes.

Red fibers had been found on the bodies and clothes of most of the earlier victims. In the following days, as investigators tracked down Dodge Magnums, the bodies of two more young women would be found, along with tiny bits of red fiber. Ultimately, the police began to focus on Long, and followed him for thirty-six hours before arresting him as he left the movie theater on November 16. He was charged with the murder of Michelle Simms, whose nude body—raped, stabbed, and tied up—had been found the previous May. She was twenty-two years old, and had been a beauty-pageant contestant in California before she moved to Florida.

On the day he was arrested outside the theater, Long, thirty-one years old, was on three years' probation for an aggravated assault charge. The previous April, a middle-aged woman had agreed to take him for a ride in her Jaguar after he stopped her outside a drugstore in Tampa and gushed about how much he liked her car. As they rode along, he pulled a gun and pointed it at her. She swerved the car, it flipped, and she was able to escape and contact the police. By July 1983, when he was sentenced in that case, the bodies of three of his murder victims had already been found, and the mystery was growing. By the end of November, Long had been charged with nine murders in two counties in central Florida, setting off jurisdictional and legal challenges that would last for decades.

Who was Bobby Joe Long? Born in 1953 in the small town of Kenova, West Virginia, he was an awkward child who had a difficult adolescence. His mother, Luella Lucas, was seventeen years old in 1952 when she married Joe Long, who was twenty-three. His parents separated in 1954 and divorced a year later. Luella disliked the long, cold West Virginia winters and dreamed of moving to Florida. When Bobby Joe was two years old, she took him and what belongings she could manage on a bus to restart their life in Florida, leaving her husband behind. She rented rooms in several homes, and worked nights as a waitress. Bobby Joe cried when she left and "was such a sad, lonely little boy back then," she told a reporter after his final arrest in 1984.

Luella and Joe remarried in 1960, but Bobby Joe's childhood was tumultuous, with several moves between states. He began first grade in Florida, but spent the last months at a school in West Virginia, where he flunked and was forced to repeat the year. During that time, he was hit by a car, leaving him with scars and protruding teeth. Bobby Joe eventually moved to Florida with his mother and some of her relatives. Again, he was a poor student. He was forced to repeat his sophomore year in high school because of poor attendance, and was ultimately dismissed from the school when he turned eighteen, never having finished his sophomore year. His mother was working long hours as a waitress at a restaurant and at a bar called Big Daddy's Lounge, where she was required to wear some skimpy clothes. Bobby Joe was disgusted by her appearance, and they argued frequently. "I almost feel like I killed him," she lamented in the 1984 interview.

But Bobby Joe had found some happiness too, with his move back to Florida as a young teenager. Living in Hialeah, northwest of Miami, he met a young girl named Cindy at a local park. "We just bonded," Cindy told an interviewer decades later for a television documentary. "It was just like an instant attraction to him." Bobby Joe made her feel that she was "just the most important thing in the world." Cindy, too, had had a

difficult childhood, and was raised by an aunt and uncle. "He made me feel like I was pretty, and I was important to somebody. I could make people laugh and make them feel good, too." He filled a void, she said, and gave her a sense that he wanted her around, and wanted to help her. They went to movies together, rode bicycles, and went scuba diving in the Florida Keys. "He swept me off my feet. I guess I just fell madly in love with him. He told me that he wanted me to be his wife when we were older, and that we would be together forever and ever."

She struggled to explain what had changed him, or what she had never understood about him. One night, while they were still dating, she fell asleep at his house, where he lived with his mother. She woke to find a gun pointed at her head. He pulled the trigger, and there was what sounded like a huge explosion. "I thought for sure I was dead," she said. But it turned out that he had fired a blank, and she heard a "sick" laugh. "It's almost like it thrilled him or something." She left the house and didn't see him for a few weeks, but he had a way of "sweet-talking," and they eventually got back together. Long was nineteen years old when he joined the U.S. Army in 1972, and they made plans to get married in January 1975. But Cindy became pregnant, and they married in January 1974. "It was like my dream come true," she said. "I was so excited to start this new life with this guy I was so madly in love with."

But less than three months after the wedding, things began to change. On the foggy morning of March 14, 1974, Bobby Joe got on his motorcycle to go to work at the base in Homestead. He sped off, and was hit by a car. The injuries to his head and leg were severe, and he spent months recovering. In 1975, their second child—a girl—was born. By then, Bobby Joe's behavior, always a bit abusive, had changed dramatically. Cindy started to worry. "He was more aggressive, more possessive. A normal noise like a clock ticking would really irritate him. Certain smells. He could not stand the smell of popcorn." He called her "fat" and "disgusting," but wanted her to have sex with him several times

a day. He became violent and, at one point, choked her and accused her of having an affair. Looking back, she said "I think that it's possible that the motorcycle accident knocked the screw loose that was holding everything together at the time."

Bobby Joe eventually got a medical discharge from the Army, and earned an associate's degree in radiology from a community college. In 1979, he worked as an X-ray technician at Parkway Medical Center in North Miami Beach. During those years, women began reporting what turned out to be a spree of rapes in the area. Typically, the rapist called phone numbers of people offering to sell household items through the classified ad sections of local newspapers. If a female voice answered, he arranged a time to view the item. If no one else was in the home when he arrived, and the conditions were right, he would tie up the woman and rape her. The mysterious attacker became known in the news media as "The Classified Ad Rapist." Before the spree was over, there were as many as fifty victims.

For Cindy, the end of the relationship came in 1980. She was so severely beaten by Bobby Joe that she had to go to an emergency room. The staff saw the hand marks on her neck and called the police, who warned her that if she did not file for divorce, they would arrest Bobby Joe. She went home and pointed a shotgun at his head while he was sleeping. He woke up and said he didn't believe she had the nerve to pull the trigger. "You're not worth losing my kids over," she replied. The next morning, she found a divorce lawyer. Bobby Joe did not contest the divorce. He lost his job at the Parkway Medical Center and eventually moved back to his parents' house in West Virginia. For a time, he worked as an X-ray technician at a Veterans Administration hospital there, and he had a steady girlfriend for a while. He also began picking up prostitutes there and raping them. In 1981, he mailed obscene photographs along with an obscene letter to a twelve-year-old girl in Tampa. She had also been getting obscene phone calls. Police traced the calls to Long,

and he eventually pleaded no contest to the charges and was placed on six months' probation.

On February 11, 1985, three months after his dramatic arrest outside the movie theater near Tampa, in Hillsborough County, Long appeared before a judge at the courthouse in Pasco County, to the northeast. Security was heavy, and camera crews had swarmed into the area. He faced rape and robbery charges there for the incident at the home in Port Richey and one charge of murder in the death of Virginia Lee Johnson, an eighteen-year-old from Tampa whose body had been found near a bridge in Pasco County on November 6, 1984. The judge appointed the county public defender's office to represent Long, who appeared calm despite the heavy security, metal detectors, and crush of news reporters and cameras.

Two months later, at another pre-trial hearing in Pasco County, prosecutors pointed out a letter Long had written recently to a fellow inmate in which Long appeared to be admitting his guilt. "I mean they had me, so I thought if I cooperated it would go better on me. I was wrong! But I learned! If I ever get out, shoot first, ask questions later and don't say shit to the POLICE! except (I want a lawyer)! Live and Learn. But I don't forget." It appeared to be a reference to a key event that happened shortly after his arrest on November 16, 1984. Long, it turned out, had given a lengthy tape-recorded confession to the nine murders in a deal with the prosecutors in Hillsborough County, where the other eight murder charges were pending.

Long's trial on the rape charge was brief. He did not testify, and his lawyer called no witnesses. He was quickly convicted by the jury. A week later, on April 22, 1985, his first murder trial began in Pasco County. Virginia Lee Johnson, the victim, was eighteen years old and was originally from Connecticut. She had been raped and strangled. The police said she was a drug user and prostitute who had last been seen on the Nebraska Avenue strip in Tampa that was frequented by prostitutes and men trying to pick them up.

Long winked at his parents and his ex-wife as they took their seats in the courtroom. His lawyers had subpoenaed them as potential witnesses. At times his mother wiped away tears. Broad publicity about the case would be an issue during jury selection, so four hundred potential jurors had been called. Those who were chosen were to be sequestered during the trial. The death penalty would also be an issue, so the jury candidates were questioned about their feelings on the subject. The biggest problem for the defense was the tape-recorded confession Long had made to the police after his arrest outside the theater in November. He had admitted to all the murders, and the recording was played for the jury. Another problem would be red carpet fibers that had been found on some of the victims and matched the fibers in Long's car. The prosecutors also had a barrette that had fallen out of Lisa McVey's hair in Long's apartment, as well as items that belonged to some of the other victims. The defense called no witnesses. Within a week, the jury voted to convict him.

The following day, with the death penalty at issue, the defense called two psychiatrists to the witness stand. They testified that several head injuries and a tumultuous childhood had caused Bobby Joe to lose his ability to function rationally. Long's mother described his troubled childhood, and her three marriages to Bobby Joe's father. When Bobby Joe was thirteen, he began to develop breasts and was deeply humiliated. He had surgery to have several pounds of tissue removed. His personality changed markedly after the motorcycle accident in 1974, she said. "He became hostile. You didn't know if you should say anything or not. I had to be careful when I talked to him. There'd been a change in his eyes. His eyes got big." Some years later, when she was visiting Bobby Joe and his family, she said, he abruptly "turned me over his knee, blistering me, pounding me for a long time." He eventually left "without saying a word," she said. "I had his hand prints on me for days." On April 27, 1985, the jurors spent thirty-five minutes considering the

sentence. They voted unanimously to recommend the death penalty. One week later, Pasco County Judge Ray E. Ulmer ordered that Long be executed.

In December 1985, jury selection began in Hillsborough County, where the only issue would be whether to impose the death penalty for one of the eight murders he had already admitted. As part of his deal with the prosecutors, he had received twenty-six consecutive life sentences for seven of the murders there. The deal left open the possibility of a death sentence for the murder of Michelle Denise Simms, a twenty-two-year-old he had stabbed, beaten, and strangled to death on May 27, 1985. But problems with the availability of witnesses forced the judge to postpone the hearing and dismiss the potential jurors. By the time the sentencing began again in July 1986, Long's public defenders had been replaced by Ellis Rubin, a flamboyant private attorney from Miami. Rubin had been appointed by the judge, and was to be paid $3,500.

Addressing a crowd of reporters outside the Hillsborough County Courthouse on July 10, 1986, Rubin described what would become known as the porn defense. "Gentlemen, Bobby Joe Long is going to be the first documented case to prove the Attorney General's Commission on Pornography right." He was referring to a nearly two-thousand-page report released the previous day by Edwin Meese, the U.S. Attorney General under President Ronald Reagan. The report said that some forms of pornography can cause sexual violence. It was pornography, Rubin said, that had driven Long to rape and murder eight women in Hillsborough County. Long, he said, suffered from "prolonged, intense, subliminal, pornographic dementia." The defense also argued that Long's mental capacity had been diminished by a traumatic childhood, head injuries, and drug use.

The prosecutor, Michael L. Benito, argued that Long was not psychotic or out of touch with reality, but was a sex maniac who consciously

planned his murders and "left a trail of women that would no longer make him feel inadequate." The jurors were told that years earlier, Long had admitted to killing a tenth victim, but in return for his cooperation he was not prosecuted for that murder. Benito called Long a "cunning, intelligent, cold-blooded killer." Michelle Simms was dead, he said, because Long had strangled her, beat her with a club, and slashed her throat with a hunting knife. "Within this man right there, there burns a violent flame . . . which must now be extinguished. You should have no resolutions about your decision. You can't hold his mother responsible. You can't hold his father responsible or *Playboy* or drugs or his well-fed dog responsible. That man is responsible."

Rubin took an unusual approach in his argument to spare Long's life. "Bobby Joe Long deserves to die," he told the jury. "So does every other person who takes a life. Bobby Joe Long is vicious. Bobby Joe Long contains a flame of violence, and Mr. Benito wants to extinguish it. And so do I." But Long, he said, was a "special breed," and should be kept alive so that he could be studied to provide more information on the growing epidemic of serial killers. "The question is to kill or not to kill? Revenge or research? Electrocution or prevention? You don't stop it by burning him alive. You put out that flame by understanding what makes it spark in the first place. I ask for an intelligent response to an epidemic." His final appeal was to the conscience of each juror: "When a jury kills, it is the same thing that Bobby Joe Long did."

After deliberating for two hours and thirty minutes on July 18, 1986—eight days after the hearing began—the jury recommended in an eleven-to-one vote that Long receive the death penalty. Long showed no reaction as the judge asked the individual jurors to confirm their votes. One week later, Hillsborough County Circuit Judge John P. Griffin sentenced Long to die in the electric chair. Now Long faced multiple consecutive life terms in prison and two death sentences.

Along the way, Long had admitted to killing a tenth victim, but prosecutors decided not to pursue the case. No one involved in the case, from the families and friends of the victims to the prosecutors, investigators, and defense lawyers, could have predicted the legal wrangling that was to come.

Two years later, on June 30, 1988, the Florida Supreme Court threw out his two death sentences and ordered a new trial in the Virginia Lee Johnson murder case in Pasco County, as well as new sentencing hearings for all the murders. Long's rights had been violated, the court said, because during his hours-long confession after his final arrest in 1984, Long paused at one point and said "I think I might need an attorney." The justices ruled that his lengthy statement was not admissible in court because the investigators ignored what amounted to a request for a lawyer and went on with their questioning. The recorded confession had been played for the jury in the 1985 Pasco County trial. Decades of legal wrangling, retrials, convictions, and appeals followed. On October 4, 1993, the United States Supreme Court turned down a request to review the case.

The end came in 2019, nearly thirty-five years after Long walked out of the theater in Florida and into the custody of the justice system. On April 23, 2019, Florida Governor Ron DeSantis ordered that Long be executed at 6 P.M. on May 23 at the Florida State Prison near Starke for the May 27, 1984 murder of Michelle Denise Simms. On May 3, 2019, ten days after the governor's order, Long's defense lawyers argued in a Hillsborough County court that the execution should be halted because the drug used to kill Long might cause him to have a seizure. The prosecution called experts who testified that a seizure would be highly unlikely, and that Long would be so deeply sedated that a seizure would not be felt. Christina Pacheco, the Florida Assistant Attorney General, put things more bluntly: "He's not entitled to a pain-free death. Michelle Simms certainly didn't have one in this case."

LISA NOLAND, WHO SURVIVED AN ATTACK AT THE HANDS OF SERIAL KILLER BOBBY JOE LONG, SPEAKS TO REPORTERS AFTER HIS EXECUTION MAY 23, 2019, IN STARKE, FLORIDA.

Long was sixty-five years old on May 23, 2019. He had no visitors that day, and no spiritual adviser stopped by for a final talk. His last meal, at 9:30 A.M., was a roast beef sandwich, bacon, French fries, and soda. He was described as "calm and quiet." He was pronounced dead at 6:55 P.M. in the death chamber at the prison in Starke. He had not said a word. Lisa McVey, the girl whose escape had led to Long's capture by police, sat in the front row. Her name was now Lisa Noland, and she was a deputy in the Hillsborough County Sheriff's Department. "I wanted to be the first person he saw," she said. More than two dozen people—many relatives of the victims—had crowded into the gallery to witness the end. Long was given a chance to offer some final words. He said nothing. The lethal drugs were administered. A reporter described his last minutes: "Soon, his breathing became disjointed, his mouth

appeared to start twisting and his breathing grew more labored. A state official pressed on his shoulders at 6:47 P.M. A minute later, Long appeared to stop breathing. His eyelids grew ashen, then his face turned white. A doctor started examining him at 6:55 P.M., and pronounced his official death a minute later."

When it was over, family members of the victims, as well as some survivors, gathered outside the prison. Noland gave an emotional statement dedicated to the memory of the victims. "I vow to carry on," she said, "and be their voice."

Later, in the television documentary, Long's ex-wife, Cindy, looked back on the decades of turmoil: "I feel like a total idiot because I didn't see any of it," she said. "I don't know if I was blind, but I never imagined in a million years that he was capable of doing the things that he has done. He was an animal, you know, and this was somebody that I loved." She has remarried and found peace with a "very supportive" husband.

## THE VICTIMS

- **Ngeun Thi "Peggy" Long.** Nineteen years old. Originally from California, she moved to Tampa in early 1984 and worked as an exotic dancer. She hoped to go back to school to study art and cinema. Her naked body, bound with a rope, was found under an overpass on East Bay Road. on May 13, 1984.

- **Michele Denise Simms.** Twenty-two years old. She had recently moved to Tampa from Fort Pierce, where she worked in a massage parlor. Her body—nude, stabbed, and tied up—was found on May 27, 1984, near Plant City. She had last been seen about 11 P.M. the night before. She had been raped, stabbed, and strangled.

- **Elizabeth Loudenback.** Twenty-two years old. She was a technician who lived with her parents in Tampa. Her body, raped and strangled,

was found on June 24, 1984, in an East Brandon orchard. She had last been seen alive about two weeks earlier.

- **Vicky Marie Elliott.** Twenty-one years old. She worked as a waitress at Ramada Inn in Tampa and was planning to return to Michigan to study to become a paramedic. She disappeared on September 7, 1984, and her body was found near Morris Bridge Road northeast of Tampa on November 16, 1984. She had been raped and stabbed.

- **Chanel Devon Williams.** Eighteen years old. She moved to Tampa in September, 1984 from Winter Haven, about fifty miles northeast of Tampa. Investigators said she had been working as a prostitute. She was last seen on Nebraska Avenue on September 30, and her nude body was found on October 7 along a road. She had been shot in the head and neck.

- **Karen Beth Dinsfriend.** Twenty-eight years old. She grew up in St. Petersburg and was working as a prostitute when she was last seen in the early morning hours on October 14, 1984. Her body was found later that day in an orange grove in Hillsborough. She had been strangled.

- **Kimberly Kyle Hopps.** Twenty-two years old. She lived in the Sulphur Springs area of Tampa and was last seen in mid-October 1984, with a group of prostitutes near Nebraska Avenue. Her body was found in a ditch along U.S. 301 north of Tampa on October 31, 1984.

- **Virginia Lee Johnson.** Eighteen years old. She had been born in Connecticut and was last seen near the Nebraska Avenue area in mid-October, and her skeletal remains were discovered on November 6, 1984, off the Morris Bridge Road in Pasco County.

- **Kim Marie Swann.** Twenty-one years old. She had worked as a dancer at a club on the Nebraska Avenue strip, but decided she wanted to change her life. She had moved into her parents' home with her year-old son and enrolled in a program to become a medical technician. She was last seen at a convenience store on November 11, 1984. The following day, her body was found under a highway overpass. She had been strangled.

# CHAPTER 5

# CHARLES NG
# AND LEONARD LAKE

California was a place of wide-open spaces and cultural revolution in the 1970s and 1980s, a magnet for the disaffected looking to begin a new and better life. The Interstate highway system, begun after World War II, provided a simple and direct way to travel from coast to coast, and hitchhiking was common. The invention of small, inexpensive transistor radios that ran on batteries and could be held in your hand or stashed in a pocket provided some entertainment along the way. And the music of the times was compelling. *California Dreamin'* by The Mamas and The Papas. *Hotel California* by the Eagles. *Good Vibrations, Surfin USA,* and

*California Girls* by the Beach Boys. The Troubadour, a nightclub in West Hollywood, was the coveted destination for emerging performers and their fans. Elton John kicked off his career there. Joni Mitchell, Carole King, James Taylor, Neil Diamond, and Linda Ronstadt were among the many who took the stage.

But California also attracted—or produced—some of the most depraved and malevolent criminals in the country's history. Juan Corona was convicted of murdering twenty-five farm workers and burying their bodies in Yuba City, north of Sacramento, in the early 1970s. Patrick Wayne Kearney—known as the "Trashbag Killer" or the "Freeway Killer"—picked up thirty-two men from 1975 to 1977 and dumped their bodies along highways from Los Angeles to Mexico. Vaughn Greenwood, the "Skid Row Slasher," was suspected of committing eleven murders in the Los Angeles area from 1964 to 1975, when he was tracked down and arrested. He was ultimately convicted of nine of the killings.

Perhaps the most spine-chilling event with its roots in California was the massacre of some nine hundred members of the People's Temple in 1978. It was a quasi-religious group—frequently called a cult—that ended up with its headquarters in San Francisco. Its leader, who called himself Rev. Jim Jones, had at times said he was the reincarnation of Jesus Christ. In 1977, when elected officials began asking questions about reports of financial and physical abuse by Jones, he abruptly moved his congregation to Guyana, on the northern coast of South America.

In November of 1978, Congressman Leo Ryan, who represented the district that included San Francisco, flew to Guyana with a group of journalists to investigate the conditions there. Ryan and four others were shot to death on an airstrip as they tried to flee the compound, called Jonestown. In the end, some of the cult members were shot to death, but Jones persuaded hundreds more to commit suicide by swallowing a cyanide-based fruit drink. More than 900 people, including babies and

children poisoned by their parents and others, died that day. Jones died from a bullet wound to the head, apparently self-inflicted.

About six years later, law enforcement and the news media were confronted with a hauntingly similar occurrence much closer to home. Leonard Thomas Lake, thirty-nine years old, was arrested outside a lumberyard in South San Francisco on June 2, 1985, after a shoplifting incident. Charles Chitat Ng, a twenty-four-year-old who had accompanied Lake, took a workshop vise from a display and walked out of the store without paying for it. He put it in the trunk of Lake's car. The store's manager, alerted by a customer, confronted Ng in the parking lot. When Lake walked outside and saw the commotion, he offered to pay the $75 price of the vise to settle the matter. But the police had been called; and as they waited, Ng quietly walked away. When the police arrived, they found a twenty-two-caliber gun, a silencer, and forty-five bullets in the trunk of Lake's car. Suspicious, they checked the car's registration and found it on a list of stolen vehicles. It had been repainted, and the license plates had been stolen. Lake's driver's license carried the name of a man who lived in San Diego, and the gun was registered in his name. Ultimately, the police determined that Lake was being sought on a federal gun-law violation. The car, it turned out, belonged to Paul Cosner, a car salesman from San Francisco who had disappeared seven months earlier after telling his sister that he was delivering a car "to that weird guy."

The weird guy was Lake, who, as he was being taken into custody outside the lumberyard, swallowed a cyanide-laced capsule. At the South San Francisco police station later that day, he asked permission to write a note to his ex-wife. In it, he asked for her forgiveness, and he forgave her. He concluded the note with the words "freedom is better than this." Then he collapsed. He died four days later, when he was taken off life support at a hospital. Cyanide-laced capsules similar to the one found during his autopsy were found in the glove compartment of the car he had been driving before his arrest.

Before the week was over, what seemed like echoes of Jonestown burst into the news in northern California and across the country. Investigators soon began finding skeletal remains in shallow graves on the grounds of a home in Wilseyville, about 150 miles northeast of San Francisco in Calaveras County. Lake's ex-wife, Claralyn Balazs, who was listed as the owner but no longer lived there, told police that Lake had stayed there off and on for years. The house, surrounded by a barbed-wire fence, was on two acres of rural land. An official told reporters that "a truck-load of bones" had been found on the property. A woman who had helped Lake waterproof a cinder-block bunker on the property said he had invited her to a meeting of a cult in San Francisco that practiced murder and believed in "life sacrifices." Investigators determined that the "bunker" had been used as a sex torture chamber. Numerous disturbing videotapes were found on the property.

Ng was nowhere to be found. A nationwide hunt was underway. "We absolutely must find him," San Francisco Police Chief Cornelius Murphy said at a news conference. Without Ng, he said, it would be impossible to determine exactly what had happened. Ng was believed to be heavily armed, and had made statements that he would not be taken alive.

Eleven days after the shoplifting arrest, a fifth body was found on the Wilseyville site, and officials said they had no idea how many more they might uncover. As the days wore on, the investigation became more difficult. It appeared that most of the bodies they discovered had been burned, then chopped into pieces with a tool similar to a pickax. John Van de Kamp, the California attorney general, lamented, "How can you identify someone when all you have to work with is a fingernail or something?" He confirmed that one of the five bodies that had been uncovered was that of a child.

A sixth body was found under two feet of dirt on June 18, and was quickly identified as Charles D. Gunnar, a thirty-six-year-old from

Morgan Hill, a city south of San Francisco in Santa Clara County. Gunnar was a former postman and drama coach who had met Lake when they served together in the Marine Corps. He had been the best man at Lake's wedding in 1981. As investigators spread out in the area around Lake's home, they learned that Lake had identified himself to neighbors as Charles D. Gunnar. In all, police had tentatively connected nineteen missing people and the three identified corpses to Lake and Ng.

On June 2, a month after the lumberyard incident, there was still no sign of Ng. Investigators learned that he had boarded a plane to Chicago that day under an assumed name. They suspected that he might be planning to cross the border into Canada. Interpol, Scotland Yard, and the Royal Canadian Mounted Police joined the search. The FBI warned that Ng was a particular danger to Asian-American men. He was known to have said that if he were ever on the run, he would kill an Asian man and take on his identity. "He has no qualms at all about killing you for his identification papers," an FBI supervisor in San Francisco warned.

On June 4, he checked into a hotel in Chicago, using a California identification card and a Social Security card with the name of an Asian man. Four days later, he was in Detroit. From there, he crossed the border into Windsor, Ontario, then took a bus to Toronto. He was seen shaving his sideburns and mustache in a public restroom there. Officials cautioned that Ng was a martial-arts expert and was also armed and dangerous. On July 7, five weeks after he'd disappeared from the lumberyard in California, Ng was arrested at a store in Calgary, Alberta, where he was attempting to shoplift some food. He fired two shots, and slightly injured a security guard. Calgary police arrived, and Ng was arrested. This time, he was carrying identification under his true name. Calgary officials kept him segregated from other inmates and under constant surveillance, concerned that he might attempt to commit suicide, as Lake had done. Ng was charged with the attempted murder of the security guard, unlawful use of a firearm, and theft.

By now, Ng's troubled background was clear. He was born in Hong Kong in 1961 to a well-to-do family, but had a troubled, rebellious childhood. For a time, he went to an upscale English boarding school, but did not do well there and returned home. He moved to California in 1978 on a student visa to attend the College of Notre Dame in Belmont, in the San Francisco Bay area, but soon dropped out. He had smashed his car into a utility pole and attempted to drive away, but was caught. He enlisted in the U.S. Marine Corps in 1979, to avoid paying restitution for the hit-and-run incident. Stationed in Hawaii, he was involved in the theft of grenade launchers and assault rifles from an armory. He then fled back to California and met Lake in 1981 through a classified ad in a survivalist magazine. Authorities traced Ng to Lake's home in Mendocino County and arrested both of them. Ng was sent to the prison at Fort Leavenworth, Kansas, but Lake posted bond and fled. Ng was released from prison in June 1984. He returned to California and reconnected with Lake, who was living in the Wilseyville cabin.

Lake, too, had a troubled background. He was born on October 29, 1945, in San Francisco, the first child of Gloria May Lake and Elgin Leonard Lake, a Seaman 1st Class in the United States Navy. His father was an alcoholic who abandoned the family several years later. When Leonard was six, his mother left him in the care of his stern grandparents and took his two younger siblings with her as she attempted to reconcile with his father. He attended Balboa High School in San Francisco, then joined the Marine Corps in 1964, when he was eighteen. In 1966, he was assigned to a ten-month tour in Vietnam. He returned home, married a young woman, and was promoted to staff sergeant. He returned to Vietnam and worked as an aviation technician in Da Nang, but was never involved in combat. He worked long, difficult shifts, frequently in pounding rain, and psychiatric problems emerged. His wife, he learned, was working as an exotic dancer in a San Francisco bar. A doctor's notes from the time said he had climbed a twenty-five-meter tower in high

winds to combat unreal feelings. He told doctors that he had fantasies about being surrounded by enemy soldiers and killing them all with his machine gun. He spent two years at the hospital at Camp Pendleton near San Diego before being discharged from the Marine Corps in 1971. A year later, his wife divorced him.

Lake moved to a ranch in northern California for a time. It was a kind of commune where members chanted while celebrating the summer solstice and fall equinox. In 1980, he was convicted of stealing building materials and was put on one year's probation. The ranch members asked him to leave. He met Claralyn "Cricket" Balazs, a teacher's aide, at a Renaissance fair, and they married in 1981. She divorced him the following year and moved away. He remained at the Wilseyville site, where he accumulated weapons, practiced survivalism, and built the bunker to protect himself from nuclear attacks. Ng eventually made his way there.

With Lake dead and Ng securely in custody in July 1985, the American and Canadian legal systems now took center stage. The deaths or disappearances of at least twenty-two people in California were at issue. In Canada, Ng was charged only with attempted murder, shoplifting, and a firearms violation. The charges in the United States were far more consequential. If convicted, Ng would surely face the death penalty. Canada had no death penalty, and a century-old agreement between Canada and the United States barred Canadian judges from ordering the extradition of anyone who might be subject to execution in the United States. Beyond the death-penalty issue, California officials needed Ng's help if they were ever to sort out what actually had happened at the Wilseyville site. During five hours of questioning on July 7 by Canadian authorities and San Francisco police, Ng offered little help. "There is nothing we didn't expect," Lt. George Kowalski, the San Francisco homicide chief said. "He's blaming the other guy, the dead guy."

Meanwhile, investigators in California continued to unearth bodies, body parts, and other evidence on the Wilseyville property. They also found bloody tools and videotapes of sexual torture. One videotape showed Ng threatening a twenty-one-year-old neighbor with a knife. She had since disappeared, and her last paycheck was found on the property. By then, the remains of eleven people and forty pounds of charred human bone fragments had been found. Investigators searching an eight-square-mile area around the site unearthed the body of Robin Scott Stapley, a twenty-six-year-old, and Lonnie Bond, a twenty-seven-year-old, from a shallow grave about a half-mile from the property. Stapley was the founder of the San Diego branch of the Guardian Angels, a private group of volunteers who patrolled high-crime areas. Their bodies, stuffed into sleeping bags and bound together with tape, had been there from three to six months. Bond, Brenda O'Connor, and their two-year-old son, Lonnie Jr., had been living in a house near Lake's property, along with Stapley, who had a room there. All four had been missing for months.

By the beginning of August 1985, the Calaveras County authorities had ended the investigation of Lake's property. In addition to the unearthed bodies, they had accumulated some two thousand bits of evidence, including forty-five charred and hacked human bones. In October, Ng was charged with eight murders in Calaveras County and one in San Francisco. Authorities believed that Ng and Lake had killed at least twenty-two people, but some of the bodies were so badly mutilated that they would never be identified. They had been hacked to pieces, burned, buried, or scattered around the rural area.

By the end of 1985, a jury in Alberta, Canada, had convicted Ng of robbery and assault in the shoplifting incident that had led to his arrest the previous July. But the jurors acquitted him of the attempted murder charge. His lawyer had argued that the gun went off accidently and Ng had not intended to shoot the security guard, who was not seriously

injured. Ng was sentenced to two years in prison for the assault charge, eighteen months for robbery, and one year for a weapons charge. The sentences, totaling four years and six months, were to be served consecutively. Ng served that time, and more, while Canada and the State of California battled over his extradition.

Angry parents of some of the victims went to Canada to urge officials there to send Ng back to California to stand trial for the murders. At a hearing in Edmonton in mid-November 1988, Dwight and Lola Stapley were among a group of Americans who urged the court to extradite Ng back to California to stand trial. The body of their son Robin, the Guardian Angels group founder, was among those found on the Wilseyville site. "We lost our youngest son, and that grief will never be alleviated," Lola Stapley, tears in her eyes, said outside a court in Edmonton. The issue before the court was whether there was sufficient evidence to send Ng back to California, where he might be sentenced to death.

The last time the Stapleys heard from their son, he said he was going camping in Yosemite National Park to "clear his head" before going back to school at San Diego State University, where he was studying for a master's degree in education. They considered themselves fortunate that his body was one of the few that were intact. He had been shot in the head three times. Soon they found that his camper truck was missing and that his apartment had been looted. A gun collection that had been mounted on the wall was gone. The Stapleys said they were in favor of the death penalty.

American and Canadian victims' rights groups sent thousands of letters to Canadian officials demanding that Ng be returned to the United States for trial. California Governor George Deukmejian, in a radio address on November 12, 1988, said he respected the sovereignty of the Canadian judicial system. "I only ask that officials in California

be given an opportunity to meet the burden of proof imposed by law," he said. "A decent respect for human life and for the right of the survivors of Ng's alleged victims compels that he be sent here without delay to answer the charges against him." On November 29, a Canadian judge ruled that there was enough evidence to justify Ng's extradition. Ng, his hands chained to his waist, sat silently in the courtroom. His lawyer was given twenty-three days to appeal. In Sacramento, Deukmejian said he was pleased by the decision, but added "My satisfaction is tempered by the fact that it will be months, if not years, before Charles Ng will be returned to face justice."

Appeals and lengthy legal arguments followed. One compelling reason for returning Ng to the United States, authorities said, was that allowing him to remain in Canada would be creating a legal shelter for American murderers who wanted to avoid execution. Ng completed his Canadian sentence in June 1990, but it wasn't until September 26, 1991, that Canadian officials agreed to return him to California, where, by then, he faced twelve murder charges and the possibility of execution. Within hours of the four-to-three decision by the Canadian Supreme Court, Ng, handcuffed and shackled, was put on a plane in Prince Albert, Saskatchewan, and flown to McClellan Air Force Base in Sacramento, then taken to an isolation ward at Folsom Prison, about twenty miles away.

Ng, awaiting trial on twelve murder charges, was caught hiding what authorities called "small weapons or escape paraphernalia" in his cell and a visiting booth at Folsom in October of 1992. During courtroom appearances, he was shackled in wrist and ankle chains and flanked by two guards. By then, discussions had begun about a change of venue, moving the trial to Orange County in southern California, where there had been far less publicity about the case. After much legal wrangling about the expected cost of the trial—at least several million dollars—it got underway in the Orange County city of Santa Ana on October 26,

1998, thirteen years after Ng fled to Canada and was arrested. So much time had passed that Ng, now thirty-seven years old, was no longer being called a "mass murderer." Instead, he was a "serial killer," a more up-to-date classification. He was charged with killing seven men, three women, and two babies. Prosecutors opened with a videotape of Ng cutting away the clothes of a woman who was bound up.

After more than four weeks of testimony by dozens of witnesses and the presentation of torture videos, the prosecution rested. Then it was time for the defense. Ng's lawyer, William Kelley, blamed the killings on Lake. "The defense in this case is simple," Kelley said. "Leonard Lake was motivated by his hatred for women, and he had a plan for murder. . . . Leonard Lake was killing women before Charles Ng was ever on the scene." The jury was shown a twenty-minute videotape of a monologue by Lake sitting in an easy chair and drinking coffee: "Life, as I am living it, is boring. I want to be able to use a woman whenever and however I want. Then lock her up." In another video shown to the jury, two women were manacled and tormented by Lake. Ng was also there. "If you don't go along with us," Lake said, "we'll probably take you into the bed, tie you down, rape you, shoot you, and bury you." In another, Lake cut the blouse and bra off a woman while she pleaded for her baby and said "He can't live without me." Lake responded "He's gonna learn." Against the strong advice of his lawyers, Ng took the witness stand. He denied that he had participated in any of the killings, but said he had helped to bury two bodies. Under tough questioning by prosecutors, he admitted that he had participated in sado-masochistic games.

The jurors—nine women and three men—deliberated for two weeks before returning their verdict on February 25, 1999, four months after the trial began. They found Ng guilty of eleven murders, but they were split seven to five on the murder of Paul Cosner, the San Francisco car dealer.

Next came the sentencing phase. They would have to decide whether to recommend the death penalty. Ng's father, Charles, flew in from Hong Kong, and pleaded for his son in halting English. He said he blamed himself, and had beaten Charles severely when he was a child. On May 3, the jury voted that Ng should be executed. On June 30, 1999, Orange County Superior Court Judge John J. Ryan sentenced Ng to death by lethal injection. Onlookers in the crowded courtroom burst into applause. The trial was estimated to have cost taxpayers more than $13 million.

More than two decades later, Ng remains on death row at San Quentin. He is among more than seven hundred death-row inmates in California, where the death penalty was suspended in 2019 by Governor Gavin Newsom. "Our death penalty, by any measure, has been a failure," Newsom said. "It has discriminated against defendants who are mentally ill, black and brown, or cannot afford expensive legal representation. It has provided no public safety benefit or value as a deterrent. It has wasted billions of taxpayer dollars. But most of all, the death penalty is absolute, irreversible, and irreparable in the event of human error."

## THE VICTIMS

- **Harvey Dubs.** Twenty-nine years old. And **Deborah Dubs**, thirty-three years old, and their son **Sean**, sixteen months old. Items from their home in San Francisco were found at the Wilseyville site.

- **Jeff Gerald.** Twenty-five years old, of San Francisco. He worked with Ng as a mover and disappeared after telling a friend he was going to help Ng move.

- **Kathleen E. Allen.** Eighteen years old, of San Jose. She was seen in a video at Lake's home. Her last paycheck was sent to a location near Lake's home.

- **Michael S. Carroll.** Twenty-three years old, of Milpitas. Kathleen Allen's boyfriend; his driver's license was found at Lake's cabin.

- **Lonnie Bond, Brenda O'Connor,** and their two-year-old child, **Lonnie Jr**. They lived on a property next to Lake's.

- **Robin Scott Stapley.** Twenty-six years old. A founder of the Guardian Angels group in San Francisco.

# CHAPTER 6

# RICHARD RAMIREZ

Murder-weary residents of California, still reeling from the horrors of Leonard Lake and Charles Ng, were confronting another frightening mystery in the summer of 1985. At least sixteen people, nearly all in southern California, had been shot, bludgeoned, or beaten to death over the previous year and a half. Some of the female victims had been raped. The killer was known by several nicknames in the news media, but was most frequently called the Night Stalker. Law-enforcement officials were

baffled. Fifty detectives from departments around the state formed a task force to share information, including sketches of the attacker drawn with the help of witnesses and live victims.

Perhaps the most valuable witness was James Romero, a thirteen-year-old boy who lived with his parents and sister in Mission Viejo, a city in Orange County, south of Los Angeles. In late August, the family returned home from a camping vacation in Mexico, just a few miles south of the California border. In the middle of the night, James left his bedroom to get a pillow he had left in the camper. He returned through the garage and realized that someone was outside and seemed to be looking for him. Terrified, James ran into the kitchen, then to a window at the front of the house. He saw a strange man there. James sneaked back out a side door and got a look at the man's car. It was an orange Toyota hatchback with a chrome roof rack. The man got in the car, drove off, made a U-turn, got a look at James, then sped away. James got a partial license plate number and quickly wrote it down: 482 T. His family, awakened by the ruckus, called 911.

A week later, on Friday, August 30, Los Angeles County Sheriff Sherman Block called a late-night news conference to announce that the so-called Night Stalker had been identified. Investigators had found an old mug shot that closely resembled the composite drawings that had been circulating based on the descriptions of victims who had survived the Night Stalker's attacks. His name was Richard Ramirez. He was a twenty-five-year-old ex-convict and drifter originally from El Paso, Texas. His most distinctive feature was rotting teeth. Authorities released the mug shot and asked for the public's help. Officials didn't mention it at the time, but James Romero's help had been a key. A car that closely resembled the one James described had been towed from a parking lot. It was orange, had a chrome roof rack, and had a license plate with the number 482 RTS. The fingerprints had been wiped—except for one on top of the steering wheel. They fed the print into a database. It belonged to Richard Ramirez.

On Saturday, August 31—within twelve hours of the news conference—Ramirez was in police custody. He had been chased and clubbed by angry residents in East Los Angeles after he attacked a woman and tried to steal a car. Suspecting that he was the Night Stalker, they held him until the police arrived.

Who was Richard Ramirez? His background quickly became clear. He had been living in a series of Skid Row hotels, and had been cited by police about a week before his arrest for driving a motorcycle without a license. He was convicted of auto theft and spent five months in jail in 1983. He frequently used aliases and spent thirty-six days in the Los Angeles County jail in 1984. The Night Stalker attacks began after he was released. Born in El Paso, Texas, on February 28, 1960, he was the youngest of five children in a working-class Roman Catholic family that frequently attended church. They lived in a small white stucco house, and his parents were strict. But as a young boy and teenager, he was a loner and a troublemaker. He began sniffing glue in eighth grade, smoked marijuana in high school, and then moved on to injecting cocaine. He enjoyed junk food and began shoplifting and stealing from his friends. He grew tall and skinny, and his love of candy—especially chocolate—contributed to his rotting and discolored teeth.

Ramirez dropped out of school in 1977, after his seventeenth birthday, having not yet completed the requirements of his freshman year. He was arrested several times on marijuana-related charges, but his only conviction came in 1982, when he pleaded guilty in return for a fifty-day suspended sentence and a fine of one hundred fifteen dollars. By then, he had begun traveling between El Paso and the San Francisco Bay area. He spent the summer of 1980 there, and remained there until 1983. Then he began injecting cocaine, moved to Los Angeles, and became fascinated with Satanism. Investigators had found satanic symbols scrawled on the walls in the homes of Night Stalker victims.

By the end of September 1985, about a month after his final arrest, the breadth of his criminal actions was clear. He was charged with fourteen murders, five attempted murders, nineteen burglaries, six robberies, seven rapes, five forcible oral copulations, seven sodomies, three lewd acts on children, and two kidnappings. The alleged crimes had begun in June 1984. Ramirez was not present in the courtroom on September 27, when the charges were formally read. Instead, audio of the session was piped into his holding cell near the courtroom. A loud disturbance from the holding cell could be heard in the courtroom. Ramirez also faced a range of charges in San Francisco, where he was wanted for the murder of Peter Pan, a sixty-year-old man, and his wife, Barbara.

By the end of October, it was clear that the legal wrangling over the case would be complex for the lawyers and judges involved, and deeply frustrating for the victims and their families. When Ramirez finally

"NIGHT STALKER" DEFENDANT RICHARD RAMIREZ DISPLAYS A PENTAGRAM SYMBOL ON HIS HAND INSIDE A LOS ANGELES COURTROOM THURSDAY, OCTOBER 24, 1985.

entered a not-guilty plea in Los Angeles County on October 24, he had already been represented by five lawyers. He was brought into the courtroom wearing leg irons and manacles. He flashed the palm of his left hand to show a pentagram, a symbol of the devil. He shouted "Hail Satan" as he was led out. In December, he was brought into court in Orange County, where he was charged with attempted murder and rape for an attack on a couple in their home in Mission Viejo three months earlier. That case was put on hold until the Los Angeles cases were finished.

In the spring of 1986, during nine weeks of preliminary hearings, the public learned the gruesome details of many of the alleged crimes. The purpose of the hearings was to establish whether the prosecutors had enough evidence to hold Ramirez for trial on the murder charges, which could lead to a death sentence. It was clear that he had some fans. A young woman named Bernadette, who had never met him, showed up in the courtroom wearing a sticker that said "I Love Your Smile."

Bernadette was a stark contrast to the victims who took the witness stand. A twenty-nine-year-old woman wept uncontrollably as she described how Ramirez had shot and killed her husband, then raped her and sexually assaulted their eight-year-old son. She had been asleep in the living room when Ramirez entered their house in Sun Valley. "He just pointed the gun on my head. . . . He just said 'Bitch, shut up.'" He walked away, she heard a gunshot, then he returned and told her he had just killed her husband. "If you don't do what I tell you," he said, "I'll kill your children." Eventually, he raped her on the bedroom floor next to her dead husband's body. He took breaks to attack her son, she said, and went into the kitchen to sip apple juice between attacks. On May 6, 1986, Judge James F. Nelson ordered that there was sufficient evidence for Ramirez to be tried for the crimes, and possibly face a death sentence.

There had been many closed sessions during the weeks of pretrial hearings. Two days after they ended, the judge unsealed the records, and a fuller, more frightening picture of Ramirez and his deeds became

public. A prison guard had testified that Ramirez admitted he had killed about twenty people in California, and said "I love to watch people die." Ramirez also told the guard "One time I told this lady to give me all her money. She said no. So I cut her and pulled her eyes out. I would do someone in and then take a camera and set the timer so I could sit them up next to me and take our picture together." The victim was Maxine Zazzara, a forty-four-year-old woman from Whittier, west of Los Angeles. Ramirez gazed around the courtroom and grinned as the testimony was read.

There would be two more years of pretrial motions and activity before jury selection began. Given the mountains of evidence and Ramirez's own statements, the only defense seemed to be not guilty by reason of insanity. But Ramirez rejected that. The first trial witness took the stand on January 30, 1989, nearly three and a half years after his arrest. Ramirez wore black sunglasses in court and refused to take them off. At one point, his father took the witness stand and testified that his son had been with him in Texas when two of the attacks occurred. Ramirez refused to enter the courtroom when the jury returned its verdict on September 20, 1989. He was convicted of thirteen murders and thirty other felonies. On October 4, the jurors voted to recommend the death penalty.

Superior Court Judge Michael Tynan held a session on November 7, 1989, to announce his decision. This time, Ramirez made a dramatic appearance in the courtroom. "You don't understand me," he said. "You are not expected to. You are not capable of it. I am beyond your experience." He went on: "I don't even know why I'm wasting my breath, but what the hell. For what has been said of my life, there have been lies in the past and there will be lies in the future. I don't believe in the hypocritical, moralistic dogma of this so-called civilized society.... You maggots make me sick. Hypocrites one and all. We are all expendable for a cause. No one knows better than those who kill for policy, clandestinely or openly as to the governments of the world, which kill in the name of God and

country." He added "I am beyond good and evil. I will be avenged. Luther dwells in us all. That's it."

Then it was Judge Tynan's turn. Ramirez, he said, had displayed "cruelty, callousness, and viciousness beyond any human understanding." The gouging out of the eyes of one victim was "obscene," he said, and he noted that Ramirez had left a pentagram—a Satanic symbol—at the scene of another murder. He sentenced Ramirez to death, which, at the time, meant in California's gas chamber. Years of appeals would follow. A number of notorious murderers had been sentenced to death in California, but none of the executions had been carried out for more than a quarter of a century. Ramirez displayed little emotion. When he was led out of the courtroom, he fussed with his long hair, glanced at the reflecting glass in a long hallway, and smiled.

On the following day, prosecutors in Orange County dropped the rape and attempted murder charges pending there against Ramirez. They said that it was no longer necessary to proceed, and they did not want to put the victims through the ordeal of testifying at a trial. Inez Erickson had been raped in her Mission Viejo home on August 24, 1985. Bill Carns, her fiancé, was shot three times in the head, but survived. Erickson had testified against Ramirez at a preliminary hearing two years earlier. She said Ramirez told her he was the Night Stalker, and made her say that she loved Satan. Carns had no memory of the incident because of his severe brain injury.

Ramirez still faced murder charges in San Francisco, and was transferred there in December 1989. He was accused of killing Peter and Barbara Pan in their home on August 17, 1985. Pretrial sessions and hearings went on for months—and years. During that time, hundreds of people, mostly women, visited him in the county jail. In 1991, jail officials cracked down and limited him to visits on just one day per month. He was never tried on the charges pending in San Francisco, and was ultimately transferred to San Quentin State Prison.

A frequent visitor over the years was Doreen Lioy, a magazine editor and a Roman Catholic, who became engaged to marry Ramirez, a Satanist. They were finally allowed to touch each other in the summer of 1996. "It was one of those defining moments," she told a reporter. "I sort of fell into his arms softly and, yes, gently." Her love for Ramirez began on the night before he was arrested in 1985. She was watching television that night when police broke into the broadcast to show a photograph of Ramirez, who they had finally identified. "They showed his mug shot in the middle of *Dallas*, and I saw something in his eyes. Something that captivated me." She sent him a birthday card, wrote him letters, and began to visit him. They married on October 3, 1996, at San Quentin, where Ramirez was on death row.

Ramirez died of lymphoma on June 7, 2013, at the age of fifty-three. He had spent twenty-three years on death row, and was the fifty-ninth California inmate to die while awaiting execution.

## THE VICTIMS

- **Jennie Vincow.** Seventy-nine years old. She was nearly decapitated and stabbed to death in her bed in her apartment in the Eagle Rock section of Los Angeles on June 27, 1984.

- **Dayle Yoshie Okazaki.** Thirty-four years old. She died after she was shot in the forehead in her condominium in Rosemead on March 17, 1985. Dayle's roommate, Maria Hernandez, twenty-four years old, was also shot, but survived.

- **Tsai-Lian Yu.** Thirty years old. She died after she was pulled out of her car in Monterey Park and shot twice on March 17, 1985.

- **Vincent Zazzara.** Sixty-four years old. And **Maxine Zazzara**. Forty-four years old. Vincent was beaten to death, and his wife Maxine

was stabbed to death, in their home in Whittier on March 27, 1985. Ramirez gouged out Maxine's eyes after he killed her.

- **Bill Doi.** Sixty-five years old. He was shot to death in his home in Monterey Park on May 14, 1985.

- **Mabel Bell.** Eighty-three years old. She died, and her eighty-one-year-old sister Florence was injured when they were bound and bludgeoned at their home in Monrovia on May 29, 1985.

- **Mary Louise Cannon.** Seventy-seven years old. She was stabbed to death in her home in Arcadia on July 2, 1985.

- **Joyce Lucille Nelson.** Sixty-one years old. She was beaten to death at her home in Monterey Park on July 7, 1985.

- **Maxon Kneiding.** Sixty-eight years old. And **Lela Kneiding**, sixty-six years old. The husband and wife were shot to death in their home in Glendale on July 20, 1985.

- **Chainarong Khovananth.** Thirty-two years old. He was shot to death in his home in Sun Valley on July 20, 1985.

- **Elyas Abowath.** Thirty-one years old. He was shot to death in his home in Diamond Bar on August 8, 1985.

# CHAPTER 7
# JOSEPH JAMES DEANGELO

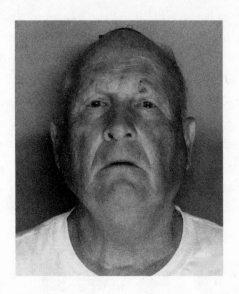

By the time the mysterious man attacked a woman in her home northeast of Sacramento on December 2, 1977, he had earned himself a menacing nickname: the "East Area Rapist." The incident began just before midnight in the Foothill Farms area. The woman, in her thirties, was asleep in her bed. She was awakened by a flashlight shining in her eyes and was taken to another room, where she was tied up. Investigators were unsure how he had gotten into the house, but they believed that he was scared off when the woman began crying and a group of teenagers outside—unaware of what was happening—became noisy. This time it turned out to be an attempted rape.

The East Area Rapist had been scared off a few times before. In all, he had entered the homes of twenty-eight women and teenagers in the suburbs east of Sacramento over the previous eighteen months, and raped nearly all of them. One attack in Stockton, about sixty miles to the south, appeared to be connected. By the summer of 1978, the number of victims had reached forty-four, including attacks in Stockton, Davis, and the San Francisco Bay area. Police in Visalia, about two hundred miles to the south, had begun to suspect that the East Area Rapist was the same man known to them as "The Ransacker." He was believed to have burglarized and ransacked more than one hundred twenty-five homes there in the early 1970s. He was also the prime suspect in the murder of a man who tried to stop him from abducting his teenage daughter.

By the summer of 1983, it had been five years since the East Area Rapist abruptly stopped. The mysterious man had been called the East Bay Rapist, the Original Night Stalker, and the Diamond Knot, a reference to the way he tied up some of the victims. The public remained

AN UNDATED PHOTO RELEASED BY THE FBI SHOWS ARTIST RENDERINGS OF A SERIAL KILLER AND RAPIST, ALSO KNOWN AS THE "EAST AREA RAPIST," THE "ORIGINAL NIGHT STALKER," AND LATER THE "GOLDEN STATE KILLER," FROM 1976 TO 1986.

fearful and wary. Law-enforcement officials persevered, but hit mostly dead ends. Sergeant Jim Bevins, who headed the investigation for the Sacramento County Sheriff's Office, expressed his frustration in an interview with the McClatchy News Service. "I want him very badly," he said. "I've got six years invested, and I'd hate to think it was all for nothing."

Although they didn't have a suspect, they had come up with a kind of profile of his actions, which did not appear to be random. At first, he broke into homes where no men were present. Later, he sought out married couples. In those cases, he awakened the couple by shining a flashlight into their faces. Armed with a gun or a knife, he forced the women to tie up their husbands so they could be forced to watch as he raped their wives. He always wore a ski mask to hide his face. Because of the five-year hiatus, Bevins speculated that the rapist might be dead or in jail.

For Michelle McNamara, the case became an obsession that evolved over the years. She was in her mid-thirties in 2006 when she launched a website called "True Crime Diary," a place for mystery buffs to delve into unsolved murder cases. She described herself as "something of a DIY detective" and "stay-at-home mom" who lived in Los Angeles with her husband, the comedian Patton Oswalt. By 2013, her website had developed a following of eight thousand people who shared her interest, offered their thoughts, and even came up with some helpful tips. The East Area Rapist seemed to have disappeared. His last known rape had been on July 6, 1979. Almost three months later, things went seriously wrong for him. At about 2 A.M. on October 1, he entered a house near Santa Barbara in southern California and attacked the couple living there. He tied the man to the bed in the bedroom, blindfolded the woman, bound her feet and hands, and placed her facedown in the living room. He moved to the kitchen, and she could hear him saying, "I'll kill 'em, I'll kill 'em, I'll kill 'em." She was able to free herself and run out the front door screaming for help. Her partner was able to hop into the backyard and hide behind an orange tree.

The attacker fled, but a witness alerted by the shouting was able to describe him to the police. He was a lean man who rode away quickly on a silver Nishiki ten-speed bicycle. After that night, the East Area Rapist never left a live victim. Three months later, and about a half-mile to the south, he seemed to strike again. The victims were Robert Offerman, a forty-four-year-old osteopath, and Debra Manning, a thirty-five-year-old psychologist. They had been shot to death. The evidence pointed to the modus operandi of the East Area Rapist. There were pry marks on the doors and windows. Twine was used to tie up the victims. Size-nine tennis shoe impressions matched those found outside the windows at the scenes of earlier attacks.

McNamara credited her True Crime Diary followers with helping to keep the case active by searching for information and clues as the Internet came alive in the decades after the killings stopped. In 2013, she decided that the flagging public interest in the case might be reawakened if the killer had a chilling nickname. After DNA tests in 2001 showed that the East Area Rapist was also the murderer they were hunting, law-enforcement agencies began referring to him as "EAR/ONS," a combination of East Area Rapist and Original Night Stalker. The simpler "Night Stalker" nickname had already been used for Richard Ramirez, the Satan-worshipping serial killer who'd terrified California in the mid-1980s.

So McNamara came up with a nickname that stuck: the Golden State Killer. She announced it in a lengthy article published in *Los Angeles* magazine in 2013. "The world has changed for the Golden State Killer in ways he could never have predicted," she wrote. "But if he's alive, he's growing old in a world where every day, more and more windows are opening around him—on computers, in smart phones, in DNA labs. He couldn't have predicted that one day we'd be able to identify people by a single skin cell." McNamara died three years later, apparently from a combination of prescription drugs and an undiagnosed heart condition. Her husband found her unresponsive in her bed on the morning

of April 21, 2016. Oswalt went on with her research and eventually completed her book about the case, called *I'll Be Gone in the Dark*. It would be two more years before the mystery was solved.

The Golden State Killer was ultimately tracked down by dogged investigators who never gave up the search. They finally identified him using a tool that could only be imagined decades earlier when he started his rape and murder sprees—DNA. Paul Holes, an investigator who specialized in the growing field of DNA evidence, played a key role. He worked for the district attorney's office in Contra Costa County, just southwest of Sacramento County. He located an evidence kit that had been stored in a freezer since the 1980 rape and murder of Charlene Smith and the murder of her husband, Lyman. Over the following decades, online services had emerged that enabled people to send in samples of their DNA so that it could be analyzed to find matches to unknown relatives. Holes sent in a sample from the Golden State Killer case. The result was at least a thousand connections to the killer. Some time-consuming research whittled down the connections to about twenty matches that might lead to distant relatives. Many of them would have died decades earlier, so some more tedious research was needed—yearbooks, gravesite locators, and eventually LexisNexis.

Eventually, they eliminated all but one—Joseph James DeAngelo. He was a seventy-two-year-old living quietly in retirement with a daughter and granddaughter in the small town of Citrus Heights. He had worked as a police officer from 1973 to 1976 in Exeter, a town about 200 miles south of Sacramento, and again as an officer in the town of Auburn, about twenty miles northwest of Sacramento. He worked there from 1976 to 1979. Some of the rapes and murders occurred during those years. He was fired from the job in Auburn in 1979 after he was charged with shoplifting a can of dog repellent and a hammer from a local store. He later went to work at a distribution center for the Save Mart chain, and retired in 2017 after twenty-seven years there.

The Contra Costa team, working with Sacramento County investigators, followed DeAngelo and were able to pick up an item he discarded. It contained his DNA. It matched samples of the killer's DNA. They watched his movements and waited. When he left his house on April 24, 2018, they quickly arrested him and took him to the Sacramento County Jail. It had been thirty-two years since the Golden State Killer's last murder, and more than four decades since his first.

Finally the details of his life were becoming clear. He was born in the town of Bath in eastern New York, about a hundred miles from Buffalo. He graduated from Folsom High School near Sacramento in 1964, then enlisted in the U.S. Navy and was sent to Vietnam. He won several military awards, including a Bronze Star. He returned to California and got an associate's degree in political science from Sierra College and a bachelor's degree in criminal justice from Sacramento State University. During his years at the Visalia Police Department, the so-called "Visalia Ransacker" burglarized more than eighty-five homes and killed a journalism professor at the College of the Sequoias. DeAngelo married Sharon Marie Huddle in 1973. They had three children, then ultimately divorced. Officials believed that DeAngelo committed his first rape after he moved to the Auburn Police Department in 1976.

The public got its first view of the Golden State Killer on the afternoon of April 27, 2018, when he was rolled into a courtroom in Sacramento in an orange jumpsuit, with his wrists shackled to his wheelchair. The judge read out the eight murder charges, and DeAngelo answered his questions in a thin, raspy voice. Then he was wheeled away. He was kept in isolation in a Sacramento County Jail cell for his own protection. Officials feared that he might be a target because of his notoriety, as well as the brutality of the crimes he was accused of committing.

By August 2018, the authorities agreed to try all the cases from around the state in Sacramento County. In addition to the rape charges, DeAngelo faced thirteen murder and kidnapping charges, with "special

circumstances" that could lead to the death penalty. Public defenders were appointed to handle the enormously complex and time-consuming case. In March 2020, they filed a motion with the court saying that DeAngelo, who was by then seventy-four years old, would be willing to plead guilty to all the charges and serve a life sentence if the prosecutors dropped their request for the death penalty. The prosecutors stood firm.

By the summer of 2020, the situation had changed dramatically for a reason no one could have predicted—the COVID-19 epidemic that was sweeping the country. The victims and witnesses in the case were, for the most part, elderly, and suffering from health conditions that would make it unsafe for them to testify in open court. In June, prosecutors in the six counties involved issued a joint statement saying that they had "a moral and ethical responsibility to consider any offer from the defense, given the massive scope of the case, the advanced age of many of the victims and witnesses, and our inherent obligations to the victims."

The Sacramento County District Attorney, Anne Marie Schubert, said "He is the real-life version of Hannibal Lecter," a reference to the psychopathic killer in the movie *The Silence of the Lambs*. She described DeAngelo as "a cruel, intelligent, sadistic serial killer," and a "sociopath" who is a "master manipulator." Todd Spitzer, the Orange County District Attorney, said "What's so frustrating is that if anyone is the poster child for the death penalty, it's DeAngelo." Spitzer said that the only reason he agreed to the deal was that he had "spoken to all the family members of the four Orange County murder victims and they agreed this was the best thing." Another reason the prosecutors agreed to the deal was that DeAngelo, seventy-four years old and in poor health, was unlikely to live through the long death-penalty appeal process. The principal cause of death on California's death row was old age.

Others thought DeAngelo was faking poor health. He sat hunched in a wheelchair in June when he quietly uttered "guilty" as the thirteen murder charges were read. He also admitted to committing fifty rapes.

Prosecutors wanted to play jailhouse recordings that showed a much fitter DeAngelo, but Sacramento County Superior Court Judge Michael Bowman denied the request. "Whether or not he can stand up on his bunk or not stand up on his bunk is of little relevance," Bowman said. In return for his guilty pleas, DeAngelo was given eleven consecutive life sentences, and prosecutors agreed not to seek the death penalty.

Over three days in August 2020, DeAngelo's victims were given their opportunity to confront him and to tell the court how he had affected their lives. His first rape victim, attacked in 1976, was unable to attend, but her sister, choking back sobs, read her statement to the court: "I went to bed . . . not knowing my life would change. The roles have now been reversed. He deserves to spend the rest of his miserable life in prison. I am not what happened to me. I am what I choose to become."

A woman who was raped in 1976 when she was fifteen years old confronted DeAngelo: "Do you feel any remorse for what you did to me? For the people whose lives you sadistically cut short or for the years of pain to your victims and their families? Do you finally feel humiliated?"

DeAngelo had displayed little reaction over the three days. He sat stoically in a wheelchair and stared straight ahead. His face was partially covered by a white mask because of the COVID-19 epidemic. By the end of the three days, forty-five victims and relatives had testified about the pain DeAngelo had caused. At the end, DeAngelo rose from his wheelchair and removed his mask. In a halting voice, he said "I have listened to all of your statements, each one of them, and I am truly sorry to everyone I have hurt. Thank you, Your Honor."

Then it was Judge Bowman's turn. He spoke directly to DeAngelo. "I was moved by their courage, their grace, their strength, all qualities you clearly lack." And, Bowman said, he "could not help but wonder, what are you thinking? Are you capable of comprehending the pain and anguish you have caused?" Bowman imposed the eleven life sentences, to be served consecutively, with no chance of parole. DeAngelo, he said,

would "ultimately meet his death" behind the walls of a state prison. "The defendant deserves no mercy," he said. The courtroom applauded.

## THE VICTIMS

- **Keith Harrington.** Twenty-four years old. And his wife, **Patty Harrington**. Twenty-seven years old. The newlyweds were bludgeoned to death at their home in Laguna Niguel, an Orange County town about fifty miles southeast of Los Angeles. Their bodies were found on August 21, 1975.

- **Claude Snelling.** Forty-five years old. He was shot to death on September 11, 1975, outside his home in Visalia, in Tulare County, about halfway between Sacramento and Los Angeles. He was awakened by some commotion at about 2 A.M. and confronted a masked man outside the door trying to kidnap his daughter. The man shot and killed Snelling, then ran. Snelling was a journalism professor at the College of the Sequoias.

- **Brian Maggiore.** Twenty-one years old. And his wife, **Katie Maggiore**. Twenty years old. They were walking their dog at about 9 P.M. on February 2, 1978, near their home in the Rancho Cordova area northeast of Sacramento when they encountered DeAngelo. He shot them in the back as they tried to get away.

- **Robert Offerman.** Forty-four years old. And **Debra Manning**. Thirty-five years old. Offerman, an osteopath, and Manning, a psychiatrist, were tied up in their home in Goleta, in Santa Barbara County, on December 30, 1977, and shot and killed at about 3 A.M.

- **Lyman Smith.** Forty-three years old. And his wife, **Charlene Smith**. Thirty-three years old. Lyman, a lawyer, and Charlene, an interior

decorator, were bound and bludgeoned in their home in Ventura, northwest of Los Angeles in Ventura County, on March 13, 1980.

- **Manuela Mitthuhn.** Twenty-eight years old. Her husband was in the hospital, and she was alone in their home in Irvine, in Orange County, on February 5, 1981, when she was bludgeoned to death.

- **Gregory Sanchez.** Twenty-seven years old. And **Cheri Domingo**. Thirty-five years old. Sanchez, an electronics technician, and Domingo, a mother of two, had an on-and-off relationship. Domingo and her children were living in a house in the Goleta area of Santa Barbara on July 27, 1981. DeAngelo broke into the house in the early morning hours and attacked the couple in a bedroom. Sanchez died of a gunshot wound to the head followed by repeated skull fractures with a blunt instrument. Domingo was then raped and beaten to death.

- **Janelle Lisa Cruz.** Eighteen years old. A restaurant cashier, she was raped and killed on May 4, 1986, in her parents' home in Irvine in Orange County while they were away. The cause of death was blows to the head.

# CHAPTER 8

# AILEEN WUORNOS

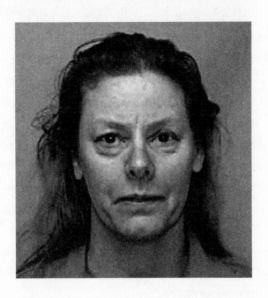

The first body turned up at the end of 1989, buried in the woods near Daytona Beach, a resort town on the Atlantic Coast in central Florida. Richard Mallory was fifty-one years old and owned an electronics repair shop in Clearwater, a city to the southwest on the Gulf Coast. Two junkyard scavengers found his decomposing remains under a piece of carpet. The pockets of his pants were turned out, and he had been shot four times.

The last body was discovered on November 19, 1990. Walter Gino Antonio, a sixty-year-old reserve deputy sheriff, had been shot three times in the back and once in the head. He was number seven. They were

all middle-aged white men who traveled alone on Interstate 75 or nearby highways in north-central Florida. Six had been shot with a small-caliber handgun. The body of one was never found. All seven of their vehicles had been abandoned; in some, condoms and long blond hairs were found on the seats or floorboards. The position of the driver's seat in some of the cars suggested that a short person had been behind the wheel.

The killer's big mistake happened on the Fourth of July in 1990. People sitting on the front porch of their home near Highway 40 in the Ocala National Forest heard the familiar sound of tires screeching that afternoon, and realized that there had been yet another wreck not far from their house, where the road curved sharply. They ran to the brushy area where the car had come to rest and saw beer cans flying in the air out into the woods. Two women had gotten out of the car and were shouting. The one with blond hair pleaded with the family not to call the police. Her father lived nearby, she said, and she would call the authorities from his house. The family went back to their porch and soon heard the car lurch away. Then they heard it slam into an iron gate and some barbed wire. They saw that the blond woman was in the driver's seat, and that the windshield was shattered. The two women got out of the car and walked off as if nothing had happened.

Later that afternoon, a local man spotted the women walking along a road, carrying a red-and-white cooler between them. The blond woman had blood all over her. He assumed they were local residents and offered them a ride. They said they had been in a bad accident and needed to get to Daytona. That was about fifty miles away. He said he wasn't going that far, and the blond woman got angry. The man drove away, but called for help. The chief of the local volunteer fire department drove around the area and finally spotted the women walking along the road. They rejected any help and hurried away. But the fire chief reported the incident to the Marion County Sheriff's Office, and deputies found the car, a gray Pontiac Sunbird, in a nearby field. There appeared to be bloodstains

on the trunk and throughout the interior. They noticed what looked like a bloody palm print. There were no license plates or tags, so they ran the car's Vehicle Identification Number through the department's computer. The results were startling.

The car belonged to Peter Siems, a sixty-five-year-old man who was classified as a missing person and an endangered adult. He had last been seen on June 6 at his home in Jupiter in southern Florida, when he headed out to visit relatives in Arkansas and New Jersey. He never turned up, and was reported missing on June 22. Marion County quickly had an artist draw up sketches of the two women who had been seen with the car and faxed them to departments around the state. The police in Jupiter sent out a nationwide alert. It said that "foul play" was suspected and mentioned the blood inside the car. Two white females "who appeared to be lesbians" were seen exiting the vehicle and walking away on foot. One was from twenty-five to thirty years old, and about five feet, eight inches tall. She was wearing blue jeans with some kind of chain hanging from the belt loop and a white shirt with the sleeves rolled up. The other was a white female in her twenties who was about five feet, four inches tall, "very overweight and masculine looking." She had dark red hair and was wearing a gray shirt and red shorts. The "victim," Siems, was described as a "devout Christian and family man who has no history of mental instability." Siems was a retired merchant seaman who was working for an outreach ministry called Christ Is The Answer.

It would be another seven months before the full picture emerged. By the beginning of January 1991, law-enforcement agencies, including the FBI, had come up with a prime suspect. For a week, investigators had secretly followed her around in the seedy areas of Daytona Beach, where she drifted from place to place with all her possessions: a suitcase, a purse, and a silver key. On the evening of January 8, a Tuesday, she sat on a bar stool at The Last Resort, a biker hangout not far from the cheap motel where she stayed sometimes when she could come up with fifteen

dollars to pay for a room. She confided to the sympathetic men sitting on either side of her that the only thing she owned of any value was the silver key clipped to the belt on her blue jeans. She had enough money to pay for a couple of beers, and she smoked a few cigarettes. As she had done many times before, she slept that night on the bar's front porch. The next day, her two bar buddies from the previous evening offered to rent her a room for one night at a nearby motel. She gratefully accepted. Then they walked her out of the bar and into the custody of uniformed cops. Her pals had been undercover officers from the sheriff's department in Volusia County, which included Daytona Beach.

Stunned, she asked them if they had a warrant for her arrest. They said they did, and they showed it to her. It was for "Lori Grody," and it described a 1986 concealed-weapon charge from Port Orange, back in Marion County. It seemed like no big deal, so she didn't put up a fight.

It was, in fact, a big deal. Investigators in Marion County believed that "Lori Grody" was an alias once used by Aileen Carol Wuornos, the thirty-three-year-old woman who, they thought, was responsible for at least seven murders in central Florida. But they did not have quite enough evidence to charge her with homicide. The break in the case had come at the end of November 1990, when Steve Binegar, the chief investigator in the Marion County Sheriff's Office, decided to release to the public the composite drawings that had been sent to law-enforcement agencies after the two women walked away from the car crash on the Fourth of July. Newspapers and television stations across the country used the sketches, and hundreds of leads poured in.

Four of the callers described the same two women, but they had used several different names over the years. Investigators spread out. A motel owner in the Daytona area said one sketch looked like a woman who had stayed there for a while, and paid for her room by pawning some of her possessions. In a check of local pawnshops, investigators found that a woman named Cammie Marsh Greene had brought in a radar detector

and a Minolta camera that belonged to Richard Mallory, whose body had been found in December 1989. At another shop, the same woman had pawned a box of tools that matched the description of the set missing from the pickup truck driven by David Spears, whose body was found on June 1, 1990. There was a thumbprint on the receipt for that transaction. It was quickly analyzed. The print matched the one taken after "Lori Grody" was arrested in 1986, when she was found in a stolen vehicle with a gun hidden under the front seat. It was also matched with the bloody palm print found in Peter Siems's Pontiac Sunbird on the previous Fourth of July.

INVESTIGATOR HOLDING UP MUG SHOTS OF MURDERER AILEEN WUORNOS AND HER FIRST VICTIM, RICHARD MALLORY.

On January 16, 1991, a week after her arrest at the bar, in Daytona Beach, Aileen Wuornos was charged with the 1989 murder of Richard Mallory. She was brought into court the following day and was assigned a public defender. She did not enter a plea, and was ordered held without bail. This was something new: a female serial killer. One investigator

said Wuornos was a part-time prostitute and described her as "a killer who robs rather than a robber who kills." News media across the country and beyond were riveted by the events in central Florida. It wasn't long before they came up with evocative nicknames. A recurring favorite was "Damsel of Death."

Property belonging to some of the victims was located in a storage unit that investigators tracked down after they arrested Wuornos and found the silver key she carried. Officials said the men were killed after picking up or stopping to help Wuornos. Hitchhiking was not uncommon in the 1970s. But by the 1980s, fear of the previous decade's notorious serial killers, who sometimes picked up their victims as they were hitchhiking along the vast system of Interstate highways, had made people more cautious about the practice. Now, the Wuornos case seemed like hitchhiking/murder in reverse: the hitchhiker was the murderer.

An important break in the case was attributed to Sergeant Brian Jarvis, the "computer whiz" of the Marion County Sheriff's Office. He had made use of emerging technology to design a program that allowed quick cross-checking of more than a thousand leads that had come in from all over the country.

Another key element had yet to emerge. Tyria Jolene Moore, a twenty-eight-year-old who was Wuornos's longtime girlfriend, had been working with investigators behind the scenes for more than a week. Moore and Wuornos had met at a gay bar in South Daytona in 1986 and lived together for four years, first as lovers, then as sisters. They had parted ways about a year before Wuornos was arrested, and Ty, as she was known, was living in Pennsylvania with her sister when the investigators tracked her down. They wanted to talk to her, but she was hesitant. They read her her Miranda rights against self-incrimination, and eventually persuaded her to fly back to Florida with them. Once there, they put her up in a motel and had her send a letter to Aileen asking her to call her

collect at the motel. They warned Ty to play along and reminded her that she could still be charged with first-degree murder.

Lee, as Aileen was known, got the letter in her jail cell and called Ty collect, as instructed. The investigators were in the motel room when the phone rang on the morning of January 14, 1991. They had warned Ty not to lie about anything. She could still be prosecuted. They had put a recording device on the phone and would be listening in. The women exchanged greetings, and Wuornos said she assumed that the police would be listening. At one point, Wuornos said that Moore had never done anything wrong and added, "You're an angel." There were numerous calls that day and the next. The investigators were getting impatient. None of the conversations had produced any kind of confession. On January 16, that changed: Moore took a different tack. She said she might go out and kill someone so that she would be put in jail and could see Wuornos again. "There's no reason," Wuornos responded. "You didn't do anything! I am the one. I am the one who did everything. And I'm gonna let them know this, all right?" Moore said "Okay."

Wuornos said she would probably die of a broken heart or a heart attack, but she didn't care. Then she became a bit cheerful. "Hey, by the way, I'm gonna go down in history. Yep. I'll be like Bundy."

Moore said "What a way to go down in history." Ted Bundy, one of the nation's most notorious serial killers, had kidnapped, raped, and murdered as many as thirty girls and young women across the country in the 1970s. He was executed in Florida in January 1989 for the rape and murder of a twelve-year-old girl.

Wuornos went on: "It's like that Ted Bundy. If I ever write a book, I'm gonna give you the money." She said she had committed the murders because she was so in love with Moore, and was afraid they would lose their apartment, and wouldn't be together anymore. "I know it sounds crazy, but it's the truth," Wuornos said.

"Yes, it does sound crazy," Moore said.

Wuornos repeatedly expressed her love for Moore, and the call ended. A short time later, Wuornos was taken to another room in the jail, where she faced a camera. "I'm here to confess to the murders," she said. She was read her Miranda rights, and began what turned into a somewhat rambling videotaped session that went on for three hours. During that time, a lawyer from the public defender's office arrived, and urged her to stop talking. She did not take his advice. She admitted to killing all seven of the men, and gave details that only the killer could have known.

She said she had had sex with thousands of men; and when she killed, it was only in self-defense because they had become violent and abusive. She described herself as "a very kind person," but added "when I get drunk, I do stupid things." Later that night—January 16, 1991— Wuornos was charged with first-degree murder in the death of Richard Mallory, the fifty-one-year-old electronics shop owner from Clearwater. Wuornos had said that she fought with Mallory before pulling a gun from her bag. "He just backed away, and I thought . . . should I, you know, try to help this guy, or should I just kill him? So I figured, well, if I help the guy and he lives, he's gonna tell on me, and I'm gonna get arrested for attempted murder, all this jazz. And I thought, well, the best thing to do is just keep shooting him."

Who was Aileen Wuornos, and how had her life reached this point? She was born Aileen Pittman on February 19, 1956, in Rochester, Michigan, about thirty miles north of Detroit. Four years later, she was legally adopted by her maternal grandparents, Lauri and Britta Wuornos. Her mother, Diane, had shown little interest in her and disappeared when Aileen was about two. Aileen and her brother Keith, who was about two years older, grew up believing that their grandparents were actually their parents, and that they had three more siblings. But the three, they would learn, were actually their grandparents' children: Diane, who was rarely spoken of; Lori, who was only a few years older than Aileen; and Barry, who was twelve years older than Aileen. When Aileen was eleven, her

grandparents told her the truth about her mother. She had remarried and had two other children. And Aileen learned that her father was a man named Leo Pittman, who was eventually convicted of kidnapping and raping a seventeen-year-old girl and sentenced to life in prison, where he committed suicide.

Lauri Wuornos, Aileen's grandfather, was abusive to Keith and Aileen. Her grandmother, Britta, was an alcoholic who did little to stop the abuse. Several times, her grandfather made her lie facedown and naked on a bed while he beat her with the leather strap. He told her she was "evil, wicked, worthless" and should never have been born. As a young teenager, Aileen performed sexual acts for boys in return for loose change, and she was known in the community as a "whore" and a "slut." She shoplifted, was often drunk and vulgar, and had frequent run-ins with the police. When she was fifteen, she gave birth to a boy, who was quickly given up for adoption at the insistence of her grandfather. Around that time, her grandmother died of liver failure. When Aileen was sixteen, she left home and began her journey to Florida. When she was twenty, she married a seventy-year-old man. He divorced her after a month and filed for a restraining order, claiming that she had beaten him with his cane.

Wuornos never had a serious job, and was frequently arrested during those years, during which she moved around a lot, spent a lot of time in bars, and used a number of pseudonyms. One day in 1981, she got drunk and decided to kill herself. She bought a gun at a pawnshop, stopped at a Kmart to buy some bullets, then headed toward Mosquito Lagoon on the Atlantic Coast south of Daytona Beach, where she planned to end it all. On the way, she stopped at a convenience store to buy some potato chips. As she checked out, she remembered that she had the gun in her purse. She aimed it at the clerk, then left the store and drove away with the potato chips. She was arrested a few minutes later when her car broke down.

A psychiatrist's report after that arrest noted that Wuornos had dropped out of school when she was in the tenth grade, and been drinking and using drugs since she was twelve years old. She had worked as a waitress, a maid, a pool hustler, and a prostitute. She had been raped and beaten numerous times as she hitchhiked around the country. The psychiatrist considered her sane, but a probation officer said she was "very unstable" and "could become a threat to the safety and well-being of others, as well as to herself." She was sentenced to three years in prison and released in June 1983.

Her criminal behavior continued, and she frequently prostituted herself. In 1984, she was arrested for trying to pass forged checks at a bank in Key West. There were more arrests to come.

When she was walked into the courtroom in Daytona Beach on January 17, 1991, the day after her long confession, it was clear that the name Aileen Wuornos would indeed reach the heights of fame achieved by Ted Bundy, John Wayne Gacy, and, perhaps, the mysterious "Jack the Ripper," who had terrified London a hundred years earlier. Stories about her court appearance referred to Wuornos as a "transient woman," a "prostitute," a "female drifter," a "strong-willed woman," and, at last, a "female serial killer."

On February 1, Wuornos was back in court. She pleaded not guilty to the Mallory murder charge, and was charged with a second murder. Charles R. Humphreys had been shot seven times the previous September. In her confession, Wuornos had said that she aimed the seventh shot at his head "to put him out of his misery." She had told one investigator that she had a line no one could cross. If you crossed that line—and the line changed—if you crossed that line by something that you said or something nasty that you did, you weren't leaving. She could do eight guys in one day and seven could get away, then one would do something that made her decide "Well, he doesn't need to live."

Despite Wuornos's long, detailed confession, her court-appointed lawyer entered a not-guilty plea, and the legal maneuvering began. Perhaps predictably, the saga of the "highway femme fatale," as one writer put it, had caused a frenzy of interest from movie producers, writers, tabloid television shows, and "assorted hucksters" looking to win the rights to her story. It was a story that was about to get a little stranger. One of the producers who contacted Wuornos was Jackelyn Giroux, from Studio City, not far from Hollywood. Giroux's mother, who lived in Ocala, Florida, was standing in line at a grocery store in late 1990 when she recognized Wuornos from the composite sketches that had been sent out by the police. She handed Wuornos her daughter's business card, and asked her to give her daughter a call. Then Giroux's mother reported the sighting to the police. A few weeks after her arrest, Wuornos called Giroux and they worked out a deal. Wuornos would receive $60 a month for the rest of her life in exchange for her permission to tell her story in a movie to be called *Angel of Death*.

Perhaps strangest of all, Arlene Pralle, a forty-four-year-old horse breeder from Colorado, legally adopted Wuornos after her arrest and began visiting her weekly at the jail in Florida. Each evening, she accepted collect calls from Wuornos. Pralle described herself as a born-again Christian. She told the *Washington Post* that she became interested in the case when she saw pictures of Wuornos in a newspaper, and peered deeply into her eyes. God prompted her to do something, so she wrote a letter to Wuornos saying she wanted to be her friend. By the end of November 1991, the adoption by Pralle and her husband was approved.

The first of what were expected to be several murder trials got underway in early 1992 at the Volusia County Criminal Court in Deland, about twenty miles southwest of Daytona Beach. It involved only the death of the first victim, Richard Mallory, whose body was found in late 1989. Newspapers across the country, and beyond, carried a story by the Associated Press wire service that summed up what was expected

to come: Aileen Wuornos was a thirty-five-year-old "self-professed highway hooker," according to authorities. She was "cold-blooded" and fit the definition of a serial killer—someone who kills at least four people over an extended period of time, and won't stop until arrested or killed. And female serial killers were very rare. Wuornos had admitted to killing seven men, but claimed it was all in self-defense because they had become violent and abusive.

A more sympathetic view came from Phyllis Chesler, the feminist author and psychologist whose book *Women and Madness* had been published in 1972. Chesler had been following the case, and arranged to have Wuornos call her collect from the county jail in Daytona Beach. As the trial was about to begin, Chesler wrote an opinion piece for the *New York Times* with the headline "A Double Standard for Murder?" She said she had learned through those calls that Wuornos had been "tortured physically and psychologically" in the jail. Wuornos had told her, and her "adoptive mother," that she spent long periods in solitary confinement, freezing and naked. She could not see very well, and her requests for a hearing aid and glasses had been ignored. She was bleeding heavily, but was not allowed to see a gynecologist. And she had lost forty pounds.

Ted Bundy, on the other hand, had been permitted to "marry, enjoy conjugal visits, and father a child in prison in Florida before he was executed in 1989." Female prisoners were routinely mistreated in Florida jails and prisons, where there was a "double-standard for violence: one for men and quite another one for women." Many male serial killers attacked women and homosexual men, and they rarely claimed that they killed in self-defense, as Wuornos had, Chesler wrote. "If we understood how many times a street prostitute is robbed, harassed, raped, beaten and murdered, we might have an easier time entertaining the possibility that a woman like Ms. Wuornos has, as she told me, lived 'on dangerous ground at all times.'"

As the trial began, Mallory was described in a story by the *Orlando Sentinel* as a "temperamental loner with a penchant for strip bars and an ongoing beef with the Internal Revenue Service." More than three hundred people, including Tyria Moore, had been listed as potential witnesses. John Tanner, the Volusia County State Attorney, had announced that he would seek the death penalty. In his opening statement to the jury, he said Wuornos had shot Mallory four times "because she didn't want to leave a witness." She liked control, he said, and had been controlling men for many years. Tricia Jenkins, an assistant public defender, said Wuornos was a terrified woman who was defending herself. "The frequency with which she met physical abuse was escalating," she said. "Time after time, she was raped. Time after time, she was beaten up and wasn't paid."

The trial didn't last long, but the testimony was powerful. The prosecution presented evidence of the six other men Wuornos was suspected of killing, and played parts of her three-hour taped confession. On January 17, as Wuornos sat at the defense table, the real drama began. The prosecutor—not the defense—called Tyria Moore to the witness stand. She testified that when Wuornos came home on December 1, 1989, and as they were sitting around, drinking beer and watching television, Wuornos said that she had just killed a man. She didn't look injured or upset. "She seemed fine." That was the day that Mallory was shot. Moore said she didn't want to believe it, and discouraged Wuornos from continuing to talk about it. And Wuornos never said that the man had done anything to her. Moore left Wuornos about a year later, she said, when she saw a police sketch of herself and Wuornos on television. During the seventy-five minutes of her testimony, Wuornos and Moore barely looked at each other. Arlene Pralle, Wuornos's adoptive mother, prayed and wept from her seat in the second row. Before prosecutors rested their case the following week, they played segments of the videotaped confession, including the part where she admitted killing Mallory and said "I deserve to die."

A week later, Wuornos, with a crucifix dangling from her neck, took the stand as the only defense witness. She said she was shy, and had been victimized many times over the years; and that after Mallory picked her up, he said "You're going to do anything I want you to do, and if you don't, I'll kill you." He tied her to the steering wheel and sodomized her, she said. "I thought to myself, I got to fight or die." And she said she had lied during the videotaped interview in order to protect Tyria Moore. But during two hours of cross-examination, she became flustered and at times refused to answer, invoking her Constitutional right against self-incrimination. It was a quick trial. On January 27, 1992, the jury of seven women and five men deliberated for an hour and thirty-five minutes before convicting Wuornos of first-degree murder. They were to return the following day to consider whether to recommend the death penalty.

As the jurors were being polled individually, Wuornos quietly said "I am innocent." But as they began to file out of the courtroom, she raised her voice. Her lawyers tried to restrain her, but she shouted "I was raped! I hope you get raped! Scumbags of America!"

Next, the jurors had to decide on whether to recommend the death penalty. After three days of arguments and testimony about Wuornos's crimes and mental state, the jurors deliberated for less than two hours before voting unanimously for the death penalty.

Four days later, on January 31, 1992, Circuit Judge Uriel Blount had to decide whether to accept the jury's decision. Arlene Pralle, who had sat through the trial, took a turn and said that her adopted daughter had never gotten a chance to grow up. She begged the judge for mercy. Wuornos spoke up, and blamed everyone but herself. She said she had been framed by law enforcement, and she was no serial killer. Alcohol withdrawal had led her to confess to murders that she hadn't committed. "I was raped or beaten thirty-nine times," she said. "What I did was what anyone else would do: I defended myself." Tyria Moore, she said,

was "lying through her teeth" when she testified. And Wuornos trashed her lawyers for mishandling the case. Blount announced his decision. He told Wuornos she would be "electrocuted until you are dead." Wuornos was quickly taken from the courtroom to be transported to Florida's death row for women in Broward County, two hundred fifty miles away. As deputies put her in a van, she yelled to reporters "Bust these crooked cops and their conspiracy, please! I'm innocent!"

By the end of 1992, Wuornos seemed to have changed her mind about everything, or at least come to a reckoning about her life. In April, she pleaded no contest to the murders of Spears, Burress, and Humphreys, the second, fourth, and sixth victims. In May, she faced the death penalty again. Arlene Pralle again begged for mercy. She told the judge, Thomas Sawaya, that Aileen had been cooperating with the authorities. Sawaya was unmoved. He sentenced Wuornos to death three more times. Wuornos responded "Thank you, and I'll be up in heaven while you all rot in hell." Then she gave him the finger. Turning to the prosecutor, Ric Ridgway, she said "May your wife and kids get raped."

Years of legal maneuvering and appeals followed. At one point, Wuornos argued that she had pleaded "no contest" not because she was guilty, but because she wanted to return to her jail cell in Broward County and avoid the stress of another trial. In October 1994, the Florida Supreme Court upheld the four murder convictions and the sentences that had put her on Death Row. It would be eight more years before things were settled. In April 2002, the Florida Supreme Court ruled in Wuornos's favor, in a way. For the previous year, Wuornos had been writing letters to the justices saying that she wanted to fire all her lawyers, end all her appeals, and be executed. The justices agreed. The nation's first known female serial killer could be executed.

Over the following months, the Florida governor, Jeb Bush, ordered a temporary stay so that experts could evaluate her mental

health. Three psychiatrists found her mentally competent, and Bush lifted the stay in October 2002. Wuornos, now forty-six years old, spent the night before her execution with a childhood friend, Dawn Botkins. She said Wuornos was in a good mood and laughed a lot. "She was looking forward to being home with God and getting off this Earth." The next day, October 9, she made her final statement. When the curtain in the death chamber opened, she lifted her head to look at the twenty-nine witnesses nearby. She seemed surprised. In her final statement, she referred to a recent film. "I'd just like to say I'm sailing with the Rock and I'll be back like *Independence Day* with Jesus, June 6, like the big movie, big mother ship and all. I'll be back." An injection was administered to her right arm, and she was pronounced dead seventeen minutes later, at 9:47 A.M. She was the tenth woman executed in the United States after the Supreme Court lifted the moratorium on capital punishment in 1976.

## THE VICTIMS

- **Richard Mallory.** Fifty-one years old. He owned an electronics repair shop in Clearwater. He was last seen alive on November 30, 1989. His fully dressed body was discovered on December 13, 1989, in the woods northwest of Daytona Beach. He had been shot three times in the chest with a .22-caliber gun.

- **David Spears.** Forty-three years old. He was a construction worker. He was last seen alive on May 19, 1990. His body was found on June 1, 1990, in a wooded area about forty miles north of Tampa. He had been shot six times with a .22-caliber gun.

- **Charles Carskaddon.** Forty years old. His body was found on June 7, 1990. He was a part-time rodeo worker. He had been shot nine times in the chest and stomach.

- **Troy "Buddy" Burress.** Fifty years old. He was a salesman. He disappeared on July 30, 1990. His body was found in Marion County on August 4, 1990. He had been shot twice in the torso.

- **Peter Siems.** Sixty-five years old. He was last seen on June 7, 1990. He was a Christian missionary. His body was never found, but his car was found on July 4, 1990, in Orange Springs.

- **Charles "Dick" Humphreys.** Fifty-six years old. He was a retired Air Force major and a child-abuse investigator. His body was found in Marion County on September 12, 1990. He had been shot seven times.

- **Walter Antonio.** Sixty-two years old. His body was found on November 19, 1990 in a remote part of Dixie County. He had been shot four times in the back and head.

# CHAPTER 9

# ARTHUR SHAWCROSS

Investigators found the body of eight-year-old Karen Ann Hill facedown and smothered in dirt under a bridge over the Black River in upstate New York, about four hours after her mother reported her missing on September 2, 1972. She had been raped and strangled not far from their home in Watertown, where they had just moved. On September 3, police arrested Arthur Shawcross, a twenty-seven-year-old employee of the Watertown Public Works Department.

Five days later, on September 7, police found the decomposed body of ten-year-old Jack O. Blake in the same area. He had been missing for four months—since May 7, 1972. The medical examiner ruled that the

case was a homicide, but that it was impossible to determine the cause of death. Only his skeleton and two small patches of flesh remained. The boy had been forced to disrobe and attempted to run away, the report said. The killer tried to conceal the child's body by covering it with long strips of tree bark and scattering his clothes around the area.

Prosecutors persuaded a grand jury to indict Shawcross for the murder of Karen Hill, but did not have enough evidence to charge him for the Blake child's death. The solution was announced in court on October 17, 1972. Although there was no direct evidence connecting Shawcross with the death of Jack Blake, Shawcross had admitted that he had caused the child's death. A deal had been worked out. The Karen Hill murder charge would be reduced to first-degree manslaughter, and the Blake death would be included in that plea. Judge Milton H. Wiltse pronounced the sentence: an indeterminate term of no more than twenty-five years. Shawcross would serve his time at Attica, the maximum-security prison in upstate New York, and he would be given psychiatric treatment. The parole board would decide when he was fit to be released.

Shawcross was back in the news seventeen and a half years later. He was arrested on January 4, 1990, and charged with the murders of eight women. He was suspected of killing several more. This time, the bodies were found in the Rochester, New York area, about seventy miles northeast of Buffalo. The women—most of them sex workers—were apparently victims of the mysterious "Genesee River Killer" spree that began after Shawcross was paroled from prison in June 1987. He had served fifteen years of his twenty-five-year sentence. Edward Elvin, the head of the State Parole Board, said Shawcross had seemed to be adapting well to life outside prison. "Superficially, he was making a good adjustment," Elvin said. During his time in prison, he was considered a "very good" inmate. In 1982, he earned his high school equivalency diploma and took a correspondence course in horticulture.

ARTHUR SHAWCROSS (CENTER) IS CHARGED WITH EIGHT COUNTS OF MURDER IN ROCHESTER IN CITY COURT.

The Shawcross case became a time of reckoning for the parole board. Howard R. Relin, the chief prosecutor in Monroe County, expressed his frustration. "We're very upset," he said. "Every prosecutor in New York can recount three or four horror stories about people who never should have been paroled, but were." The state senate began working on legislation to change the parole system. Relin began to push for a law that would allow prosecutors and the families of victims to testify at parole hearings.

After his parole, Shawcross lived in Binghamton, then in the small town of Delhi, but was forced to move away because the residents of each place protested about his living in their communities. The parole board helped him move to Rochester in 1987. He took a job making salads at a food wholesaler, and married a woman named Rosemary who had been writing him letters in prison. They lived in a three-story apartment building, where neighbors described him as helpful. His wife had a car,

but he rode a bicycle around town. In the months before he was arrested, he was soft-spoken, generous, and kind. But he was also quick to lose his temper and turn to violence. In the last weeks of December 1989, the final weeks before his arrest, he baked Christmas cookies and murdered three women.

Shawcross ultimately came into focus for the police on January 3, 1990, when state police in a helicopter saw him in the car of a female friend on a country bridge over Salmon Creek. Shawcross was alone and eating a salad. Under the bridge, the troopers saw the body of a woman later identified as that of a thirty-four-year-old prostitute. Officers in patrol cars followed him as he drove to the nursing home where his girlfriend worked, and questioned him. The next morning, they found the body of a twenty-year-old prostitute about two miles away from where they had spotted him the day before. After more questioning, police quickly found two more bodies in the woods northwest of Rochester.

Shawcross was eventually charged with eleven murders, and pleaded not guilty by reason of insanity, seemingly the only defense available in the face of the considerable evidence of his guilt that the authorities had compiled. During jury selection in September 1990, his defense attorneys warned prospective jurors that he had engaged in cannibalism and mutilation. The lawyers, Thomas Cocuzzi and David Murante, said Shawcross had been sexually abused as a child, and had raped and cannibalized two women while serving in Vietnam. And, they said, Shawcross had eaten body parts of ten-year-old Jack Blake in 1972.

Shawcross said he killed out of anger. One prostitute, for instance, had made fun of his sexual prowess. In his lengthy confession, made public on September 21, 1990, Shawcross said he knew what he was doing was wrong. He said he killed two of the women because he was unable to perform sexually. He said if he were ever to be freed, he would kill again. Shawcross also told the police that a headless body found the previous October by two teenagers fishing on an island in the Genesee River was

that of Dorothy Keeler, his fifty-nine-year-old mistress, who had threatened to tell his wife about their affair.

As is the case with many serial killers, Shawcross and his lawyers decided that a plea of not guilty by reason of insanity would be their best option. But that plea comes with a critical difficulty: serial killers are, by definition, able to control their behavior. Would they, for instance, commit their crimes if a police officer were standing there watching them? If the answer is "no," then the insanity plea fails. Shawcross's lawyers suggested that he had been sexually abused as a child, suffered from "altered states," a kind of multiple-personality disorder, and had post-traumatic stress disorder as a result of his service in Vietnam. The prosecution psychiatrist testified that he had not suffered from PTSD and was faking mental illness in an attempt to avoid prison.

Shawcross never took the witness stand during the three-month trial. The jury found him guilty of ten murders after deliberating for six hours on December 13, 1990. Shawcross stared straight ahead and showed no emotion, as he had done through much of the trial. On February 1, 1991, Judge Donald J. Wisner sentenced him to a minimum of two hundred fifty years in prison. The death penalty was not an option in New York at the time.

Relatives of the victims, jurors from the trial, and police officers and investigators packed the courtroom. "For far too long, you have held center stage in this community," Wisner said. "It's time to put all of this behind us." Wisner asked Shawcross if he wanted to say anything. He replied "No comment at this time." His lawyers did not ask the judge for leniency.

The prosecutor, Charles Siragusa, said he was pleased by the sentence and called Shawcross "a totally immoral individual" who should never have been paroled in the first place. In March, Shawcross pleaded guilty to one murder charge in nearby Wayne County, bringing the total to eleven.

Shawcross emerged in the news again in 1999 when he was sent to solitary confinement for two years for selling his autograph and artwork on the Internet site eBay. That meant that he could no longer receive packages, make phone calls, or purchase items in the prison store at the maximum-security Sullivan Correctional Facility in Fallsburg, New York. He was also barred from the prison's arts-and-crafts program.

Shawcross was sixty-three years old when he died on November 10, 2008. He had complained of leg pain that morning, and was transported from the prison in Fallsburg to a hospital in Albany. The cause of death was cardiac arrest.

## THE VICTIMS

- **Karen Ann Hill.** Eight years old. She lived in Watertown, New York, where she was raped and strangled to death on September 2, 1972.

- **Jack O. Blake.** Ten years old. Disappeared from his home in Watertown, New York, on May 7, 1972. His skeletal remains were found on September 7, 1972.

- **Dorothea Blackburn.** Twenty-seven years old. Disappeared on March 18, 1988. Her body was found on March 24, 1988.

- **Anna Marie Steffen.** Twenty-eight years old. Disappeared on July 9, 1988. Her body was found on September 11, 1988.

- **Dorothy Keeler.** Fifty-nine years old. Disappeared on July 29, 1989. Her body was found on October 21, 1989.

- **Patricia Ives.** Twenty-five years old. Disappeared on September 29, 1989. Her body was discovered on October 27, 1989.

- **June Stott.** Thirty years old. Disappeared on October 23, 1989. Her body was found on November 23, 1989.

- **Marie Welch.** Twenty-three years old. Disappeared on November 5, 1989. Her body was found on January 5, 1990.

- **Frances Brown.** Twenty-two years old. Disappeared on November 11, 1989. Her body was found on November 15, 1989.

- **Kimberly Logan.** Thirty years old. Disappeared on November 15, 1989, and her body was found the same day.

- **Elizabeth Gibson.** Twenty-nine years old. Disappeared on November 25, 1989. Her body was found on November 27, 1989.

- **Darlene Trippi.** Thirty-two years old. Disappeared on December 15, 1989. Her body was found on January 5, 1990.

- **June Cicero.** Thirty-four years old. Disappeared on December 17, 1989. Her body was found on January 3, 1990.

- **Felicia Stephens.** Twenty years old. Disappeared on December 28, 1989. Her body was found on December 31, 1989.

# CHAPTER 10

# DENNIS RADER

When three of the Otero children returned home from school on the afternoon of January 15, 1974, they were surprised to find that the front door was locked. They got no answer when they knocked and pounded, so they finally forced it open. There was no one in the kitchen or living room, which seemed odd, so they ran to their parents' bedroom. Their mother was on the bed and their father was on the floor. Cords had been tied around their necks, hands, and ankles. Carmen, who was thirteen, and Danny, who was fourteen, tried to cut the cords, but couldn't. They tried to call for help, but the phone line was dead. Charlie, who at fifteen was the oldest of the five Otero children, ran to the house next door on their quiet residential street in Wichita, Kansas. He asked the neighbors to call the police.

As the children waited, police searched the house. The officers found that their father, Joseph Otero, had his ankles tied with a white cord and his hands bound behind his back. One of the children had cut the rope that held a plastic bag over his head. There was a knife next to his body. Julie Otero, the children's mother, had her ankles tied together and her hands tied behind her back. Both bodies were cold and stiff.

But there were more horrifying discoveries to come. While the children waited, the police found the body of their nine-year-old brother, Joseph Jr., in another bedroom. A pillowcase had been placed over his head, which was covered with plastic bags and a T-shirt. His hands and ankles had been bound with a cord. In the basement, an officer searched around with a flashlight and bumped into a body hanging from a sewer pipe. It was their eleven-year-old sister, Josephine. Her ankles and knees were wrapped in cords, and her hands were tied behind her back. Her panties had been pulled down. There was dried semen on her leg and around the area. The officers collected some samples.

Outside the house, police saw that the telephone line had been cut. The family's car, an Oldsmobile Vista Cruiser, was missing. The officers found two witnesses who said they had seen a man driving the Vista Cruiser. They described him as "dark or swarthy." The police found the car that evening in a grocery store parking lot about half a mile away. The keys were gone. The officers lifted some fingerprints, but couldn't find a match.

Decades later, Charlie reflected on that horrifying time. "I thank God every day that I didn't find Joey and Josie, because I don't know how I could have handled it," he said. "My heart just got ripped out of my chest. My life changed instantly." Of course, in 1974 he could not have known that the samples taken at their house would eventually emerge as significant evidence in the mystery of what had happened to his family.

Wichita, the largest city in Kansas, had a population of about 280,000 in 1974, at the time of the inexplicable murders. It was a quiet Midwestern town that ranked 51st in the 1970 census. Abruptly, the Otero murders had residents making sure to lock their doors, close their windows, and forgo walking anywhere alone, especially at night. But there was more trauma on the way that would make Wichita the focus of national attention and network news broadcasts.

When Kevin Bright and his sister, Kathryn, walked into her house on East 13th Street in Wichita on the evening of April 4, 1974, they found an intruder. He was armed with a knife, and he told them that he was a fugitive wanted in California. Then he pointed a gun at Kevin and forced him to tie up Kathryn. The man demanded money. He locked Kevin in the bathroom, and he could hear his sister crying in pain. Kevin was shot twice. He decided their only hope would be for him to run for help. He was able to get out of the house and run to a neighbor's home.

When the police arrived, they found Kevin with a white cord hanging from his neck. He was barely alive. Kathryn was lying in a pool of blood, and was in terrible pain. Nylon stockings were tied around her wrists and ankles. A scarf and a thin cord had been tied around her neck. She showed them her stab wounds, and was able to tell them her name and age. She begged for help, then passed out. Kathryn made it to the hospital that night, but died in surgery. She was twenty-one years old. In all, she had eleven stab wounds and she had been strangled. Kevin barely survived. But he was able to give the police a description of their attacker that ran in the newspapers and was broadcast on television.

This sort of thing did not happen in Wichita. Now it had happened twice. Was there a connection to the Otero murders? No one knew. In the fall of 1974, six months after the Bright attacks, Wichita got a chilling clue. News stories appeared about the police questioning one of three sex offenders who had hinted that they might have information about the Otero family murders. Don Granger, a columnist for the *Wichita*

*Eagle*, got a phone call on October 2 from a man with a gruff voice. He didn't give his name, but he told Granger to go to the Wichita Public Library and get a book called *Applied Engineering Mechanics*. The caller told Granger precisely where the shelf was. Inside the book, he said, there would be a typed letter describing the Otero murders in detail, therefore proving that the three men in custody had nothing to do with the case.

Granger alerted the police about the call, and they quickly found the clumsily written letter:

> Those three dude you have in custody are just talking to get publicity.... They know nothing at all. I did it by myself and with no oneshelp.... [He describes the Otero crime scene in detail.]
>
> I'm sorry this happened to the society.... It hard to control myself. You probably call me "psychotic with sexual perversion hang-up." Where this monster enter my brain I will never know. But, it here to stay. How does one cure himself? If you ask for help, that you have killed four people, they will laugh or hit the panic button and call the cops.
>
> I can't stop it so, the monster goes on, and hurt me as well as society. Society can be thankfull that there are ways for people like me to relieve myself at time by day dreams of some victim being tortore and being mine. It a big complicated game my friend of the monster play putting victims number down, follow them, checking up on them waiting in the dark, waiting, waiting... the pressure is great and somt-times he run the game to his liking. Maybe you can stop him. I can't.
>
> He has already chosen his next victim or victims. I don't know who they are yet. The next day after I read the paper I will Know, but it too late. Good luck hunting.
>
> YOURS, TRULY, GUILTILY.

P.S. Since sex criminals do not change their M.O. or by nature cannot do so, I will not change mine. The code words for me will be . . . bind them, torture them, kill them, B.T.K., you see he at it again. They will be on the next victim.

There was more in the letter, including details of the crime scenes that only the killer could have known. The police did not want to give anyone the ability to imitate the killer's signature, so it was withheld from the public, as were the signatures on other letters sent to the media and the police in the following weeks. Investigators now knew with certainty who the killer was. They just didn't know his name or where to find him. For the people of Wichita and its quiet suburbs, the era of B.T.K. had begun, and there was no end in sight.

Two and a half years later, on March 17, 1977, B.T.K. struck again. This time, it was at a home on South Hydraulic Street in central Wichita, about four miles south of where Kathryn Bright had been attacked. A neighbor called the police after some very upset young boys said they had seen the body of a nude woman with a bag over her head inside their house. The police found that the woman was facedown on the bed, and the plastic bag had been tied in place with a pink nightgown. Black electrical tape had been wrapped around her arms and ankles. Her hands had been tied behind her back with a white cord. Another white cord was wrapped around her neck. The cord ran down her body and tied around her wrists and ankles.

The victim was Shirley Vian Relford, who was twenty-six years old. The boys who had run to the neighbor's house were her sons, who were six and eight years old. They had been forced into their home's bathroom and tied up along with their younger sister as their mother was attacked and killed. After the killer left, Steve, the six-year-old, was able to break a window in the bathroom and get out. He told the police that he had seen the man earlier on his street. The man had been knocking on a door and

holding a photograph of a woman and a child. The man showed him the photo and asked him if he knew the people. He said he didn't.

Nearly nine months later, there was another attack. A police dispatcher got a call from a pay phone in Wichita just after 8:15 in the morning of December 9, 1977. A male voice said "Yes, you will find a homicide at 843 South Pershing, Nancy Fox." At the phone box, they found the receiver dangling off the hook. At the address, a pink duplex, the front door was locked. The phone line had been cut, and a back window had been damaged.

Inside, they found the body of Nancy Fox, a twenty-five-year-old, facedown on a bed, covered with a pink sweater. Her ankles had been tied with a yellow piece of clothing, and her hands had been tied behind her back with a red piece of clothing. There was a burnt cigarette in an ashtray, and her purse had been dumped out on a table. Jewelry boxes had been disturbed, and a pair of pantyhose was on the floor. Her panties had been pulled down, and two pairs of pantyhose had been wrapped around her neck. A nightgown near her bed had what turned out to be semen stains. It appeared as though she had been strangled. There were pry marks on the window lock. But there was a new and significant clue: the phone call had been recorded by the police.

The killings seemed to stop after that. But B.T.K. had not finished tormenting the public and the police. For nearly eight years, Wichita lived in fear bolstered by taunts from the mysterious murderer. In February 1978, B.T.K. sent a letter to a local television station claiming responsibility for the two previous murders as well as the murder of another victim he did not name. In response, Richard LaMunyon, the Wichita Police Chief, called a news conference to warn that Wichita was dealing with an unidentified serial killer who had threatened to kill again.

During those years, the Wichita Police Department, the Kansas Bureau of Investigation, the FBI, and other law-enforcement agencies formed a task force to work on the case. In all, B.T.K. sent five

communications to the police, individuals, and the news media from 1974 to 1988 claiming credit for some of the killings. Then he went silent for sixteen years. He reappeared on March 19, 2004, when the *Wichita Eagle* received a letter containing a copy of a driver's license belonging to Vicki Wegerle, whose death had never been connected to B.T.K. The mailing also included some photographs that appeared to have been taken by her killer on September 16, 1986.

When Gordon Wegerle headed home for lunch that day, he saw someone driving what looked like their car, a gold 1978 Monte Carlo, going in the opposite direction. When he arrived at his house on West 13th Street, he saw that their car was missing. Inside, he found the body of his twenty-eight-year-old wife, Vicki, on the bedroom floor. Her hands had been tied behind her back, and her feet were bound with a leather lace. Her jeans were unzipped, and her breasts were exposed. There was a pocketknife near her head. Gordon used it to cut a nylon stocking and leather shoelace from around her neck, but there was no response. Their two-year-old son seemed to be unharmed. Wegerle called the police, and they tried to revive Vicki, but their attempts failed. The Monte Carlo was found in a store parking lot a few blocks away. The photocopies included with the 2004 letter contained a clue that B.T.K. had used before—the letter "B" shaped to resemble female breasts. Vicki's driver's license had been missing from her home since the day she was killed.

Kerri Rawson slept late on the morning of February 25, 2005. She was a twenty-six-year-old substitute teacher in Detroit, Michigan, and she had taken the day off. A little after noon, she noticed a car parked next to the dumpster behind the apartment building where she lived with her husband. The man in it seemed to be staring up into their window on the second floor. Her father had taught her to be fearful of strangers. Suddenly, there was someone pounding on her door. She decided to pretend that there was no one home. Then she looked through the peephole

and saw a man who appeared to be in his fifties, wearing a dress shirt and a tie. She asked him what he wanted. He said he was from the FBI and he needed to speak to her. She opened the door a crack and asked him to show his badge. He did. Then she let him in. He was carrying a yellow legal pad and a pencil.

He asked her if she was Kerri Rawson, and whether her maiden name was Rader. She answered yes to both. "Have you heard of B.T.K.?" he asked. Yes, she had heard of him. He was the murderer they were looking for in Wichita. "Has something happened to my grandma?" she asked. "Has my grandma been murdered?" The agent assured her that her grandmother was fine. "No. It's your dad," he said. "What is my dad?" she asked. "He's been arrested," the agent replied. "Your dad is wanted as B.T.K. Wanted for murders in Kansas." She seemed confused. He repeated: "B.T.K. Wanted. Arrested. Can we sit down? I need to ask you some questions." Later, she remembered that she was shaking and the room was spinning. "I was falling into a black hole, with no idea of how I was ever going to get out."

Kerri's husband, Darian, arrived home for lunch and saw what was happening. "What's going on?" he asked. "Who are you? Why are you here?" The agent told him why he was there, but Darian didn't believe him and asked to see his badge. Still skeptical, he went off to a bathroom and called the Detroit office of the FBI. They confirmed that the agent was from the FBI. Darian returned to the living room and sat down on the couch next to Kerri, who appeared dumbfounded. "I've been sent here by my office to notify you that your father has been arrested, and to ask you some questions," the agent said. She listened for a time, but eventually told the agent "That's not possible." What he was saying made no sense. "I talked to Dad on the phone last night. He hasn't ever done anything wrong. He's a good guy." She told the agent about her father's time in the military, his jobs over the years, and the fact that he was a church president and a Boy Scout leader.

Eventually, the agent turned the conversation to something that had happened in the mid-1980s. Did she remember anything? Yes, their neighbor Mrs. Hedge was murdered. She lived down the street, on the way to Kerri's grandparents' house. They never found her killer. The agent went to another room and made a phone call. When he returned, he asked her if she would agree to take a DNA test. In the kitchen, she rubbed the inside of her mouth with a cotton swab and dropped it into a plastic bag. Then the agent left.

On the following day, Saturday, February 26, 2005, all of Kansas, and the rest of the world, would hear the news. B.T.K. was Dennis L. Rader, a fifty-nine-year-old who had been living in Park City, a quiet suburb on the edge of Wichita, for more than thirty years. The police said they had pulled him over in his car about a block from his home just after noon on Friday. The arrest was uneventful. He had been suspected of killing eight people, but officials said they anticipated that he would soon be charged with ten murders. He was being held at an undisclosed location.

The broad feeling of relief across the region was matched by a sense of deep shock. B.T.K. was not some twisted transient living on the fringe of society. He was an upstanding citizen, president of the church council at Christ Lutheran Church in Wichita. He, along with his wife, son, daughter, and other relatives had attended the church for decades.

Perhaps most disquieting was the revelation that he was currently working as a municipal compliance officer for Park City, and had been for a decade. He wore a uniform and drove around in a marked city vehicle, checking yards and driveways for code violations, for which, people recalled, he had little tolerance. Before that, he had worked for ten years as a security officer for ADT Security Services. In the early 1970s, he'd been an assembly line worker for Coleman, an outdoor equipment company. Two of his early victims, Josephine Otero and Katherine Bright,

worked at Coleman during those years. From 1966 to 1970, he was on active duty in the U.S. Air Force and served at bases in Texas, Alabama, Okinawa, and Japan.

Rader's ultimate mistake was that he had trusted the police, and, in particular, Ken Landwehr, the Wichita lieutenant who headed the multi-agency task force that had been hunting for B.T.K. for so many years. Some weeks before his arrest, Rader left a package at a Home Depot store with a message for the police, but he got no response. He waited a while, then sent a postcard to a television station directing them to another package he had left by the side of a road. That package was found. It contained detailed descriptions of the Otero family killings, along with some jewelry and a doll with a rope around its neck.

The postcard also mentioned the package he had left at the Home Depot. Police searched the store and found nothing. But a store employee mentioned that a few weeks earlier, a strange package had been found in the back of his pickup truck. It was presumed to be garbage. Police searched the trash and found the package. One of several documents inside included a question apparently from B.T.K. He asked the police whether, if he sent them a floppy disk, they would be able to trace it back to a particular computer. Rader instructed the police to respond to him by placing a classified ad in a local newspaper. The ad should read: "Rex, it will be OK." The police placed the ad and waited. They also reviewed the store's security tapes, which showed a black Jeep Grand Cherokee pulling up to the employee's pickup truck and walking beside it. It was the make and year of Rader's vehicle.

Rader sent the disk to a local television station. The police soon traced it back to the Christ Lutheran Church, where it had been saved by someone named "Dennis." The church's website said Dennis Rader was the president of the congregation. Investigators drove past Rader's house and saw a black Jeep Grand Cherokee in his driveway. They got a subpoena for a tissue sample from a pap smear taken from his daughter

when she was a student at Kansas State University. Her DNA showed that she was the daughter of B.T.K.

Landwehr later told the American Bar Association Journal that Rader sending the disk is what cracked the case. "If he had just quit [killing] and kept his mouth shut, we might never have connected the dots." Soon after his arrest in 2005, Rader began what would be thirty hours of questioning that ultimately turned into a confession. At first, he expressed shock that police would deceive him about sending a floppy disk. "I need to ask you, how come you lied to me? How come you lied to me?" Landwehr responded "Because I was trying to catch you." Later, Rader returned to the issue of the floppy disk. "I really thought Ken was honest when he gave me—when he gave me the signal that it can't be traced," he said. "The floppy did me in." For a while during the session, Rader referred to the killer as B.T.K., but eventually gave full, detailed confessions to the eight murders they had connected to him, and two more as well. And he acknowledged that he had been planning an eleventh murder when he was arrested.

One of the newly connected victims was Marine Hedge, who lived down the street from the Rader home in Park City. She had failed to show up for her job at the Wesley Medical Center coffee shop in Wichita on April 27, 1985. It was so out of character for the fifty-three-year-old that one of her co-workers telephoned Hedge's son. He went to her home and saw that her car was gone. He wasn't too worried; but when there was still no sign of her the next day, he called the police. They went to the house and found that the telephone line had been cut. They contacted a male friend of hers who had been with her on the night of April 26. He said he left her at her home at about 1 A.M. on the 27th.

The days wore on, and there was no sign of her. Then on May 2, her car was found in a shopping-center parking lot in Wichita. It was

locked, and had been there since April 27. The car was muddy, but someone had partially wiped it clean. Inside, the police found two bed covers, a purple bedspread, a curtain, and an electric blanket. The next day, they found her purse some miles away. Ultimately, they found her body in a ditch covered with grass and twigs and a small tree. She had been strangled, and a pair of pantyhose was nearby. At the time, the police saw no obvious connection to B.T.K., so her male friend became the chief suspect.

The other previously unconnected victim was Dolores Davis, a sixty-two-year-old who, like Marine Hedge, lived in Park City. On the afternoon of January 19, 1991, a friend stopped by Davis's house to do some work on her car. He thought it was odd that the curtains were closed and the outside light was on. Her car was in the driveway, but she always left it in the garage. The door between the house and the garage was open, and a phone cord in the kitchen had been pulled out. Broken window glass and a cinder block were on the living room floor, and the sheets had been stripped from the bed in the bedroom.

He couldn't find Dolores anywhere, so he called for help, and detectives from the Sedgwick County Sheriff's office went to the scene. They found a purple hairnet in the hedges outside. A neighbor pointed out a set of car keys on the roof of the garage. About a quarter mile north, a detective found sheets and a mattress pad stuffed into a culvert. Two weeks later, a boy walking his dog on a street a few miles to the north saw a frozen body faceup under a bridge. Pantyhose were wrapped tightly around the neck and the knees. Animals had eaten parts of the face, hands, and feet. Investigators were unable to identify the body at the time, but they later determined that they had found the remains of Dolores Davis.

On Sunday, February 27, 2005, the day after the world heard about Rader's arrest, confusion, tears, and disbelief swept over the congregation at Christ Lutheran Church in Wichita. Two days earlier, police officers

had shown up at the church with a search warrant. Rader, his wife, Paula, and other relatives had been members there for three decades. Paula was in seclusion, and Rader was in the Sedgwick County Jail, where he was being held on a $10 million bond. During his lengthy confession, Rader told the investigators about a locked file cabinet at his City Hall office where he kept copies of his communications, mementos of his victims, and photographs. They would also find some chapters of the book he was writing—"The B.T.K. Story."

Four months later, Rader pleaded guilty to the ten murders in a Wichita courtroom and calmly described each one in detail. "I had never strangled anyone before, so I really didn't know how much pressure you had to put on a person or how long it would take," he said, referring to his first victims—the Oteros and two of their children in 1974. He described masturbating over eleven-year-old Josephine after hanging her in the basement. Steve Osborn, Rader's lawyer, said later that Rader pleaded guilty because he basically wanted to take responsibility for his actions. They had determined than an insanity defense was unrealistic, he said. "Pretty much everything that came from Dennis we did not help him prepare for," Osborn told reporters. "We didn't expect this." Relatives and friends of the victims sat quietly through Rader's graphic descriptions of the murders. The following month, Rader's wife, Paula, who worked at a convenience store, was granted an emergency divorce. The judge agreed that her mental health was at risk and waived the usual sixty-day waiting period.

In August of 2005, Rader's lengthy sentencing hearing got underway, and investigators took the opportunity to present horrifying and graphic evidence of the murders. In Rader's home, office, and a camper, they had also found hundreds of index cards to which Rader had attached pictures from magazines along with details of his sexual fantasies. One showed a little girl posing in a swimsuit. Another showed the actress Meg Ryan. Lieutenant Landwehr, who had headed the investigation, asked

the judge for an order that Rader be denied crayons and markers during his years in prison.

Jeff Davis, whose mother was killed by Rader, said Rader was "a rotting corpse of a wretch of a human being hiding under a human veneer." He said he had been waiting for five thousand three hundred twenty-six days to "confront the walking cesspool" and that "there could be no justice harsh enough or pain bitter enough." He added "The world would have been better off if your mother had aborted your demon soul."

Rader addressed the court for half an hour on August 18, the second day of the hearing, his voice seeming to choke with emotion: "I hope some day God will accept me. The dark side was there, but now I think light is beginning to shine. People will say I'm not Christian, but I believe I am. I know the victims' families will never be able to forgive me, I hope somewhere deep down that will happen." At times his eyes seemed to be filled with tears.

Rader could not be executed, because Kansas did not have the death penalty in effect at the times of the murders. Nola Fouston, the Sedgwick County District Attorney, asked that Rader's sentences be carried out one after the other, "until there is no light at the end of the tunnel." People like Rader, she said, "who lead lives built around sexual perversions, just are not built like the rest of us." Judge Gregory Waller imposed the maximum possible sentence: ten consecutive life terms in prison with no possibility of parole.

But Rader found a way to keep himself in the news. He collaborated with Katherine Ramsland, a professor of forensic psychology at DeSales University, a Catholic college about fifty miles north of Philadelphia. Ramsland, who had written many true-crime books, began contacting Rader in 2010, and the two communicated in phone calls and lengthy letters. The result was *Confession of a Serial Killer—The Untold Story of Dennis Rader The BTK Killer*. Published in 2016, the book contained grisly new details of each of the murders, as well as a bit of news. He

had been planning an eleventh killing when he was arrested. He had intended to hang a woman upside down, and described precisely how he had intended to torture her. Ramsland said that about eighty percent of the book's content was provided by Rader. The other twenty percent was her commentary. Any profits from the book were to go into a trust fund for the families of the victims.

## THE VICTIMS

- **Joseph Otero.** Thirty-eight years old. **Julie Otero.** Thirty-four years old. **Josephine Otero.** Eleven years old, their daughter. **Joseph Otero Jr.** Nine years old, their son. The Oteros, originally from Puerto Rico, met and married in New York City. They had five children, and moved to Wichita in 1973 after Joseph retired from the U.S. Air Force, where he was a master sergeant.

- **Kathryn Bright.** Twenty-one years old. She graduated from Valley Center High School near Wichita in 1971, attended the University of Kansas for a semester, then returned to Wichita and took a job at Coleman, the outdoor gear company.

- **Shirley Vian Relford.** Twenty-six years old. She was the mother of three young children who were locked in a bathroom while she was attacked and killed.

- **Nancy Fox.** Twenty-five years old. She graduated from Wichita South High School and worked full-time as a secretary at a construction company, and part-time at a jewelry store in the Wichita Mall.

- **Vicki Wegerle.** Twenty-eight years old. She was the mother of two young children. She met Bill Wegerle in high school and they eventually married.

- **Marine Hedge.** Sixty-two years old. She worked in the coffee shop at the Wesley Medical Center in Park City. She had four children and was a grandmother.

- **Dolores Davis.** Sixty-two years old. A mother and grandmother, she lived alone in Park City, not far from Rader's home. She retired in 1990 from the Lario Oil & Gas Company, where she worked as a secretary.

# CHAPTER 11
# JEFFREY DAHMER

In September 1988, Jeffrey Dahmer met a boy on a street in Milwaukee and persuaded him to pose for photographs at his apartment nearby. Dahmer told the boy that he had a new camera he wanted to try out, but no one would help him. He offered the boy fifty dollars. The boy was fifteen years old. Dahmer was twenty-eight. The boy followed Dahmer inside and accepted a cup of coffee, unaware that it had been laced with a drug. Dahmer fondled the boy, who eventually escaped and was able to stumble his way home. The police were called, and Dahmer claimed that if the boy was drugged, it must have been an accident. Perhaps the boy had somehow ingested a prescription drug left on the kitchen counter. But investigators didn't believe Dahmer's version of things, and he was

arrested. After a week in jail, he was released on bail and allowed to return to his job at the Ambrosia Chocolate Company, a candy factory.

Nine months later, Dahmer pleaded guilty to second-degree sexual assault and enticement of a child for immoral purposes. The judge, William D. Gardner, sentenced him to eight years in prison, but stayed the sentence. Instead, he ordered that Dahmer serve five years' probation and spend one year in a prison work-release program that would allow him to keep his job at the candy factory. He said Dahmer had a better chance of getting the appropriate treatment for a sex offender outside of the prison system. He ordered Dahmer to have no contact with juveniles, and not to hang around schools or playgrounds.

Gale Shelton, the prosecutor, argued strongly that the deal was inappropriate, and that there was little hope that Dahmer's behavior would change if he were allowed to live on his own. She urged that he be sent to prison for five or six years, and then released on probation. Dahmer, she said, believed that his only mistake had been choosing a victim who was too young. She pointed out that Dahmer had been arrested in 1986 for urinating in front of children, and he still believed there was nothing wrong with that behavior. In that case, he had been charged with lewd and lascivious behavior, but was eventually convicted of disorderly conduct and put on probation for a year. The doctor who oversaw his therapy sessions reported that Dahmer was basically uncooperative, denying that he even had a problem. "In my judgment, it is absolutely crystal clear that the prognosis for treatment of Mr. Dahmer within the community is extremely bleak," Shelton said.

Gerald Boyer, Dahmer's lawyer, argued that he would be healthier if he got treatment rather than a prison sentence. He said Dahmer was basically "alone in the world," and was "monastic" and "Spartan." He said Dahmer was not a multiple offender. "I believe he was caught before it got to the point where it would have gotten worse." Dahmer, too, made his case to the judge. He said he had sexual problems and acknowledged

that he was a homosexual. He also said he was an alcoholic who some-times drank too much. "This is a nightmare come true for me," he said. "If anything would shock me out of my past behavior patterns, it's this." Dahmer asked the judge for a chance to prove himself, and said the entic-ing of the fifteen-year-old was "the climax of my idiocy." . . . "I can't stress enough that I want to change my conduct for the rest of my life."

After ten months in custody, Dahmer was released. He rented an apartment in Milwaukee, and a worker from the sex-crime unit was sup-posed to visit him there twice a month. Those visits never happened. The worker asked to be excused because of her overly large caseload, and her request was granted. Dahmer was basically on his own. No one knew that he had already killed five young men. He would go on to mutilate, kill, and dismember twelve more men and boys.

Jeffrey Dahmer was a standout among serial killers. Born in Milwaukee on May 21, 1960, he would learn about John Wayne Gacy, who killed thirty-three young men and boys during the 1970s and buried most of their bodies under his house about seventy-five miles south of Milwaukee in a suburb of Chicago. The horrifying details of the Gacy murders became known in December 1978, after he was arrested and confessed in gruesome detail. His defense was insanity, blamed largely on his abusive, alcoholic father. Gacy was ultimately convicted and sen-tenced to death.

Dahmer, by contrast, was raised by a caring—if troubled—family. He was born less than a year after his father, Lionel, and mother Joyce, married in 1959. During her pregnancy, they moved from their apart-ment in Milwaukee to the home of Lionel's parents in the suburb of West Allis. Lionel was a graduate student at Marquette University, where he studied analytical chemistry. Joyce worked as a teletype instructor, but had to quit her job because of a difficult pregnancy that brought nausea, seizures, difficulty walking, and other problems. At times, her doctor gave her injections of barbiturates and morphine. When Jeffrey was four

months old, Joyce's continued illness and the tension in the home led the couple to move with their new son to an apartment in Milwaukee. They lived there for two years, and, in Lionel's view, Jeffrey was a happy and playful child. In 1962, Lionel took a job at Iowa State University in Ames, Iowa, and the family moved into a small house there.

The family moved again in 1966 after Lionel got his Ph.D. and accepted a job as a research chemist in Akron, Ohio. In December 1966, their second son was born after another difficult and painful pregnancy. By then, their marriage was faltering and Jeffrey was having trouble in school. His first-grade teacher considered him extremely shy. He was polite, she said, but avoided engaging with other children and seemed profoundly unhappy.

Over the following years, Jeffrey developed a fascination with bones, and collected the bodies of dead animals. He once mounted a dog's head on a stake. He did only what he had to at school, and seemed to have no friends and no interest in anything, including his life after high school. Unnoticed by his parents, whose marriage was dissolving, he had also become a full-fledged alcoholic. His mother filed for divorce in 1977 and won custody of their younger son. Jeffrey remained at the house, and Lionel moved to a room at a motel. Eventually, Jeffrey's mother and younger brother moved away, leaving Jeffrey alone in the house. Lionel moved back in when he learned what had happened. Of course, he did not know that Jeffrey had already committed his first murder.

In June 1978, Jeffrey had picked up an eighteen-year-old hitchhiker who had just graduated from Coventry High School in Akron, Ohio. He had attended a rock concert at Chippewa Lake Park in Bath, Ohio, near Akron. Jeffrey bludgeoned and strangled him, then dismembered the body and spread the remains in the woodland around the Dahmer home in Bath Township.

In the fall of 1978, Lionel drove Jeffrey to Ohio State University in Columbus, where he had been accepted as a freshman after help and

prodding from his father. Lionel's optimism turned out to be unrealistic. Jeffrey ended the first semester with a grade point average of 0.45 and only two hours of credit. Back home, Jeffrey was arrested after getting drunk at a shopping mall. With a push from his father, Jeffrey enlisted in the Army in 1979, and was assigned to Fort McClellan in Alabama for training as a military police officer. He also received training as a medical specialist at Fort Sam Houston in Texas. Later, he was stationed in Germany. He had enlisted for six years, but was discharged three years early because of chronic alcoholism. He eventually returned to Ohio and rejoined his father, who had remarried. Jeffrey continued drinking, and was arrested after attacking police officers who had been called to remove him from a local mall.

Ultimately, Lionel and his new wife, Shari, decided that Jeffrey should leave Ohio for a while and visit his grandmother at her house in West Allis, Wisconsin, a suburb of Milwaukee. As things turned out, they got along well. She cooked meals and did his laundry. He did chores and mowed the grass. He also got a job at the Milwaukee Blood Plasma Center and joined Alcoholics Anonymous. In 1985, he got the job at the Ambrosia Chocolate Factory, and seemed to be doing well there. At home, there were some disturbing signs. His grandmother found a male mannequin from a department store hidden in Jeffery's closet. He said he had stolen it as a prank. He had disassembled the mannequin, put the pieces in shopping bags, then took them home, where he reassembled it. There were other signs during those years that hinted at a darker side of Jeffrey. Twice, a rancid odor came from the garage, and each time he had explanations: experiments with chemicals on chicken parts, and the dissection of a dead raccoon. By the fall of 1988, unknown to anyone, he had already killed four people—two in the basement of his grandmother's house.

Jeffrey moved out of the house on September 26, 1988, and into an apartment on North 24th Street in Milwaukee. That was the day he enticed the fifteen-year-old boy, Somsack Sinthasomphone, to come

inside, where he drugged and sexually molested him. Under the conditions of his bail, he had to return to his grandmother's house, where he remained until he was sentenced in the plea agreement. After ten months in custody, and with his grandmother growing frail, he moved into the Oxford Apartments on North 25th Street in Milwaukee, where he had an elaborate security system installed in his unit.

The full extent of Jeffrey Dahmer's depravity became known to law enforcement, his family, and the public after his arrest late on Monday, July 22, 1991. Two police officers on patrol at about 11:30 P.M. saw a man running on West Kilbourn Avenue with handcuffs dangling from his wrists. He told the officers that he thought the man in the apartment he had just visited intended to kill him. Dahmer let the officers into the apartment, and they smelled a stench so overpowering that they had probable cause to search it. One officer opened the refrigerator and found three preserved human heads. Elsewhere, they found body parts strewn on the floor and a large drum filled with acid that was being used to dissolve body parts. They also found photographs of mutilated dead bodies. The oversize headline in the *Milwaukee Journal* the next day summarized the events: "BODY PARTS LITTER APARTMENT." The *Milwaukee Sentinel* followed the next day with a bigger splash: "HORROR UNFOLDS: 11 SKULLS FOUND; SUSPECT CONFESSES."

The man who escaped, a thirty-one-year-old, told the police that he had met Dahmer at a shopping mall, and Dahmer invited him to his apartment for a beer. At the apartment, Dahmer handcuffed him and threatened to kill him with a butcher knife. Some of Dahmer's neighbors told the police that they heard sawing coming from the apartment at all hours. The smell coming from the apartment the previous spring was so strong that some neighbors had complained about it. A week before his arrest, Dahmer had been fired from his job at the Ambrosia Chocolate Factory for chronic lateness and absenteeism. He had been working as a laborer in the manufacturing department.

Amid the cascade of revelations in the days after Dahmer's arrest was the identification of the body of his final victim, Konerak Sinthasomphone. He was fourteen years old, the younger brother of the boy who had been assaulted by Dahmer in 1988. It was that case that had led to Dahmer's arrest, trial, and eight-year suspended sentence. On May 26, 1991, Konerak had been on his way to soccer practice when he encountered Dahmer. He later escaped from Dahmer's apartment and was seen running naked in a nearby alley, bleeding from his buttocks. Neighbors called the police, and two officers interviewed the boy, then returned him to Dahmer, who told them that the boy was nineteen years old, and was a house guest who had had too much to drink.

Not long after his arrest on July 22, 1991, Dahmer began talking to the police, who believed he might have killed as many as seventeen people. Dahmer told them that he had drugged, strangled, and dismembered the victims, and photographed their body parts at various stages. He also boiled some of their skulls. He kept one heart in a freezer so that he could eat it later. He said he met one of the victims at a gay bar in Chicago and another at a Gay Pride activity in Chicago in the summer of 1991. He invited them back to his apartment in Milwaukee, and each was drugged, strangled, and dismembered. The body parts were kept in a vat, refrigerator, or freezer. For weeks, his neighbors in the apartment building complained about what seemed like the stench of rotten meat wafting through the halls. Sometimes they heard the hum of a buzz saw and other odd noises coming from Dahmer's one-bedroom apartment on the second floor. "How could we know he was collecting dead bodies?" one resident told a reporter. "I didn't know what a dead body smells like."

Investigators also learned that Dahmer's family members had found a vat filled with bones and slime at his grandmother's house three years earlier, but did not know whether any of the remains were human. In all, he had killed eleven people at his apartment and six others elsewhere.

One skull found at the apartment belonged to a victim he had killed at his grandmother's house.

With the eyes of the nation on the bizarre, unfolding case, official actions came quickly. On July 26, three police officers who had allowed Dahmer to take Konerak Sinthasomphone back to his apartment two months earlier were suspended. The Milwaukee police chief, Philip Arreola, said he was "taken aback" by the officers' actions and called their behavior "a matter of grave concern to me and the entire department." The officers never filed a report about the incident and failed to check Dahmer's background.

As the days went on, Dahmer kept talking. Authorities searched his boyhood home in Ohio and found what appeared to be the remains of his first victim, Steven Hicks, the hitchhiker. Dahmer had told them that he'd picked up Hicks, driven him to his house, and offered him a beer. When Hicks said he wanted to leave, Dahmer hit him on the back of the head and then strangled him with a barbell. Police said they found a substantial amount of blood and a bloody handprint in the crawl space. Dahmer told them that he had dismembered Hicks's body, put the pieces in trash bags, and buried them in the backyard. Later he dug them up, smashed the bones, and scattered them in a ravine behind his house.

At long last, the friends and families of the missing had some answers. Each victim had been lured by a charming, seemingly harmless young man who offered them drinks at his apartment, money to pose for photographs, or a chance to watch some sex videos. Tracy Edwards was one of the fortunate. He was thirty-two when he met Dahmer, who "seemed so normal," at a shopping mall. Dahmer invited him to a party, and he accepted. Once there, "it was like I was confronting Satan himself." He smelled what seemed like the stench of dead bodies, saw a large knife under Dahmer's bed, and fled the apartment with a handcuff dangling from his wrist.

When the homicide cases first got to court on September 10, 1991, Dahmer pleaded not guilty to fifteen murder charges. His lawyer was

Gerald P. Boyle, who had represented him in the 1988 case involving the Sinthasomphone boy, whom he drugged and sexually abused. Boyle indicated that an insanity defense was under consideration. Four months later, Boyle notified the court that Dahmer's plea would be guilty but insane. That set the stage for a two-part process in which the judge would accept the guilty plea, and a jury would be chosen to decide on the issue of insanity. That would give Dahmer the possibility of being confined in a hospital rather than a prison. If the jury rejected the insanity plea, Dahmer would spend the rest of his life in prison. Wisconsin had abolished the death penalty in 1853.

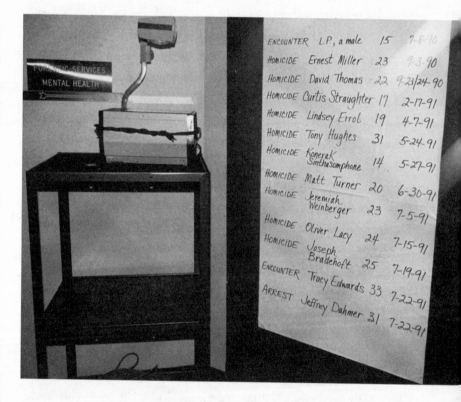

A LIST OF VICTIMS' NAMES AND THE DATES OF THEIR MURDER HANGS NEXT TO AN OVERHEAD PROJECTOR DURING THE TRIAL OF JEFFREY DAHMER.

Jury selection got underway in January 1992. Lawyers warned potential jurors that they might hear testimony about cannibalism, dismemberment, and sex with corpses. "You're going to hear about things you probably didn't know existed in the real world. Will you be able to handle that?" Boyle asked a woman during individual interviews in the chambers of Judge Lauren Gram Jr. The prosecutor, District Attorney E. Michael McCann, said "The issue is not whether he slept with a dead body or whether he tasted a dead body. The issue is whether he was responsible for the killings that occurred."

At the sentencing hearing, Tracy Edwards, who had escaped from Dahmer's apartment, told the jurors about his encounter. After Dahmer handcuffed him and held a knife, he rocked back and forth on a bed with Edwards and chanted while he watched a videotape of *The Exorcist III*. At one point, Dahmer forced him to lie on the floor. Then Dahmer put his head on Edwards's chest and told him he was going to eat his heart. Dahmer also showed him a human hand he kept in a file cabinet and forced him to look inside a refrigerator where he kept a human head. Eventually, Edwards was able to hit Dahmer in the head and run out the door.

The jurors also heard from Dennis Murphy, a homicide detective who described the sixty hours of interviews Dahmer had with the police after his arrest. Dahmer told the police that he sometimes ate parts of his victims, but "only the people he really liked and wanted to keep with him." He said Dahmer acknowledged that he was a homosexual who performed sex acts on corpses before dismembering them. He also said that he had a "high-risk lifestyle." Dahmer described once meeting a man at a gay bar and passing out drunk. He said that when he awoke, he was hog-tied in the man's apartment and suspended by ropes hooked into the ceiling fan; the man sexually assaulted him with a candle. The man ultimately freed him. He dismissed the incident as a danger of his "high-risk lifestyle."

The key issue with the insanity defense was whether Dahmer could control his behavior when he needed to. It's a particular problem for serial killers, who by definition manage to kill repeatedly, always in secret. In essence, would they perform the actions if a policeman were standing there, watching? The prosecution pointed out that Dahmer had, in fact, used condoms while having sex with some of the bodies because he wanted to avoid sexually transmitted diseases.

Boyle, Dahmer's lawyer, argued that he suffered from necrophilia, and therefore could not control his desire to have sex with dead bodies. Several psychiatrists testified for the defense that Dahmer was delusional. In closing arguments, Boyle described Dahmer as an insane "steamrolling killing machine." He said Dahmer "couldn't stop killing because of a sickness he discovered, not chose." In his closing argument, McCann, the prosecutor, said Dahmer was sane and sacrificed others for his own sexual pleasure. "Please, please, don't let this killer fool you with this special defense." The jurors were instructed to base their decision on two questions. Did Dahmer suffer from a mental illness? If so, did he have "the capacity to appreciate the wrongfulness" of his conduct or "the ability to conform" to the law?

The answer came on the following day, February 15, 1992. As they waited, relatives of some of the victims held hands and prayed quietly. Two of the twelve jurors voted that Dahmer was legally insane, but the votes of ten of the twelve jurors were sufficient for a finding of insanity under Wisconsin law. In the courtroom, relatives of some of the victims wept, gasped, and embraced each other. Two days later, Milwaukee County Judge Lauren C. Gram Jr. sentenced Dahmer to fifteen consecutive life terms in prison with no chance of parole, the longest sentence possible.

Relatives of some of the victims were in the courtroom. Dahmer sat stone-faced. His lawyer said they had no plan to appeal. At the end, Dahmer made his own unexpected statement. He said, in part, "I take all the blame for what I did," and told the judge he wished he could be put to

death for the "holocaust" he had created. It was the first time he had spoken out in court. He said he had pleaded not guilty by reason of insanity not to gain his freedom, but for understanding. "I wanted to find out just what it was that caused me to be so bad and evil," he said. "The doctors have told me about my sickness, and now I have some peace." He said he had turned again to God since his arrest. "I should have stayed with God. I tried and I failed, and I created a holocaust," he said. "I feel so bad for what I did to those poor families, and I understand their rightful hate."

On May 1, 1992, Dahmer pleaded guilty in Ohio to a charge of aggravated murder for the beating death and dismemberment of his first victim, Steven Hicks, in 1978. At the time of the killing, Ohio had no death penalty.

The end came for Dahmer on November 28, 1994, when he was killed in a Wisconsin prison at the age of thirty-four. His body was found in a pool of blood that morning in the toilet area near a prison gym. A bloody broomstick was found nearby. Dahmer and two other inmates had been assigned to clean the toilets in the area and had been left unattended for about twenty minutes. Dahmer had spent his first year in prison in protective custody to prevent just such an attack. In September 1995, his remains, except for the brain, were cremated, and each of his parents got half the ashes. His parents, who were divorced, argued about what to do with the brain. His mother, Joyce Flint, wanted to have it studied to see whether biological factors were to blame for his actions. In December 1995, a judge ordered the brain destroyed.

## THE VICTIMS

- **Steven Hicks.** Eighteen years old. June 18, 1978. He had just graduated from high school in Akron, Ohio, and was hitchhiking to a rock concert when Dahmer picked him up. He was beaten, strangled, and dismembered, and his remains were scattered in a ravine behind Dahmer's home in Ohio.

- **Steven Tuomi.** Twenty-four years old. November 20, 1987. He worked at a restaurant in Milwaukee, and was killed in a hotel room and dismembered at the house in West Allis, Wisconsin. No remains were found.

- **James Doxtator.** Fourteen years old. January 16, 1988. Dahmer met him at a bar in Wisconsin and persuaded him to pose for nude pictures in return for fifty dollars. Dahmer killed him and dismembered the body in the basement.

- **Richard Guerrero.** Twenty-two years old. March 24, 1988. He was drugged, strangled, and dismembered at Dahmer's grandmother's house in West Allis. His flesh was dissolved and his head was kept on a spear for a time, then disposed of.

- **Anthony Sears.** Twenty-four years old. March 25, 1989. He was the first victim killed at Dahmer's apartment in Milwaukee. An aspiring model, he may have been lured to the apartment by Dahmer's request to photograph him.

- **Raymond Smith**, also known as **Ricky Beeks**. Thirty-three years old. May 29, 1990. He was raised by his grandmother in Rockford, Illinois, and was the first victim killed at Dahmer's apartment on N. 25th Street.

- **Edward W. Smith.** Twenty-seven years old. June 14, 1990. He lived in Milwaukee and was an acquaintance of Dahmer. His brother reported him missing in June 1990, after he failed to return from a Gay Pride parade in Chicago. Dahmer had invited him to his apartment, where he drugged and strangled him, then put his body in the freezer. He accidentally destroyed the skull when he placed it in the oven to dry out, and it exploded. No remains were found.

- **Earnest Miller.** Twenty-four years old. September 2, 1990. He lived in Chicago and was visiting relatives in Milwaukee over the Labor Day weekend. He said he was going out to eat, then back to Chicago. His carotid artery was severed and his body was dismembered.

- **David C. Thomas.** Twenty-two years old. September 21, 1990. He lived on Birch Street in Milwaukee. A photograph of his body was found in Dahmer's apartment, and, after his arrest, Dahmer identified him as one of the victims. He had been drugged, strangled, and dismembered. No remains were found.

- **Curtis Straughter.** Eighteen years old. March 7, 1991. He lived with his grandmother in Milwaukee. He was drugged, strangled, and dismembered in Dahmer's apartment, where his body parts were saved.

- **Errol Lindsey.** Nineteen years old. April 7, 1991. He lived with his family and left home to walk to a key shop near Dahmer's apartment. Dahmer injected him with hydrochloric acid and drilled his skull. When he awoke, Dahmer strangled him to death.

- **Tony Hughes.** Thirty-one years old. May 24, 1991. A deaf-mute who lived in Madison, he had known Dahmer for two years and was visiting Milwaukee the day he disappeared. He was strangled and his body was dismembered. His skull was retained, and he was identified from dental records.

- **Konerak Sinthasomphone.** May 27, 1991. Fourteen years old. He was the younger brother of a boy assaulted by Dahmer in 1988. He was drugged and his skull was drilled and injected. He wandered into the

street and the police were called, but he was returned to Dahmer's apartment, where his head was found after Dahmer's arrest.

- **Matt Turner.** June 30, 1991. Twenty years old. Also known as **Donald Montrell,** he left his home in Flint, Michigan, in 1990 and lived in a halfway house in Chicago. He was picked up by Dahmer at the Chicago Pride Parade and lured back to Milwaukee. Dahmer drugged him, killed him, and kept his head in the freezer.

- **Jeremiah Weinberger.** July 6, 1991. Twenty-three years old. He was last seen alive on July 6, when he met Dahmer at a gay bar in Chicago. Dahmer offered him money to pose for photographs and watch videos at his apartment in Milwaukee. Dahmer injected boiling water into his head, decapitated him, and placed the body in a 57-gallon drum.

- **Oliver Lacy.** July 15, 1991. Twenty-four years old. He had moved to Milwaukee four months earlier, to be near his two-year-old son. A track star in high school, he got a job at a cleaning company in Milwaukee and was engaged to be married. He disappeared after stopping at a mall for ice cream after work. He was drugged, strangled, and decapitated. His head and heart were in Dahmer's freezer.

- **Joseph Bradehoft.** July 16, 1991. Twenty-five years old. A married father of three, he had recently moved to Milwaukee to live with his brother and look for a job. Dahmer said he met Bradehoft at a bus stop near Marquette University and offered him money to pose for photographs at his apartment. His head was found in the refrigerator, and his body was in the 57-gallon drum.

# CHAPTER 12
# GARY LEON RIDGWAY

The revelation came thirty-seven years after she disappeared. Her remains were found in a swampy, wooded area next to a baseball field near the Seattle-Tacoma International Airport on March 21, 1984. A dog that belonged to the groundskeeper had done some digging and brought a leg bone home. At first they called the body "Bones 10." Later it was renamed "Jane Doe B10." In January 2021, the puzzle was solved using advanced DNA technology. She was Wendy Stephens, a fourteen-year-old who had run away from her home in Denver, Colorado, in 1983. She was the youngest victim of Gary Leon Ridgway, the mysterious "Green River Killer" who had terrified the Seattle-Tacoma area near the Pacific Coast in the 1980s.

The first five bodies, weighted down by rocks, were pulled out of the Green River in King County in 1982. After that, bodies were found in wooded areas. By 1986, investigators had formed the Green River Task Force, which tied the Green River Killer to the deaths of thirty-four girls and women, as well as the disappearances of eleven more. Most were described as runaways, transients, or prostitutes. Officers began going out each night to talk to women in the red-light district of South Seattle to gather tips and warn the women about the dangers. Ridgway had been arrested and charged with prostitution in that area in May 1982 when he approached a police decoy during a sting operation. For a time, officials suspected that the Green River Killer was one of four serial killers working in the area, independent of each other. Ridgway became a Green River suspect in 1984, and was interviewed by the police but let go.

In 1985, the FBI, which had been assisting the local police, formally entered the investigation. It appeared that two of the victims had been kidnapped in Seattle, then taken to a suburb of Portland, Oregon, before they were killed. The crossing of state lines was a violation of federal kidnapping laws. By 1986, Seattle's Green River Task Force had grown to include more than forty detectives. Each night, they walked the streets of the red-light district, looking for tips and warning the women about the danger. During that time, prostitution dropped dramatically in the area. Things were different now. Everyone seemed like a suspect. When undercover officers tried to handcuff women and make an arrest, suspected prostitutes often demanded that a uniformed officer be present. Some of the women acknowledged that they were heroin addicts and had no other way to earn the money they needed. A young woman named Tonya told a reporter that her mother was overjoyed when she told her she was in jail. "My mom sounded like she was going to cry this morning because she was happy I was in jail and not dead. She said, 'Tonya, what's it going to take for you to learn?'"

Ridgway remained on the radar, and, after an extensive background investigation, he was interviewed by the task force again in 1987. He agreed to give a saliva sample by chewing on a piece of gauze. Again, he was let go. By the end of 1990, the deaths of forty-nine victims had been attributed to the Green River Killer, but investigators suspected that the number was much higher. Hundreds of women who were thought to be missing in the Seattle area from 1982 to 1984 could not be found, despite the continued efforts of the task force. Bones that could not be identified had been found in the area where the killer had been active. Investigators reviewed lists of women who were reported missing and examined court records in cases where women had been arrested on prostitution-related charges but failed to turn up for court appearances. In the summer of 1990, they compiled a list of one hundred twenty women who police agencies had tried—but failed—to find. Eventually, the list of missing women reached more than three hundred.

Ridgway was interviewed several times throughout the 1980s. He was viewed as cooperative. He admitted "dating" prostitutes, and said he had assaulted one, Rebecca Garde, because she bit him. She got away. He denied killing anyone, and he passed a polygraph test. The investigators looked deeply into his background. He was born on February 18, 1949, in Salt Lake City, Utah. His family moved to the Seattle area eleven years later. He was held back two grades in school, and graduated from Tyee High School in 1969. He enlisted in the Navy and married his first wife in 1970, before he was sent to the Philippines, where he first encountered prostitutes. While he was overseas, his wife became involved with another man. When Ridgway returned, she sought a divorce, and he called her "a whore." The divorce was finalized in January 1972.

Soon after he returned from the Philippines, Ridgway got a job as a painter at the Kenworth Truck Company in a suburb of Seattle. He remarried in 1973, and in 1975 they had a son. The marriage deteriorated over the years, as Ridgway was frequently gone in the evenings

without explanation. He sometimes returned home dirty and wet. At least once, he grabbed his wife by the neck. They divorced in 1981, and she got primary custody of their son, who stayed with his father on alternate weekends. In November, Ridgway bought a house a few blocks from an area notorious for prostitution on Pacific Highway South. He lived there alone until 1985, except for six months when renters lived there. In 1985, he met a woman at a meeting of Parents Without Partners, and she moved into the house. They married in 1988, and they moved several times in the Seattle area over the years.

For Ridgway, the beginning of the end came on April 8, 1987. The task-force investigators got a search warrant for his home, his work locker, and several vehicles. They seized hundreds of items of evidence, including carpet fibers, ropes, paint samples, and tarps, and compared them with evidence found with the victims. Then the investigation stalled.

Things picked up in March 2001, after a much smaller task force was revived by King County Sheriff Dave Reichart, who had worked on the case when he was a young officer decades earlier. The investigators submitted biological evidence from victims to the state forensic labs for DNA analysis. There were four suspects. The new analysis and improved testing showed a match—Gary Ridgway had had sex with three of the victims. But the matches did not prove that he killed them.

On November 10, 2001, Ridgway was driving on a street in Seattle when he saw a woman who appeared to be a prostitute. He offered her money for sex. In fact, she was an undercover vice officer, and she was unaware that they were being watched by members of the Green River team. They swooped in and arrested him. He was charged with loitering for the purpose of prostitution and was released on bail, still unaware of what was happening behind the scenes. The team secretly followed him for a time, but they were afraid that he might start killing again. They were mindful of the fact that he had begun killing prostitutes decades earlier after he was charged with soliciting a prostitute.

On November 30, 2001, the team arrested Ridgway at the Kenworth Truck Company, where he had been working since his discharge from the trucking company in a Seattle suburb, where he worked painting vehicles and had been employed for thirty-two years. Ridgway went quietly that day, officials said. Now fifty-two years old, Ridgway was suspected of involvement in the deaths of dozens of women and teenage girls. Sheriff Reichert called a news conference and said it was "one of the most exciting days" in his career. "I cannot say with certainty that Gary Ridgway is responsible for all of those deaths," he said, "but boy, have we made one giant leap forward." It was the saliva sample—preserved by the authorities—and the emergence of DNA technology that finally led to his arrest. Ridgway had long been a prime suspect. Now he was conclusively linked to the remains of three of the victims.

KING COUNTY SHERIFF DETECTIVES SEARCH FOR EVIDENCE IN THE BACKYARD OF THE HOME OF GARY LEON RIDGWAY, IN AUBURN, WA, MONDAY, DECEMBER 3, 2001.

Years earlier, the FBI had joined the Green River investigation, calling it "Major Case 77, GREENMURS." Over time, the investigators had collected more than eight thousand pieces of evidence, and the task force had developed several psychological profiles. One theory suggested that the killer was a police officer or a security guard. Another said he was someone who had very strong feelings of inadequacy, believed that women couldn't be trusted, and, when he sees women openly prostituting themselves, "it makes his blood boil." Ridgway and his second wife, Judith, had moved into a house on a one-acre property in Auburn, a quiet suburb of Seattle, four years before his arrest. Some of his neighbors told reporters that he was a "nice guy" who chopped wood for his fireplace; walked his dog—a poodle; and doted on Judith. They also had two cats. Others said they were a bit leery of him. They had been angered when he chopped down a stretch of trees at the back of the property, then spent many hours using a chipper and chainsaw.

On December 5, 2001, Ridgway was formally charged with the murders of four women, but prosecutors did not say that he was definitively the Green River Killer. They did say that DNA technology had allowed them to match semen on three victims to Ridgway. His court-appointed lawyers argued that the DNA match did not necessarily mean he was the killer, and pointed out that Ridgway had a history of sex with prostitutes. The three victims were Marcia Chapman, thirty-one years old; Cynthia Hinds, seventeen years old; and Opal Mills, sixteen years old. Their bodies had been discovered in or near the Green River in August 1992. The fourth victim was Carol Ann Christensen, a twenty-one-year-old whose body was discovered in May 1983 in a wooded area nearby.

The next two years were a bit of a mystery, at least to the public. Behind the scenes, the reassembled Green River Task Force searched for more information and evidence. Eventually, they agreed to a deal with

Ridgway and his lawyers. They would drop their request for the death penalty if Ridgway would help them locate the bodies of the rest of the victims. To avoid the difficulty of moving Ridgway in and out of a jail cell each day, he was quietly transferred to a room at the team's headquarters. They spent five months interviewing him, always with the unspoken threat of the death penalty in the background.

The sprawling, complex case was resolved on November 5, 2003. Ridgway pleaded guilty to forty-eight murders. "I killed so many women, I have a hard time keeping them straight," he said in an eighty-page statement read aloud by Jeff Baird, the prosecutor in the case. "My plan was to kill as many women I thought were prostitutes as I possibly could. I picked prostitutes as my victims because I hate most prostitutes and I did not want to pay them for sex. I also picked prostitutes for victims because they were easy to pick up without being noticed."

In most cases, he did not know their names. He said he killed most of them in his house, and others in his truck not far from where he had picked them up. He described how he had had sex with dead bodies. Relatives of the victims listened and wept as the details of each killing were read. Ridgway stood quietly before the courtroom, showing little emotion, and repeated the word "guilty" forty-eight times. But he did tear up a bit now and then and asked forgiveness from his family. He expressed remorse for "the ladies who were not found" and said "May they rest in peace. They need a better place than where I gave them."

Richard Jones, the King County Superior Court Judge hearing the case, was unmoved. He lambasted Ridgway and said he had shown "callous indifference" over the previous two years as prosecutors interviewed him. "As you spend the balance of your life in your tiny cell surrounded only by your thoughts, please know that the women you killed were not throwaways or pieces of candy in a dish placed upon this planet for the sole purpose of satisfying your murderous desires."

Norm Maleng, the King County prosecutor, told reporters it had been excruciating to decide early on whether to prosecute Ridgway for the seven murders they were certain about and pursue the death penalty, or spare him the death penalty in return for more information about the victims. "Here we have a man presumed to be the most prolific serial killer. A man who preyed on vulnerable young women; and I thought, as many of you did, if any case screams out for the death penalty, this was it," Maleng said. They finally gave in, he said, because the possibility of giving forty-one other families the chance to learn what had happened to their children or siblings was more important than exacting "the ultimate punishment."

Ridgway's lengthy confession provided a wealth of insight into his life and character. He had a low IQ—somewhere in the eighties—and often wet his bed at night. His father was a bus driver and his mother was a sales clerk at a department store in Seattle. He had two brothers, one older and one younger. He had sexual fantasies about his mother, who sometimes bathed him after he wet his bed. He contemplated killing his mother and his second and third wives. His second wife, the mother of his son, divorced him in 1981 in part because he liked to sneak up and scare her, and once tried to choke her. He killed at least forty-two women and teenagers in the three years before he met his third wife in 1985. They were still married when he was arrested in 2001, and she began divorce proceedings.

On December 18, 2003, families of the victims got their day in court. Nancy Gabbert, whose seventeen-year-old daughter Sandra was killed in 1983, addressed Ridgway, who turned slightly from the defense table as she and other speakers had their say. "Gary Ridgway is an evil creature who I would condemn to many, many long years of anguish and despair." He seemed to show no emotion. He did react to Robert Rule, whose sixteen-year-old daughter Linda was killed by Ridgway in 1982. Rule, with a long white beard and wearing rainbow suspenders, sometimes

played Santa Claus. He said "Mr. Ridgway, there are people here who hate you. I am not one of them. I forgive you for what you have done." Ridgway seemed to wipe away tears.

As the session was broadcast live on television, Ridgway also addressed the court. "I have tried hard to remember as much as I could to help the detectives find and recover the ladies," he said. He paused frequently and wiped his eyes. "I'm sorry for killing these ladies. They had their whole lives ahead of them." He cried at times, and asked forgiveness from his family.

King County Superior Court Judge Richard Jones had the last word. Ridgway, he said, displayed "Teflon-coated emotions," adding "There is nothing in your life that was significant other than your own demented, calculating, and lustful passion of being the emissary of death."

Ridgway had shown an uncharacteristic degree of humanity in 2002, when one of his lawyers, Michele Shaw, told him that his brothers and his son did not want him to be executed. He "just broke down and sobbed profusely," she said. Anthony Savage, another of his lawyers, said Ridgway remained a mystery. "Gary breaks the mold in a lot of different directions. The man is obviously off the rails, around the bend, down the river, whatever you want to call it. I don't think we'll ever know what fueled his anger."

In 2011, Ridgway was led back into a courtroom to plead guilty to a forty-ninth murder. The victim was Rebecca Marrero, a twenty-year-old who was last seen in 2003 leaving a motel in the Sea-Tac area, where she worked as a prostitute. Her skull was found on December 21, 2010, under a log near a ravine, about a hundred feet from where the remains of another victim had been found. Under the terms of his original plea deal, he could not be executed.

Superior Court Judge Mary Roberts addressed Ridgway, who was led into the courtroom in his orange jumpsuit, looking considerably older. "Usually when I sentence an individual, even for the most serious

of crimes, I try to reach out in some way. In this case, I cannot. I can find no compassion for you. Instead, my heart is completely filled with sympathy for the family of Rebecca Marrero, and despair to know that a person is capable of this sort of crime." Ridgway had little to say. He responded "yes" or "no" to questions from the prosecutor.

Rebecca's sister, Mary Marrero, got her turn: "What does it take to get the death penalty in the state of Washington? My sister is victim number forty-nine. I don't agree with this deal to spare his pathetic life. It makes me sick to my stomach that he beat the system. He's worthless and he's not going to give any more victims up. He knows where they all are, and what he did to them. He will never give those innocent victims up for nothing. He's a waste to society and he's a waste of space." She had more to say. "If I had one thing to ask you today, it would be to kill him. I know he will burn in hell, because he can't beat God. God will take care of him if the system fails to do so. Forty-nine women—aunts, mothers, sisters, cousins—we're talking about a whole generation! I hate your guts, Gary Ridgway, and your day is coming soon."

Ridgway was given a chance to respond. He said "I'm sorry," but was promptly interrupted by a man sitting with the Marrero family who cut him off. "Just shut your . . . mouth, just sit the . . . down! Shut up, nobody wants to hear . . . from you!"

In June of 2012, there was another discovery. The victim known only as "Bones 16" was identified as Sandra Denise Major, a twenty-year old whose bones were found near a cemetery in Auburn on December 30, 1985. She had last been seen on December 24, 1982, getting into a truck with a man. Advances in DNA technology led to the finding.

Ridgway turned seventy-three in February 2022, and was still serving his time at the Washington State Penitentiary in Walla Walla. He claimed to have killed dozens more women than he was ever charged with—so many that he'd lost count.

# THE VICTIMS

- **Wendy Lee Coffield.** Sixteen years old. July 8, 1982. She ran away from the home of her foster family in Tacoma, Washington, and her body was found a week later.

- **Wendy Stephens.** Fourteen years old. She ran away from her parents' home in Denver, Colorado, in 1982. She was killed in 1983, and her body was found in 1984.

- **Gisele Lovvorn.** Seventeen years old. She disappeared on July 17, 1982, and her body was found on September 25, 1982.

- **Debra Lynn Bonner.** Twenty-three years old. She disappeared on July 25, 1982, and her body was found on August 12, 1982.

- **Marcia Gaye Chapman.** Thirty-one years old. She disappeared on August 1, 1982, and her body was found on August 15, 1982.

- **Cynthia Jean Hinds.** Seventeen years old. She disappeared on August 11, 1982, and her body was found on August 15, 1982.

- **Opal Charmaine Mills.** Sixteen years old. She disappeared on August 12, 1982, and her body was found on August 15, 1982.

- **Sandra Denise Major.** Twenty years old. She disappeared on December 24, 1982, and her remains were found on December 30, 1985.

- **Terry Rene Milligan.** Sixteen years old. She disappeared on August 29, 1982, and her body was found on April 1, 1984.

- **Mary Bridget Meehan.** Eighteen years old. She disappeared on September 15, 1982, and her body was found on November 13, 1983.

- **Deborah Lorraine Estes.** Fifteen years old. She disappeared on September 20, 1982, and her body was found on May 30, 1988.

- **Linda Jane Rule.** Sixteen years old. She disappeared on September 26, 1982, and her body was found on January 31, 1983.

- **Denise Darcel Bush.** Twenty-two years old. She disappeared on October 8, 1982, and her skull was found on June 12, 1985. The rest of her body was found on February 10, 1990.

- **Shawnda Leea Summers.** Seventeen years old. She disappeared on October 9, 1982, and her body was found on August 11, 1983.

- **Shirley Marie Sherrill.** Eighteen years old. She disappeared in October or November 1982, and her body was found on June 14, 1985.

- **Colleen Renee Brockman.** Fifteen years old. She disappeared on December 24, 1982, and her body was found on May 26, 1984.

- **Alma Ann Smith.** Eighteen years old. She disappeared on March 3, 1983, and her body was found on April 2, 1984.

- **Delores LaVerne Williams.** Seventeen years old. She disappeared on March 8, 1983, and her body was found on March 31, 1984.

- **Gail Lynn Mathews.** Twenty-four years old. She disappeared on April 10, 1983, and her body was found on September 18, 1983.

- **Andrea M. Childers.** Nineteen years old. She disappeared on April 16, 1983, and her body was found on October 11, 1989.

- **Sandra Kay Gabbert.** Seventeen years old. She disappeared on April 17, 1983, and her body was found on April 1, 1984.

- **Kimi-Kai Pitsor.** Sixteen years old. She disappeared on April 17, 1983, and her skull was found on December 15, 1983. More remains were found in January 1986.

- **Marie Malvar.** Eighteen years old. She disappeared on April 30, 1983, and her body was found on September 29, 2003.

- **Carol Ann Christensen.** Twenty-one years old. She disappeared on May 3, 1983, and her body was found on May 8, 1983.

- **Martina Theresa Authorlee.** Eighteen years old. She disappeared on May 22, 1983, and her body was found on November 19, 1984.

- **Cheryl Lee Wims.** Eighteen years old. She disappeared on May 23, 1983, and her body was found on March 22, 1984.

- **Yvonne Shelly Antosh.** Nineteen years old. She disappeared on May 31, 1983, and her body was found on October 15, 1983.

- **Carrie Ann Rois.** Fifteen years old. She disappeared between May 31 and June 13, 1983. Her body was found on March 10, 1985.

- **Constance Elizabeth Naon.** Twenty-one years old. She disappeared on June 8, 1983, and her body was found on October 27, 1983.

- **Kelly Marie Ware.** Twenty-two years old. She disappeared on July 19, 1983, and her body was found on October 29, 1983.

- **Tina Marie Thompson.** Twenty-two years old. She disappeared on July 25, 1983, and her body was found on April 20, 1984.

- **April Dawn Buttram.** Seventeen years old. She disappeared on August 18, 1983, and her remains were found on August 30 and September 2, 2003.

- **Debora May Abernathy.** Twenty-six years old. She disappeared on September 5, 1983, and her body was found on March 31, 1984.

- **Tracy Ann Winston.** Nineteen years old. She disappeared on September 12, 1983, and parts of her body were found near the Green River on March 27, 1986. Her skull was found on an old logging road in Issaquah, Washington, in 2005.

- **Maureen Sue Feeney.** Nineteen years old. She disappeared on September 28, 1983, and her body was found on May 2, 1986.

- **Mary Sue Bello.** Twenty-five years old. She disappeared on October 11, 1983, and her body was found on October 12, 1984.

- **Pammy Avent.** Sixteen years old. She disappeared on October 26, 1983, and her body was found on August 16, 2003.

- **Delise Louise Plager.** Twenty-two years old. She disappeared on October 30, 1983, and her body was found on February 14, 1984.

- **Kimberly Nelson,** also known as **Tina Thompson** and **Linda Lee Barkey.** Twenty-six years old. She disappeared on November 1, 1983, and her body was found on June 14, 1986.

- **Lisa Lorraine Yates.** Twenty-six years old. She disappeared on December 23, 1983, and her body was found on March 13, 1984.

- **Mary Exzetta West.** Sixteen years old. She disappeared on February 6, 1984, and her body was found on September 8, 1985.

- **Cindy Ann Smith.** Seventeen years old. She disappeared on March 21, 1984, and her body was found on June 27, 1987.

- **Patricia Michelle Barczak.** Nineteen years old. She disappeared in October 1986, and her body was found in 1993.

- **Roberta Joseph Hayes.** Twenty-one years old. She disappeared in 1987, and her body was found on September 12, 1991.

- **Marta Reeves.** Thirty-seven years old. She disappeared in 1990, and her body was found in September of that year.

- **Patricia Ann Yellow Robe.** Thirty-eight years old. She disappeared in 1988 and her body was found on August 6 of that year.

- **Rebecca Marrero.** Twenty years old. She disappeared in December 1982 after leaving a motel in the Seattle-Tacoma area. On December 21, 2010, her skull was found in a ravine.

# CHAPTER 13

# SAMUEL LITTLE

When American justice caught up with Samuel Little in 2014, he was seventy-four years old, and he was enraged. "I didn't do it!" he shouted from his wheelchair in a Los Angeles courtroom. Three weeks earlier, he had been convicted of the murders of three women during the 1980s. Sentencing day was September 25, 2014, and relatives and friends of his victims finally had their chance to confront him. By the time Mary Louise Frias took the witness stand, Little had heard enough. She was the goddaughter of Guadalupe Apodaca, who was killed in 1989 when she was forty-six years old. She said Little had "no conscience, no soul." After

Little's outburst, she said "God will judge you." When Apodaca's son, Tony Zambrano, got his turn, he said "You took something very dear to me, sir." Little swore at Zambrano, and the exchange of vulgarities escalated.

Superior Court Judge George Lomeli had had enough. He stopped the shouting match and sentenced Little to three terms of life in prison with no possibility of parole. A death sentence would have meant prolonged litigation and years of appeals that Little appeared unlikely to survive, given his fragile health.

Little had sat quietly during the trial weeks earlier, showing no interest when prosecutors projected photographs of the youthful Samuel Little on a screen in the courtroom. At six feet, three inches tall, and weighing more than two hundred pounds, he had been an imposing figure. The emergence of DNA technology had finally been his undoing, as it had for other murderers and an increasing number of serial killers in the second half of the twentieth century. Little's DNA had been found on the bodies of Apodaca and two other women who were beaten and strangled in the late 1980s. Their bodies had been dumped within a few miles of each other. Apodaca's body was found on September 13, 1989, in an abandoned commercial garage. The body of thirty-five-year-old Audrey Nelson was found in a dumpster in a parking lot on August 14, 1989. The body of forty-one-year-old Carol Alford was found in an alley on July 13, 1987.

The jurors were shown crime-scene photographs of the women, in which their bodies were naked except for a shirt or sweater pushed up around their shoulders. They appeared to have been strangled. Before the jury was sent to deliberate, the prosecutor, Deputy District Attorney Beth Silverman, left them with a final thought—all the women had something in common. "They were women who law enforcement at the time were unlikely to take seriously." That trial was the beginning of the end for Little. Law-enforcement agencies believed that he might have

been responsible for dozens of murders across the country, and that he preyed on vulnerable women, including prostitutes and drug addicts. Now the hunt was on.

By the beginning of 2015, investigators had put together a timeline that tracked Little across the country, beginning with his birth in Reynolds, Georgia on June 7, 1940. He was raised by his grandmother in Loraine, Ohio. In 1956, when he was sixteen years old, he was arrested on a burglary charge in Omaha, Nebraska, and served time with a youth authority. From 1957 to 1975 he sometimes used the name Samuel McDowell, and was arrested twenty-six times in eleven states, from Massachusetts to California and Oregon. The range of charges included shoplifting, rape, DUI, and aggravated assault on a police officer. In December 1976, he was sentenced to three months in prison for assaulting a woman with intent to rape in Sunset Hills, Missouri. He was then given credit for the three months he had spent in jail, and freed.

The ultimate revelation came in the spring of 2018, when the FBI's Violent Criminal Apprehension Program, known as ViCAP, notified Texas investigators that they had found a case that sounded like the work of Little. Christina Palazzolo, a ViCAP crime analyst, and Angela Williamson, a Department of Justice liaison, traveled to Los Angeles along with James Holland, an officer from the Texas Department of Public Safety, commonly known as the Texas Rangers. In exchange for a move to Texas, Little was willing to talk.

As Palazzolo and Williamson went through records, Little opened up to Holland. Little went through each city and state, describing the number of people he had killed: one in Jackson, Mississippi; one in Cincinnati, Ohio; three in Phoenix, Arizona; one in Las Vegas, Nevada. He chose marginalized women, such as drug addicts and prostitutes, some of whose bodies were left unidentified and whose deaths were left uninvestigated. Often, there were no obvious signs of homicide. He

often knocked the women out with powerful punches or strangled them. There were no stab marks or bullet wounds.

Little was charged with the murder of Denise Christie Brothers, who was strangled to death in the west Texas city of Odessa in 1994. Little was moved to Texas in the fall of 2018, and investigators from around the country traveled there to interview him. Every day for weeks, Little was escorted in a wheelchair from his cell to an interview room under heavy guard. He was seventy-eight years old and suffered from diabetes and heart disease.

Eventually, Little confessed to more than ninety murders going back nearly fifty years. By then, investigators had tied Little to thirty of the murders. His victims were, in general, poor, marginalized drug addicts or alcoholics whose disappearances frequently went unnoticed. Investigators said he seemed to enjoy the attention he was receiving as he recited details only the killer could know. He also seemed to prefer the Ector County jail in Texas over the somewhat chaotic state of the jail in Los Angeles County. Investigators said he showed no signs of remorse as he recalled the killings in minute detail. One interviewer said he wondered aloud how Little had avoided arrest for so many years. Little responded "I can go into my world and do what I want to do." His world, he said, was one where poverty, drug addiction, and murders were common.

By June 2019, investigators had linked more than sixty killings in at least fourteen states to Little, who had been returned to California to serve his life sentences there. In failing health, he continued to cooperate with investigators. He was charged in June with the 1981 killing of a Cincinnati woman and the killings of two women in Cleveland. On October 6, 2019, the FBI announced that Little was the most prolific serial killer in United States history. He had confessed to ninety-three murders and had been matched to fifty of those cases.

Officials released sketches drawn by Little of five women he claimed to have killed, along with information about where he met each one. The sketches were among dozens of detailed portraits he had drawn using chalk pastels. One of the five depicted was a transgender woman named Marianne, whom he met in Miami in the early 1970s. Little said he did not know the names of many of his victims, or only knew their first name or nickname. Investigators said his drawings had been quite accurate, and had helped to match him to several cold cases. In videotaped interviews released by the FBI, Little smiled and laughed as he described some killings. He expressed no remorse.

DRAWINGS BY SERIAL KILLER SAMUEL LITTLE BASED ON MEMORIES OF HIS MURDER VICTIMS. LEFT: UNMATCHED CONFESSION; BLACK FEMALE; KILLED IN 1987 IN LOS ANGELES, CALIFORNIA. RIGHT: UNMATCHED CONFESSION; BLACK FEMALE; KILLED IN 1984 IN FORT MYERS, FLORIDA.

Little died on December 30, 2020, at a Los Angeles area hospital. He was eighty years old. A little more than half of his victims had been verified and identified.

On September 21, 2021, the skeletal remains of a body found by a group of hunters in Mississippi in December of 1977 were identified. Her name was Clara Birdlong. She had long been known to investigators as "Escatawpa Jane Doe" because her remains had been found near the Escatawpa River Marsh Coastal Preserve. Little had admitted killing her, but did not know her name. Investigators had tried over the years to match her DNA, but had gotten no results. She was born in 1933 in Leflore County, so would have been about forty years old when she was killed.

## THE VICTIMS

- **Mary Brosley.** Thirty-three years old. She was estranged from her family in Massachusetts. She met Little at a bar near Miami on New Year's Eve, and by New Year's Day, 1971, he had choked her to death.

- **Clara Birdlong.** About forty years old. Her remains were found in a marsh area in Mississippi in 1977.

- **Patricia Ann Mount.** Age unknown. Her body was discovered in Forest Grove, Florida, on September 12, 1982.

- **Melinda LaPree.** Age unknown. Her body was found in a cemetery in Gautier, Mississippi, in October 1982.

- **Carol Alford.** Forty-one years old. Her body was found in an alley in Los Angeles on July 13, 1987.

- **Audrey Nelson.** Thirty-five years old. Her body was found in a trash bin in downtown Los Angeles on August 14, 1989.

- **Guadalupe Apodaca.** Forty-six years old. Her body was found in an abandoned commercial garage in Los Angeles on September 3, 1989.

- **Denise Christie Brothers.** Thirty-eight years old. Odessa, Texas, 1994.

- **Melissa Thomas.** Twenty-four years old. Her body was found under a tree in a cemetery in Opelousas, Louisiana, in January 1996.

# EPILOGUE

## FEMALE SERIAL KILLERS AND SERIAL KILLERS ON DEATH ROW

Until the late 1980s, the notion that a woman could be a surreptitious—and prolific—serial killer was largely the stuff of fiction. The 1970s had produced a surge of male serial killers across the United States whose brutality was sometimes focused on women. Rodney Alcala, for one, emerged into the national news when he was arrested in 1979. He had appeared on an episode of *The Dating Game* in 1978, and was chosen as the winner. By then, he had already murdered at least four women and raped an eight-year-old girl. He went on to kill more. Ted Bundy was sentenced to death in 1979 for killing two sorority sisters at a college in Florida, and was suspected of killing dozens more across the country. The mysterious "Hillside Strangler" murdered girls and young women in southern California in the late 1970s. The strangler turned out to be two cousins—Kenneth Bianchi and Angelo Buono.

The world first became aware of Dorothea Puente at the end of 1988, when she became known as "The Death House Lady." She ran what amounted to a care home for the elderly in Sacramento, California, not far from the state capitol building. She killed nine of the residents—four of them men—and buried most of their bodies in the backyard before she was caught. Her motives were a bit murky, but she had profited over

the years by continuing to collect their Social Security checks and other benefits. A jury convicted her of all the murders, but could not agree on the death sentence. Instead, she got life in prison.

Aileen Wuornos, who came to be called "The Damsel of Death," committed her first murder in 1989 and her seventh in November, 1990. She was a prostitute who solicited men along highways in Florida, then killed them. She was arrested two months after the seventh murder largely because the FBI and a "computer whiz" in a Florida sheriff's department, using emerging technology, identified her as the likely killer. She was convicted, sentenced to death, and executed by lethal injection in 2002, nearly twelve years after her arrest.

By the 1990s, what had been seen as the Golden Age of serial killers seemed to be coming to an end. DNA technology, widespread automobile and cell-phone tracking, broad communication among police departments, and data analysis by the FBI had made it quite difficult for repeat killers to avoid detection. There were, however, exceptions. Reta Mays, a nursing assistant who worked for the Veterans Administration hospital in Clarksburg, West Virginia, was sentenced to seven consecutive life terms in prison after pleading guilty to charges that she had killed elderly men by injecting them with lethal doses of insulin she found in supply rooms and unsupervised carts around the hospital. She worked overnight shifts and had little supervision. None of the victims had been near death when she injected them, and some were on the verge of being released from the hospital. At her sentencing in 2021, Thomas Kleeh, the federal judge handling the case, said "You're the monster no one sees coming."

The 1980s cases of Wuornos and Puente, the two most infamous female serial killers, illustrate the continuing difficulties encountered by the American justice system when grappling with the cases of prolific killers and the issue of capital punishment. Puente spent nearly twenty-three years in prison before she died of natural causes in 2011. Wuornos spent

over eleven years in prison before she was executed. Execution, if it comes at all, happens many years—even decades—after the crimes. Alcala, the "Dating Game Killer," was first sentenced to death on June 20, 1980. Decades of appeals and litigation followed. He died of natural causes forty-one years later, on July 24, 2021, at a hospital near the Corcoran State Prison in central California. Technically, he was still under a death sentence, but in 2019 California Governor Gavin Newsom had signed an executive order imposing a moratorium on all executions in the state. He said the death penalty had been a failure.

## EXECUTED SERIAL KILLERS

**Bobby Joe Long.** Sentenced to death in May 1985, and again in July 1986, he was executed in Florida thirty-four years later. He had been convicted of the May 27, 1984, murder of Michelle Denise Simms, one of nine young women he killed in Florida in the 1980s. Long was sixty-five years old on May 23, 2019, when the lethal injection was administered. He had no visitors that day, and no spiritual adviser stopped by for a final talk. His last meal, at 9:30 A.M., was a roast beef sandwich, bacon, French fries, and soda. He was described as "calm and quiet." He was pronounced dead at 6:55 P.M. in the death chamber at the prison in Starke. He had not said a word.

**Aileen Wuornos.** Sentenced to death on January 31, 1992, she was executed in Florida nearly eleven years later, on October 9, 2002. She was forty-six-years old. She had been arrested on January 9, 1991, when she was thirty-three years old. She eventually admitted killing seven middle-aged men in Florida in 1989 and 1990. A jury convicted her of one murder on January 7, 1992, then voted unanimously that she should be executed. The judge ruled on January 31, 1992, that she would be electrocuted. As deputies put her in a van, she yelled to reporters "Bust these crooked cops and their conspiracy, please! I'm innocent!" Later that year, she pleaded

no contest to three other murders, and received three more death sentences. In October 1992, the Florida Supreme Court confirmed the four death sentences. Jeb Bush, then the Florida governor, stayed the execution so that experts could evaluate her mental health. The stay was lifted in October 2002. On October 9, an injection was administered to her right arm, and she was pronounced dead seventeen minutes later.

**Ted Bundy.** Sentenced to death on July 31, 1979, he was executed in Florida nine years later on, January 24, 1989. He was forty-two years old. He had been convicted of killing two Florida State University students in their sorority house in 1978. A year later, he was convicted of murdering a twelve-year-old girl and was again sentenced to death. Nearly ten years of litigation followed. As his execution date approached, Bundy began to cooperate with investigators and confessed to at least sixteen other murders. Florida Governor Bob Martinez refused to delay the execution, saying he would not "negotiate with a killer." Bundy was executed in Florida's electric chair on January 24, 1989. The precise number of murders committed by Bundy was never known. Investigators concluded that Bundy may have committed about thirteen murders in Utah, Colorado, and the state of Washington. Additionally, Bundy had provided information about fourteen murders in Washington, Utah, Idaho, California, Vermont, and Pennsylvania, and about twenty more cases around the country going back to 1969.

**William Bonin.** Sentenced to death in 1982, and again in 1983, he was executed in California fourteen years later, on February 23, 1996. He was forty-nine years old. A truck driver who lived in southern California, Bonin—along with his friend Vernon Butts—was the mysterious "Freeway Killer" who terrorized California in 1979 and 1980. Butts hanged himself in his jail cell in 1981 after telling investigators the gruesome details of Bonin's attacks on the victims. Bonin had sexually

molested a twelve-year-old and three teenage boys in the 1960s. He was declared a mentally disordered sex offender and was eventually released from prison, but then he attacked another teenager, went to prison, and was paroled in 1978. In 1982 a Los Angeles County jury convicted him of ten murder charges and recommended the death penalty. Bonin was sentenced to die in California's gas chamber for murders that the judge called "sadistic, deliberate, and unbelievably cruel." Next, Bonin was tried on four murder charges in Orange County. In August 1983, he was again sentenced to death. More than twelve years later, on February 23, 1996, Bonin spent his last day visiting with friends, and ordered a final meal of two large pepperoni and sausage pizzas, three pints of coffee ice cream, and three six-packs of Coca-Cola. California had abandoned gas-chamber executions, and Bonin received a lethal injection.

**John Wayne Gacy.** Sentenced to death on March 13, 1980, he was executed in Illinois fourteen years later, on May 10, 1994. He was fifty-two years old. A building-repair contractor and local politician, he had sexually molested and killed at least thirty-three young men and boys, some of whom he had enticed by offering them jobs. He strangled most of the victims and buried most of the bodies in the crawl space under his house in a Chicago suburb. He was convicted of thirty-three murders by a jury on March 12, 1980. On the following day, the jury voted to recommend the death penalty. The final decision was up to the trial judge, Louis B. Garippo. He sentenced Gacy to death. Gacy spent fourteen years on Death Row, where he produced oil paintings that he offered for sale, and generally seemed content. He never explained why he'd committed the murders, or expressed remorse. On execution day, he ordered a final meal of fried chicken and French fries, but he changed his mind and notified the staff that he wanted fried shrimp or lobster instead. A few hours later, he was executed by lethal injection through an intravenous line. The decision to sentence Gacy to death had been a difficult one for Judge

Garippo. "I've never been a fan of the death penalty. It's a political remedy to a social problem, and it's inadequate," he said in an interview in 2016, several weeks before his death. "I see no moral prohibition; however, it's a political solution to problems that legislatures can't solve." He considered overruling the jury's unanimous vote for death, but decided against it because of the "rumpus" it would cause.

## SERIAL KILLERS WHO WERE SENTENCED TO DEATH

**Gerald Gallego.** Sentenced to death in California in June 1983, and again in Nevada in June 1984, he died of cancer in a Nevada prison hospital on July 18, 2002. He was fifty-six years old, and his appeals were pending, nearly twenty years after his first death sentence. He and his wife, Charlene, were involved in ten murders in California and Nevada in the 1970s and 1980s. Charlene negotiated a deal with prosecutors and testified against him. She was released from prison in 1997 after serving sixteen years and eight months.

**Charles Ng and Leonard Lake.** Ng was sentenced to death in California on June 30, 1999. He was thirty-nine years old. More than two decades later, he remains on death row in California, where the death penalty was suspended in 2019 by Governor Gavin Newsom. On February 25, 1999, a jury in Orange County found him guilty of eleven murders committed during the 1980s, from San Francisco in the north to Orange County in the south. Leonard Lake was thirty-nine years old when he was arrested on June 2, 1985. He committed suicide several days later.

**Richard Ramirez.** Sentenced to death in California on November 7, 1989. He was twenty-nine years old. He was twenty-five when he was arrested on August 31, 1985, as the mysterious "Night Stalker." He was charged with fourteen murders, five attempted murders, nineteen burglaries, six robberies, seven rapes, five forcible oral copulations, seven

sodomies, three lewd acts on children, and two kidnappings. The alleged crimes had begun in June of 1984. On September 20, 1989, he was convicted of thirteen murders and thirty other felonies. On October 4, the jurors voted to recommend the death penalty. On November 7, the judge imposed the death sentence. After twenty-three years on Death Row, Ramirez died of lymphoma. He was fifty-three years old.

**Rodney Alcala.** Sentenced to death in California on June 20, 1980. He was thirty-six years old. Known as "The Dating Game Killer," he was convicted of killing a twelve-year-old girl in Huntington Beach, in southern California. Decades of appeals, retrials, and additional murder charges followed. He was ultimately convicted of six more murders, bringing the total to seven. Two of the murders took place in New York. Alcala was seventy-seven years old and still sentenced to death when he died of natural causes in a California hospital on July 24, 2021.

## SERIAL KILLERS SENTENCED TO PRISON

**Dorothea Puente.** Charged with nine murders in Sacramento, California, during the 1980s, she was arrested in November 1988, when she was fifty-nine years old, and was ultimately charged with nine murders. Most of the bodies were buried in the yard behind the boarding house she operated. The victims ranged from fifty-five to seventy-eight years old. She was sixty-three years old by the time her trial began in 1992. The jury convicted her of three murders, and was deadlocked on the rest. The jurors spent six weeks deliberating on whether to sentence her to death, but ultimately deadlocked on that too. Puente died of natural causes on March 27, 2011, at the Central California Women's Facility in Chowchilla. She was eighty-two years old.

**Robert Christian Hansen.** Killed at least seventeen women and adolescent girls in Alaska during the 1970s and 1980s. Many of the victims were

sex workers. Hansen, the congenial owner of a bakery in Anchorage, was arrested in February 1984. Officials said he'd hunted his victims down as if they were big-game animals. He eventually pleaded guilty to four murders and agreed to help investigators locate and identify the bodies of missing victims. In return, he would be sentenced to three hundred seventy-seven years in prison, plus life without parole. He would not face charges for any additional murders. Alaska did not have a death penalty. Hansen died of natural causes in 2014. He was seventy-five years old.

**Joseph DeAngelo.** Killed seven women and six men in California in the late 1970s and early 1980s. Known as the Golden State Killer, he was tracked down and arrested near his home in the small town of Citrus Heights in 2018 by investigators using preserved evidence and new DNA matching technology. He was seventy-two years old, and it had been thirty-two years since his last murder. He was in poor health. The principal cause of death on California's Death Row is old age. In return for his guilty pleas, DeAngelo was given eleven consecutive life sentences, and prosecutors agreed not to seek the death penalty.

**Arthur Shawcross.** Killed an eight-year old girl and a ten-year-old boy in upstate New York in 1972. Later that year, prosecutors, who had a weak case, worked out a deal. Shawcross, twenty-seven years old, would plead guilty to both charges, serve a term of no more than twenty-five years in prison, and receive psychiatric treatment. He was released from prison in 1987 and arrested again in 1990. This time he was charged with the murders of ten women, most of them sex workers. The jury found him guilty of the ten murders after deliberating for six hours. On February 1, 1991, Judge Donald J. Wisner sentenced him to a minimum of two hundred fifty years in prison. The death penalty was not an option in New York at the time. Shawcross was sixty-three years old when he died of cardiac arrest on November 10, 2008.

**Dennis Rader.** Killed ten people, including two children, in Kansas during the 1970s and 1980s using the initials B.T.K., standing for "Bind. Torture. Kill." He was arrested, tried, and convicted in 2005, then sentenced to ten consecutive life terms in prison with no possibility of parole. The death penalty was not in effect in Kansas at the time of the murders. Rader is still alive at the age of 77 as of the writing of this book.

**Jeffrey Dahmer.** Killed seventeen young men and boys in Ohio and Wisconsin, and kept some body parts in his apartment in Milwaukee. He was sentenced to fifteen consecutive life terms in prison in Wisconsin, which had no death penalty. He also pleaded guilty to one murder charge in Ohio. He was beaten to death by fellow inmates in Wisconsin on November 28, 1994.

**Gary Leon Ridgway.** Killed at least forty-nine women and girls in the states of Washington and California in the 1980s and early 1990s. In a deal to avoid the death penalty, he agreed to help locate the bodies of the missing victims. In November 2003, he pleaded guilty to forty-eight murders, and said, in a written statement, "I killed so many women I have a hard time keeping them straight." He focused on prostitutes because he didn't want to pay for sex, and the disappearance of a prostitute was less likely to be noticed. Norm Maleng, the prosecutor in the case, said "if any case screams out for the death penalty, this was it," and the decision to spare Ridgway the death penalty in return for more information about victims had been "excruciating." They took the death penalty off the table, he said, because the possibility of giving forty-one other families the chance to learn what had happened to their children or siblings was more important than exacting "the ultimate punishment." In 2011, Ridgway pleaded guilty to a forty-ninth murder after the skull of a young woman was uncovered about a hundred feet from where the remains of another victim had been found. Under the terms of his plea deal, he

could not be executed. Ridgway turned seventy-three in early 2022, and was still serving his time at the Washington State Penitentiary in Walla Walla. He claimed to have killed dozens more women—so many that he had lost count.

**Samuel Little.** Convicted of three murders in 2014, he eventually confessed to more than ninety murders committed in several states over nearly five decades. He killed marginalized people whose disappearances often went unnoticed. Investigators said he showed no signs of remorse. On October 6, 2019, the FBI announced that Little was the most prolific serial killer in United States history. He had confessed to ninety-three murders and had been matched to fifty of those cases. He assisted the FBI by drawing sketches of some of the women he had killed. He was eighty years old when he died on December 30, 2020, at a hospital in southern California.

**Juan Corona.** Killed twenty-five people in northern California's Sacramento Valley during the early 1970s. Most of the bodies were buried and unearthed. All the victims were male, and four of the bodies never were identified. Some of the victims were transients who were disconnected from their families. His 1973 conviction on all counts was overturned on appeal. He was convicted again on all charges at a retrial in 1982 and given twenty-five life sentences. His requests for parole were denied. In 2011, he admitted the crimes. By then, he had been attacked by inmates, stabbed thirty-two times, and lost his left eye. He died on March 4, 2019, in a hospital near the state prison in Corcoran, north of Bakersfield in central California.

**Dean Corll, Elmer Wayne Henley, and David Owen Brooks.** Known as "The Candy Man" because he once ran a candy shop, Corll sexually molested and killed twenty-seven teenagers and young adults in the

early 1970s in the Houston, Texas, area. He was thirty-three years old on August 8, 1973, when he was shot and killed at his home by Henley, his seventeen-year-old accomplice, who wanted to stop him from killing a young couple he was molesting and torturing. Henley led investigators to a boat-storage lot in Houston where they found nine more bodies buried in a shed. Brooks, Henley's eighteen-year-old friend, came forward and said he had witnessed some of the killings and helped to bury some of the bodies. Henley was sentenced to six life terms in prison. Brooks died of COVID-19 at a prison hospital in Galveston, Texas, on May 28, 2020. He was sixty-five years old and had served forty-five years of a life sentence.

**Edmund Kemper.** Known as "The Co-ed Killer." He shot and killed his grandparents in 1964 when he was fifteen years old and living with them in California's Central Valley. He was sentenced to life in prison, then turned over to the California Youth Authority and committed to the Atascadero State Hospital for the criminally insane. He was held there for four years, and received little psychiatric treatment. After another year in custody, the parole board discharged him as "cured," over the objections of the prosecutor. There were no psychiatrists or psychologists on the board. After he was released, he won a court order to have his record expunged. Nine years after the killings, Kemper was a tall burly twenty-four-year-old living with his mother in a small town near Santa Cruz on the Pacific coast. He killed his mother and a friend of hers who was visiting. He had cut off his mother's right hand, decapitated her, then placed her head on a bookshelf. During those years, five female college students had been decapitated. The body of a sixth had never been found. Kemper was arrested and soon admitted killing the six young women. He directed the investigators to a site where they soon found a putrefied human head. Kemper was charged with eight murders. In 1973, a jury rejected his insanity defense. He was convicted and sentenced to life in

prison. The death penalty was not an option at the time. In 2017 his request for parole was rejected, but the board ruled that he could apply again in 2024.

**David Berkowitz.** Known as "Son of Sam." He pleaded guilty to a string of six seemingly unrelated murders and seven attempted murders that terrified the New York City area in the 1970s. As he carried out his murders, he communicated with the city's newspapers, hinting at his intentions. He was finally arrested on August 10, 1977. On August 11, New York City Mayor Abraham Beame held a news conference at police headquarters and said "I am very pleased to announce that the people of New York can rest easy tonight because police have captured a man they believe to be the Son of Sam." Seven months of legal maneuvering followed. In 1978, Berkowitz pleaded guilty to six murder charges and seven attempted murders. He was sentenced to terms of twenty-five years to life in prison for each murder. The death penalty was not an option in New York. Berkowitz has been living a relatively quiet life in the New York prison system. At a parole hearing in 2016, he told the board that he had been a "wonderful" inmate and said, "I was constantly putting myself out there to help other individuals, with kindness and compassion." He said he was "deeply sorry" for what he had done, was working as a "caregiver" for other inmates, and reaches out to those who had psychiatric problems. "I believe that's my calling," he said. He had surgery in Albany in 2018 after suffering a heart attack. He acknowledged that his hopes for parole were not "realistic."

**Vaughn Greenwood.** Known as "The Skid Row Slasher." He killed inhabitants of the skid row area in downtown Los Angeles by slashing their necks in the mid-1970s. In January 1976, a grand jury indicted him for eleven murders, two in 1964, and nine in 1974 and 1975.

The unsolved 1964 killings matched the pattern of "slasher" killings. All the victims had had their throats slashed from ear to ear. A jury convicted him of nine murders and was deadlocked on the other two. In January 1977, Superior Court Judge Earl C. Brody sentenced Greenwood to nine terms of life in prison, and said that he hoped Greenwood "would never again be released into society." He bemoaned the fact that the law would not allow him to make the sentences consecutive. "I do not have the power to sentence him to life without parole," he said. Greenwood's most recent hearing was on December 20, 2012, when he was sixty-eight years old. The parole board told him he could try again in fifteen years. He will be eighty-three years old in 2027.

**Herbert W. Mullin.** He was convicted of ten murders in Santa Cruz, on California's central coast, between October 1972 and February 1973, and admitted to three others. He was twenty-five years old at the time. He testified at his trial that he committed the killings to avert the great earthquake, and had therefore saved thousands of lives. One of the victims was a Catholic priest who walked out of a confessional while Mullin was sitting in the church. Mullin said he got a telepathic message from himself and stabbed the priest to death. Mullin had been in and out of mental institutions over the years, and was diagnosed as a paranoid schizophrenic. The judge gave him the maximum sentence—life in prison for two of the murders and five years to life for the other eight. He has applied for parole eight times since his conviction, and was turned down each time. He can apply again in 2028.

**Kenneth Bianchi and Angelo Buono.** Known as "The Hillside Strangler." The mysterious pair began killing girls and young women in the Los Angeles area in 1977. Bianchi, a twenty-seven-year-old security guard, was arrested in Bellingham, Washington, in January 1979 on a

burglary charge. Two weeks later, he was charged with the strangulation murders of two young women in Bellingham. He had lived in the Los Angeles area when the "Strangler" murders were committed. His forty-four-year-old cousin, Angelo Buono, who lived in the Los Angeles area, was also a suspect. Bianchi eventually agreed to a deal in which he would drop his insanity defense and plead guilty to the two murders in Washington as well as five of the "Hillside Strangler" murders in Los Angeles. In return, the Washington prosecutors would drop their pursuit of the death penalty. A week later in Los Angeles, he pleaded guilty to five of the "Hillside Strangler" murders and charges of conspiracy and sodomy. He was sentenced to six life terms in prison. Buono was arrested in a Los Angeles suburb and charged with ten murders. Years of recantations and arcane litigation followed. The longest trial in the nation's history ended in November 1983, two years after it began. The jury had decided against recommending the death penalty. The judge, Roger M. George of the Los Angeles County Superior Court, sentenced both men to life in prison. "I would not have the slightest reluctance to impose the death penalty," he said. "If there was ever a case for which the death penalty was appropriate, it is this case." Buono was sixty-seven years old when he died in prison in 2002. Bianchi was returned to Washington after the trial. He has been denied parole over the years and will be eligible to apply again in 2025.

**Patrick Wayne Kearney.** Known as "The Trashbag Killer." In 1977 he pleaded guilty to the murders of three young men in Riverside County, California, and was eventually charged in Los Angeles with eighteen more murders. After working out another plea bargain, he was convicted of those murders, too. The identified victims were young and single. Some were drifters. Their bodies were found in trash bags along California freeways. Superior Court Judge Paul G. Breckinridge Jr. called Kearney "an insult to humanity" and sentenced him to life in prison.

He said Kearney should never be released. He has been denied parole six times over the decades since his conviction. The last denial came in January 2012. He was told that he could try again in January 2027, when he would be eighty-seven years old.

**Coral Eugene Watts.** Known as the "Sunday Morning Slasher." A week before he died in 2007, Watts got an unusual piece of bad news. He had just been sentenced to life in prison for killing a college student in Michigan in 1974. Until then, he had had some perversely good luck. In 1982, he had made a favorable deal with prosecutors in Texas. He would confess to the murders of twelve young women and, in return, would be allowed to plead guilty to a single charge of robbery with intent to commit murder. He would be sentenced to sixty years in prison, but he could, at some point, apply for parole. It had been a difficult decision for the prosecutors and the judge in the case. They believed that Watts was, in fact, the mysterious "Sunday Morning Slasher," who had committed his first murder in 1974. Over the years, he had become a suspect in the murders of dozens of women. But no one had been able to prove it.

# SOURCES

## 1. DOROTHEA PUENTE

"Accused Mass Killer Got Drugs from Therapist." *United Press International,* March 25, 1989.

Bishop, Katherine. "Suspect in 7 Killings Denies Charges." *New York Times,* November 18, 1988.

Capps, Steven A. "Probation Fouled up on Puente. U.S., State, Local Officials Failed to Cross-Check." *San Francisco Examiner,* November 18, 1988.

"Daughter Pleads for Dorothea Puente's Life." *Associated Press,* September 22, 1993.

Fleeman, Michael. "Murder Suspect a Friendly, Gray-Haired Widow to Police Tipster." *Associated Press,* November 17, 1988.

Gaines, John. "In Death Garden of Sacramento Boarding Home, Roses Flourished." *San Diego Union-Tribune,* November 18, 1988.

Grubb, Kathleen. "Police Find a Sixth Corpse in Rooming House Yard." *Associated Press,* November 14, 1988.

———. "Police Find Fifth Body in Yard Of Boardinghouse for Elderly." *Associated Press,* November 12, 1988.

Kole, Bill. "Tipster in Boardinghouse Murders Reunited with Family." *Associated Press,* December 9, 1988.

Marine, Craig. "A Different Town, but Same Old Game." *San Francisco Examiner,* November 17, 1988.

Mathews, Jay. "Landlady Says 'I Have Not Killed Anyone'; Murder Charge Filed; Bail Is Denied." *Washington Post,* November 18, 1988.

Miller, Max. "How Roomer Tipped Cops to Suspect." *McClatchy News Service,* November 15, 1988.

Online Archive of California. Center for Sacramento History.

"Prosecution Opens in Boarder Deaths; Accused Appears Grandmotherly."
Hamilton Spectator, February 16, 1993.

Willis, Doug. "Landlady Captured in Boardinghouse Murder Cases, Protests
Innocence." Associated Press, November 17, 1988.

## 2. GERALD AND CHARLENE GALLEGO

Alters, Diane, and Paul Avery. "Couple's Fugitive Odyssey." Sacramento Bee,
November 19, 1980.

———. "Gallego Escape at Trial Feared." Sacramento Bee, January 15, 1981.

———. "Gallego Lashes Out: 'We're Not Animals.'" Sacramento Bee,
November 22, 1980.

———. "Star-Crossed Couple—And Death." Sacramento Bee, February 15, 1981.

Avery, Paul. "Gallego Linked by His Wife to Killing of 8 More Women."
Sacramento Bee, July 20, 1982.

———. "Slaying Suspect Blamed God for Kin's Death." Sacramento Bee,
November 11, 1980.

Avery, Paul, and Bill Wilson. "Suspects Sought in Northwest." Sacramento Bee,
November 8, 1980.

Brooks, Clark. "Charlene Gallego Plea Deal Accepted." Sacramento Bee, July 21,
1982.

"Cash Gifts to Help County Hold Trial." New York Times, April 5, 1984.

"Convicted Killer Faces Nevada Trial in Deaths of 2 California Teen-Agers."
United Press International, March 31, 1984.

"Defense to Test Credibility of Gallego's Wife." Associated Press, June 5, 1984.

"Gallego Sentenced to Death in Nevada for Two Murders." Associated Press,
June 13, 1984.

Malnic, Eric. "People Chip In to Assure Killer Is Brought to Justice." Los
Angeles Times, March 11, 1984.

"Man Guilty in Two Deaths; Prosecution Aided by Donations." Associated
Press, June 9, 1984.

"Nevada Upholds Death Sentence for Murderer of 2 Teen-Age Girls."
    *Associated Press,* December 22, 1985.

"PEOPLE v. GALLEGO." Supreme Court of California, In Bank. The
    Plaintiff and Respondent, v. Gerald Armond GALLEGO, Defendant
    and Appellant. No. S004561. Decided: December 20, 1990.

Taylor, Michael. "Sex-Slave Killer Dies of Cancer in Nevada Prison Hospital."
    *San Francisco Chronicle,* July 20, 2002.

Wilson, Wayne. "Gallego Sex Fantasy Described." *Sacramento Bee,* May 25,
    1984.

———. "Killer's Ex-Wife to Be Released from Prison." *Sacramento Bee,* July 16,
    1997.

———. "Sobbing Charlene Gallego Says She Deserves to Die." *Sacramento Bee,*
    May 31, 1984.

## 3. ROBERT CHRISTIAN HANSEN

"Alaska Man Confesses Killings of 17 Women." *Reuters/The New York Times,*
    February 28, 1984.

"Alaska Serial Killer Robert Hansen Dies at 75." *Associated Press/Bismarck
    Tribune,* August 22, 2014.

"Alaskan Says He Killed 17." *Washington Post,* February 29, 1984.

Andrews, Laurel, and Kyle Hopkins. "Serial Killer Hansen Dies; 'World Is
    Better Without Him,' Trooper Says." *Anchorage Daily News,* September 28,
    2016.

Discovery Channel. *The Butcher Baker: Mind of a Monster,* 2020.

D'Oro, Rachel. "Robert Hansen, Convicted Serial Killer in Alaska, Dies at 75."
    *Washington Post,* August 22, 2014.

Douglas, John, and Mark Olshaker. *The Killer Across the Table: Unlocking the
    Secrets of Serial Killers and Predators with the FBI's Original Mindhunter.*
    New York: HarperCollins, 2019.

———. *Mindhunter: Inside the FBI's Elite Serial Crime Unit.* New York: Simon &
    Schuster, 1995.

Haines, Max. "Serial Killer Lived a Double Life." *Ontario Packet and Times,*
December 20, 2003.

"Killer of 17 Calls Deaths Summer Project. Murderer Had Been Arrested
Twice on Rape Charges and Freed." *Associated Press/New York Times,*
February 28, 1984.

Krajicek, David J. "Robert (Bob the Baker) Hansen Blamed His Tortured
Adolescence for the Rape and Murder of Dozens of Women in Alaska in
1970s." *New York Daily News,* August 30, 2014.

Sharp, Rachel. "Prosecutor Reveals How Notorious Alaska Serial Killer
'Butcher Baker' Who Killed at Least 17 Women and Raped Another 30
Acted Like a Hunter and Only Confessed When He Was Playing Good
Cop." *Daily Mail,* November 1, 2020.

Shedlock, Jerzey. "'Butcher Baker' Robert Hansen Moved to Anchorage for
Medical Treatment." *Alaska Dispatch,* May 22, 2014.

"Slayer in Alaska Was Jailed In Other Cases, Judge Notes." *New York Times,*
February 29, 1984.

Smith, Jack. *The Butcher Baker. Life of Serial Killer Robert Christian Hansen.*
Createspace Independent Publishing Platform, 2017.

Watts, Marina. "'Butcher Baker' Prosecutor Frank Rothschild Shares the Serial
Killer's Breaking Point." *Newsweek,* September 2, 2020.

## 4. BOBBY JOE LONG

Berger, Daniel. "Pasco Jury: Long Should Be Executed." *The Tampa Tribune,*
April 28, 1985.

Calise, Gabrielle. "Tampa Serial Killer Bobby Joe Long Is Scheduled to Be
Executed Tonight. We Remember the Victims." *Tampa Bay Times,* April 25,
2019; Updated May 23, 2019.

Danielson, Richard. "Long's Trial Begins Again." *St. Petersburg Times,*
November 2, 1988.

Flynn, Meagan. "A Rape Victim Helped Police Catch a Serial Killer. Nearly 35 Years
Later, Sat Front Row at His Execution." *Washington Post,* May 24, 2019.

Geyelin, Milo. "Porn Drove Long to Murder, His Attorney Says." *St. Petersburg Times,* July 11, 1986.

Glidewell, Jan. "Pasco Trial Dates Set for Accused Killer Bobby Joe Long." *Pasco Times,* February 12, 1985.

*I Lived With a Killer.* REELZ documentary, 2019.

King, Larry, and Christopher Smart. "Accused Killer Led Troubled Life with Women." *St. Petersburg Times,* November 25, 1984.

Marks, Ed. "For the Victims, There Was No Chance to Escape Their Fate." *St. Petersburg Times,* November 25, 1984.

———. "Man Charged in Women's Slayings." *St. Petersburg Times,* November 17, 1984.

Nathan, Jean, and Carol Jeffares. "Judge Rejects Bid to Move Long Trial." *Tampa Tribune,* April 12, 1985.

Sullivan, Dan. "Judge Clears Lethal Injection." *Tampa Bay Times,* May 7, 2019.

Troxler, Howard. "Jury Selection Starts in Long Murder Case." *Tampa Tribune,* December 10, 1985.

Troxler, Howard, and Gwen Fariss. "Long Jury Voted for Death." *Tampa Tribune,* July 19, 1986.

Varn, Kathryn. "Bobby Joe Long Execution: One Family Has Waited 34 Years for Justice." *Tampa Bay Times,* May 23, 2019.

———. "Tampa serial Killer Bobby Joe Long Has No visitors on Day of Execution." *Tampa Bay Times,* May 23, 2019.

———. "Tampa Serial Killer Bobby Joe Long Is Executed in Silence." *Tampa Bay Times,* May 23, 2019.

## 5. CHARLES NG AND LEONARD LAKE

Andersen, Patrick. "FBI: Ng May Kill Asian Men: Mass Killing Suspect Last Seen in Canada." *Asian Week,* July 5, 1985.

Bishop, Katherine. "Murder Suspect's Bid to Stay in Canada Tests Pact." *New York Times,* February 13, 1991.

Burns, John F. "With Death at Issue, Can Canada Wash Its Hands?" *New York Times,* November 1, 1988.

Decker, Cathleen, and Mark A. Stein. "Mass Murder Suspect Seized by Canadians." *Los Angeles Times,* July 7, 1985.

Howard, John. "Suspected Mass Killer Leaves Trail of Mystery." *Associated Press,* June 16, 1985.

Mecoy, Laura. "Jury Convicts Ng." *Modesto Bee,* February 25, 1999.

Molina, Rick. "Dead Man Is No. 1 Witness for Defense." *Calgary Herald,* November 21, 1998.

———. "A U.S. Fugitive's Day of Reckoning." *Ottawa Citizen,* September 21, 1991.

Owens, Greg, and Tom Barrett. "New Ng Murder Evidence Found." *Edmonton Journal,* September 11, 1989.

Sahagun, Louis, and Mark A. Stein. "Sixth Body Unearthed at Murder Site. *Los Angeles Times,* June 19, 1985.

Staples, David. "'Lightning Rod' Battle for Defence Lawyer. Jury Recommends Death Penalty for Killer." *Edmonton Journal,* May 4, 1999.

Stein, Mark A. "Home Searched in Probe of Killings. Three Agencies Seize Items From Ex-Wife of Suspect Lake." *Los Angeles Times,* June 23, 1985.

———. "More Bones Found at Death Site." *Los Angeles Times,* June 14, 1985.

Turner, Wallace. "At Least 5 Bodies Found At Sierras Torture Site." *New York Times,* June 13, 1985.

Weaver, Nancy. "Recalling Horror That Was Wilseyville." *McClatchy News Service,* September 29, 1991.

Wolinski, Leo C., and Mark A. Stein. "3 Bodies Found on California Farm; Suspect in 8 Disappearances Kills Himself, Another Sought." *Los Angeles Times,* June 8, 1985.

Yi, Daniel. "Ng's Father Blames Self, Begs Jurors to Spare Son." *Los Angeles Times,* April 21, 1999.

## 6. RICHARD RAMIREZ

Buchanan, Paul. "How a 13-Year-Old Boy Brought Down L.A.'s Most Notorious Serial Killer." *Los Angeles Magazine,* May 15, 2017.

Chambers, Marcia. "Defendant In 'Night Stalker' Case Denies Killing 14 in California." *New York Times,* October 25, 1985.

———. "Suspect Quoted: 'I Love to Watch People Die.'" *New York Times,* May 9, 1986.

Feldman, Paul. "For Ramirez, Trial's Ritual a Tedious One." *Los Angeles Times,* April 14, 1986.

———. "Victim Points to Ramirez as Killer, Rapist." *Los Angeles Times,* April 15, 1986.

Hicks, Jerry. "Concern for Victims Prompts O.C. to Drop Case Against Ramirez." *Los Angeles Times,* November 9, 1989.

Holley, David. "Recalling Ramirez: Even Friends Didn't Trust Him." *Los Angeles Times,* September 8, 1985.

Molinski, Michael. "Police Identify Night Stalker Suspect." *United Press International,* August 31, 1985.

Stuart, Robert W. "Stalker Suspect Ramirez Charged in 13 More Deaths." *Los Angeles Times,* September 28, 1985.

Timnick, Lois, and John H. Lee. "'Stalker' Sentenced to Die, Warns, 'I Will Be Avenged.'" *Los Angeles Times,* November 8, 1989.

Warrick, Pamela. "I Saw Something . . . That Captivated Me." *Los Angeles Times,* October 3, 1996.

Wild, Danelia. "The Alleged Night Stalker, a Pot-Smoking Drifter and Reported Satanist." *United Press International,* September 2, 1985.

## 7. JOSEPH JAMES DEANGELO

Barry, Dan, Tim Arango, and Richard A. Oppel, Jr. "The Golden State Killer Left a Trail of Horror with Taunts and Guile." *New York Times,* April 28, 2018.

Egel, Benjy. "Who Is the East Area Rapist? Police Say It's This Ex-Cop Who Attended Folsom High." *Sacramento Bee,* April 25, 2018.

Espino, Jenny, and Gretchen Wenner. "At Least a Dozen Men and Women Died Because of the Golden State Killer. Here's Who They Were." *USA TODAY Network,* April 28, 2018.

Fuller, Thomas, and Christine Hauser. "Search for 'Golden State Killer' Leads to Arrest of Ex-Cop." *New York Times,* April 25, 2018.

Haag, Matthew. "What We Know About Joseph DeAngelo, the Golden State Killer." *New York Times,* April 26, 2018.

Held, Amy. "'Golden State Killer,' Suspected of Terrorizing California for Years, Arrested." *National Public Radio,* April 25, 2018.

Jouvenal, Justin. "To Find Alleged Golden State Killer, Investigators First Found His Great-Great-Great-Grandparents." *Washington Post,* April 30, 2018.

Levenson, Michael. "Golden State Killer Sentenced to Life in Prison Without Parole." *New York Times,* August 21, 2020.

McNamara, Michelle. *I'll Be Gone in the Dark.* New York: HarperCollins, 2018.

——. "In the Footsteps of a Killer." *Los Angeles,* February 27, 2013.

Shelton, George. "In California, the Death Penalty Is All but Meaningless. A Life Sentence for the Golden State Killer Was the Right Move." *Los Angeles Times,* July 2, 2020.

Simon, Darran, Cheri Mossburg; and Paul Vercammen. "Golden State Killer Suspect to Be Tried in One Trial in Sacramento." *CNN,* August 21, 2018.

St. John, Paige. "Golden State Killer Suspect Agrees to Guilty Plea in a Deal that Spares Him Death Penalty. *Los Angeles Times,* June 15, 2020.

——. "Golden State Killer Suspect Would Plead Guilty if Death Penalty Is Off the Table, Lawyers Say." *Los Angeles Times,* March 3, 2020.

——. "Prosecutors Challenge Golden State Killer's Apparent Frailty, Say He Chooses Not to Show Remorse." *Los Angeles Times,* August 17, 2020.

St. John, Paige, and Luke Money. "Victims of Golden State Killer Finally Confront Him in Court with Stories of Pain and Survival." *Los Angeles Times,* August 18, 2020.

Wright, Tom. "Monterey Peninsula Native Greg Sanchez Among Victims of
    Golden State Killer." *Monterey Herald,* June 29, 2020.

## 8. AILEEN WUORNOS

Arrigo, Bruce A., Ph.D., and Ayanna Griffin, B.A. "Serial Murder and the Case
    of Aileen Wuornos: Attachment Theory, Psychopathy, and Predatory
    Aggression." *Behavioral Sciences and the Law,* 2004.

Brazil, Jeff. "Ex-Lover Paints Picture of Cold-Hearted Killer." *Orlando Sentinel,*
    January 17, 1992.

Chesler, Phyllis. "A Double Standard for Murder?" *New York Times,* January 8,
    1992.

Clary, Mike. "A Mother's Love." *Los Angeles Times,* December 17, 1991.

Damman, Sara Gay. "Friend: Violence Filled Accused Killer's Life." *Chicago
    Tribune,* January 16, 1992.

"'Damsel of Death' Convicted of Murder." *United Press International,* January 28,
    1992.

"Ex-Prostitute, Charged with Killing 5 Men, Goes on Trial." *Associated Press,*
    January 13, 1992.

"Execution Stays Issued For 2 Florida Inmates." *Associated Press,* October 1,
    2002.

"Jurors Recommend Death Penalty for Florida Woman Who Killed 7."
    *Associated Press,* January 30, 1992.

"Jury Finds Florida Prostitute, 35, Guilty of Killing Would-Be Client."
    *Associated Press,* January 28, 1992.

Reynolds, Michael. *Dead Ends: The Pursuit, Conviction, and Execution of
    Female Serial Killer Aileen Wuornos, the Damsel of Death.* New York:
    St. Martin's Paperbacks, 2004.

Schmich, Mary T. "Serial Killer Suspect Led Nightmarish Life." *Chicago
    Tribune,* March 17, 1991.

Smothers, Ronald. "Woman Is Arrested in a Series of Killings in Florida." *New
    York Times,* January 18, 1991.

"Transient Woman Accused in Florida Serial Killings." *Associated Press,*
January 18, 1991.

"Trial Starts for Alleged Florida Serial Killer." *Orlando Sentinel,* January 13, 1992.

"Woman Confesses to Killing 2 Men Along Florida Roads." *Associated Press,*
February 6, 1991.

"Woman Held in Interstate Killings." *Knight-Ridder Newspapers,* January 18, 1991.

Word, Ron. "Woman Who Killed 6 Executed in Florida; Her Life Spawned
Books, Movies." *Chicago Tribune,* October 10, 2002.

## 9. ARTHUR SHAWCROSS

"City Girl Strangled, Man Held." *Rochester Democrat and Chronicle,*
September 4, 1972.

Foderaro, Lisa W. "A Serial-Murder Trial. On TV, Grips Rochester." *New York
Times,* December 2, 1990.

Hanley, Robert. "Parole Board Under Scrutiny In Murder Suspect's Release."
*New York Times,* January 13, 1990.

———. "Rochester Slaying Suspect Is Called Kind but Violent." *New York
Times,* January 13, 1990.

Hevesi, Dennis. "Arthur J. Shawcross, Serial Killer in Rochester, Dies at 63."
*New York Times,* November 10, 2008.

Hyland, Bruce. "Man Accused of Serial Murder Also Accused of Cannibalism,
Lawyer Says." *United Press International,* September 18, 1990.

"Imprisoned Serial Killer Is Punished for Art Sales." *Reuters,* September 18, 1999.

"Parolee in Girl's '87 Death Held in 8 Serial Murders." *Associated Press,* January 5,
1990.

"Police: Suspect Told Them Body Was of His Mistress." *United Press
International,* October 2, 1990.

Ressler, Robert K., and Tom Shachtman. *Whoever Fights Monsters.* New York:
St. Martin's Press, 1992.

"Rochester Jury Convicts Parolee In Serial Killings." *Associated Press,*
December 14, 1990.

"Serial Slayer of 10 Women Gets 250-Year Prison Term." *Associated Press,*
    February 2, 1991.

Strom, Bob. "Shawcross Sent to Attica in Child's Death." *Syracuse Post-*
    *Standard,* October 18, 1972.

"Suspect in 10 Sexual Murders Is Portrayed as Unremorseful." *Associated Press,*
    September 21, 1990.

## 10. DENNIS RADER

"BTK Killer Gets Maximum Life Sentence." *Associated Press,* August 18, 2005.

Coates, Sam. "Rader Gets 175 Years For BTK Slayings." *Washington Post,*
    August 19, 2005.

Davey, Monica. "Relief, and Bewilderment, Over Arrest in Kansas Killings."
    *New York Times,* February 28, 2005.

———. "Suspect in 10 Kansas Murders Lived an Intensely Ordinary Life." *New*
    *York Times,* March 6, 2005.

Davey, Monica, and Glen Sharp. "After Years of Taunts and Clues, Arrest Is
    Made in Kansas Killings." *New York Times,* February 27, 2005.

Hansen, Mark. "How the Cops Caught BTK: Playing to a Serial Killer's Ego
    Helped Crack the Case." *American Bar Association Journal,* May 1, 2006.

"My Father BTK." *ABC News, 20-20,* February 1, 2019.

Ramsland, Katherine. *Confession of a Serial Killer: The Untold story of Dennis*
    *Rader, the BTK Killer.* Lebanon, New Hampshire: ForeEdge, University
    Press of New England, 2016.

Rawson, Kerri. *A Serial Killer's Daughter.* Nashville, Tennessee: Nelson Books,
    HarperCollins Christian Publishing, Inc., 2019.

Shteir, Rachel. "The Serial Killer's Co-Author." *New York Times,* September 15,
    2016.

Wichita Eagle Staff. "Who is Dennis Rader aka the BTK Serial Killer?"
    *Wichita Eagle,* January 25, 2019.

Wilgoren, Jodi. "Kansas Suspect Pleads Guilty in 10 Murders." *New York*
    *Times,* June 28, 2005.

## 11. JEFFREY DAHMER

Barron, James. "Milwaukee Police One Queried Suspect." *New York Times,* July 27, 1991.

Christopulos, Mike. "Earlier Prosecutor Urged Prison for Dahmer." *Milwaukee Sentinel,* July 26, 1991.

"Dahmer Tells Judge He Blames Nobody But Himself." *Associated Press,* February 17, 1992.

Dahmer, Lionel. *A Father's Story.* Brattleboro, Vermont: Echo Point Books & Media, 2021.

Dvorchak, Robert. "Families Struggle to Understand How Their Loved Ones Fell Prey." *Associated Press,* July 27, 1991.

"Hints of Horror at Dahmer's Jury Selection." *Associated Press,* January 29, 1992.

Johnson, Dirk. "Milwaukee Jury Says Dahmer Was Sane." *New York Times,* February 16, 1992.

"Jury Deliberates Sanity of Dahmer. Panel Weighs Whether Killer of 15 Is Sent to Prison or to a Mental Hospital." *Associated Press,* February 14, 1992.

Lavin, Cheryl. "Defending Dahmer." *Chicago Tribune,* October 13, 1991.

Mendoza, Manuel. "'89 Transcripts of Dahmer Case Hint at Trouble." *Milwaukee Journal,* July 26, 1994.

Schwartz, Anne E. "Body Parts Litter Apartment." *Milwaukee Journal,* July 23, 1991.

———. "Fleeing in Terror: Woman Says Police Gave Boy Back to Dahmer." *Milwaukee Journal,* July 26, 1991.

Walsh, Edward. "Man Describes Hours-Long Ordeal Before Police Apprehended Dahmer." *Washington Post,* February 1, 1992.

Wilkerson, Isabel. "Parts of Many Bodies Found in a Milwaukee Apartment." *New York Times,* July 24, 1991.

## 12. GARY LEON RIDGWAY

Booth, William. "Man Held in Deaths Tied to Serial Killer." *Washington Post,* December 1, 2001.

"Green River Killer Confesses. 'I Killed So Many Women I Have a Hard

Time Keeping Them Straight.'" *Seattle Post-Intelligencer Staff and News Services,* November 5, 2003.

Harden, Blaine. "The Banality of Gary: A Green River Chiller." *Washington Post,* November 16, 2003.

"Higher Victim Toll Possible in Northwest Serial Murder Case." *Seattle Times,* November 22, 1990.

Johnson, Gene. "Genetic Genealogy Helps ID Denver Girl Decades After She Was Killed by the Green River Killer." *Associated Press,* January 25, 2021.

Kershaw, Sarah. "In Plea Deal That Spares His Life, Man Admits Killing 48 Women." *New York Times,* November 6, 2003.

Lamb, Kevin. "DNA Puts a Name to One of the Last Unidentified Victims of the Green River Killer." *Seattle Times,* January 25, 2021.

Newman, Maria. "In Plea Deal, Man Admits 48 Green River Killings." *New York Times,* November 5, 2003.

Preusch, Matthew. "Families Speak as Green River Killer Gets 48 Life Terms." *New York Times,* December 19, 2003.

PROSECUTOR'S SUMMARY OF THE EVIDENCE. SUPERIOR COURT OF WASHINGTON FOR KING COUNTY. STATE OF WASHINGTON, Plaintiff, vs. GARY LEON RIDGWAY, Defendant, Norm Maleng, Prosecuting Attorney.

Rule, Ann. *Green River Running Red.* New York: Pocket Books, 2005.

Ryckman, Lisa Levitt. "Fear Walks Streets with Prostitutes." *Associated Press,* January 5, 1986.

Semple, Kirk. "Green River Killer Sentenced to Life." *New York Times,* December 8, 2003.

Spar, Penny. "FBI Joins Probe in Green River." *United Press International,* September 20, 1985.

Verhovek, Sam Howe. "Suspect Charged in 4 Green River Slayings." *New York Times,* December 6, 2001.

———. "Suspect Held in Northwest Serial-Killings Case." *New York Times,* December 1, 2001.

Whale, Robert. "Green River Killer Pleads Guilty to 49th Murder." *Auburn Reporter,* February 18, 2011.

———. "Green River Murder Victim Remains Identified." *Auburn Reporter,* June 18, 2012.

## 13. SAMUEL LITTLE

Berman, Mark, Wesley Lowery, and Hannah Knowles. "Indifferent Justice Part 2: Through the Cracks." *Washington Post,* December 2, 2020.

Confessions of a Killer: FBI Seeking Assistance Connecting Victims to Samuel Little's Confessions. Federal Bureau of Investigation, October 6, 2019.

Gerber, Marissa. "L.A. Serial Killer Gets Three Life Terms, Screams, 'I Didn't Do It!'" *Los Angeles Times,* August 31, 2014.

Kim, Victoria. "Women's Testimony Called 'Blueprint' to Serial Killer Suspect's Behavior." *Los Angeles Times,* August 31, 2014.

Knowles, Hannah, Wesley Lowery, and Mark Berman. "Indifferent Justice Part 3: Still Unsolved." *Washington Post,* December 4, 2020.

Lowery, Wesley, Hannah Knowles, and Mark Berman. "Indifferent Justice Part 1: The Victim." *Washington Post,* November 30, 2020.

"Timeline Retraces the Whereabouts of a Career Criminal, Alleged Serial Killer." *Associated Press,* January 13, 2015.

Warren, David. "Inmate Confesses to 90 Deaths; Investigators Corroborate 30." *Associated Press,* November 15, 2018.

———. "Prosecutor: More than 60 Deaths Now Linked to Serial Killer." *Associated Press,* June 7, 2019.

Williams, Timothy. "He Says He Got Away With 90 Murders. Now He's Confessing to Them All." *New York Times,* November 26, 2018.

Williams, Timothy, and Karen Zraick. "Samuel Little Is Most Prolific Serial Killer in U.S. History, F.B.I. Says. Mr. Little, 79, has confessed to 93 murders, and the agency believes 'all of his confessions are credible.'" *New York Times,* October 7, 2019.

# APPENDIX 1

## FBI DOSSIER ON JEFFREY DAHMER

*Freedom of Information*
*and*
*Privacy Acts*

Subject: <u>Jeffrey Dahmer</u>
File Number: <u>7-MW-26057-Section 2</u>

*Federal Bureau of Investigation*

FD-302 (REV. 3-10-82)

- 1 -

FEDERAL BUREAU OF INVESTIGATION

Date of transcription    9/11/92

JEFFREY L. DAHMER, white male, date of birth May 21, 1960, was interviewed by Special Agents (SAs) ███████████ and ███████████ who identified themselves as Special Agents of the Federal Bureau of Investigation (FBI). At the outset of the interview, DAHMER was asked if he had any objection to being interviewed by the FBI for Behavioral Science purposes, and for the purposes of Law Enforcement learning from a serial killer. DAHMER stated that he had no objection to being interviewed. DAHMER was advised of his rights, and DAHMER declined to have an attorney present during the interview. The interview took place in the segregation of the Columbia Correctional Center in Portage, Wisconsin.

DAHMER advised that he first realized his sexual orientation when he was 13 years old, realizing that he was homosexual. DAHMER stated that this bothered him a little, because he was different from other people. DAHMER stated that he had a lonely childhood in that his only sibling was a brother which was six years younger than him, and he never really had any close personal friends. DAHMER was asked by the interviewing agent what his relationship was with his parents, and DAHMER stated that his parents were average, but did not show much affection.

DAHMER stated that when he was 13 and 14 he started fantasizing about sex with a dead body, and he then turned to heavy masturbation. DAHMER was asked what he meant by heavy masturbation, and he stated that he would masturbate three to four times a day. DAHMER stated that he also started drinking heavily to try to suppress his fantasies, but that did not help.

DAHMER stated that he had a fascination with death and when he was around 14 he used to bring home road kill, and then dissect it, because he liked to look at the internal organs. DAHMER stated that he got sexually aroused when he would look at the internal organs. DAHMER stated that he never had sex with any animals.

Investigation on    8/3/92    at    Portage, Wisconsin    File #   7-MW-26057- 83

SA ███████████ /dkc

by    SA ███████████    Date dictated    9/11/92

FD-302a (Rev. 11-15-83)

7-MW-26057

DAHMER was asked by the interviewing agents if he had
ever killed an animal, and DAHMER stated that he intended to on
one occasion, where he had found an Irish Setter and brought it
home and was going to kill it and then skin it and dissect, but
when the dog looked at him with its eyes, DAHMER could not kill
it, so he just let the dog go.

DAHMER advised that he started turning to pornography
and heavy masturbation to try and satisfy his fantasies, but at
around age 16 he started having the violent fantasies of sex with
a dead body. DAHMER stated that he actually started fantasizing
about striking someone on the back of the neck and making them
unconscience and then having sex with the body. DAHMER stated
that when he was in the ninth grade, approximately age 15, he was
assaulted by a group of youths, who struck with a black jack on
the back of the neck. DAHMER stated that he started fantasizing
about retaliation, and this aroused him sexually.

DAHMER talked about his "mind set" which was constant
and he was trapped in this obsession and need to dominate.
DAHMER called it a prison in his own mind, which was always
constant. DAHMER stated that he was totally obsessed with his
need for physical pleasure. DAHMER stated that he never hated
his victims nor did he ever want his victims to suffer. DAHMER
stated that he never wanted to cause any pain, but just wanted to
satisfy his own selfish pleasures. DAHMER stated that he never
tortured any of his victims. DAHMER stated that he was totally
obsessed with the need to dominate and control, and have total
control over a body. DAHMER did not look at his victims as
people, but just as objects for his own selfish pleasure. DAHMER
advised that this sense of total control and total domination
increased the sexual thrill. DAHMER stated that knowing that he
had total control over his victims, and could do with them as he
pleased was his motivation.

DAHMER was asked how he would entice his victims, and
DAHMER stated that he met all of his victims in gay bars,
bathhouses, or pornographic shops and he would just offer them
money for sex or invite them back to his apartment for sex and
photographs in exchange for money.

DAHMER stated that his fantasy and obsession was with
the perfect male body, what DAHMER described as the "Chip and
Dale", the gymnasts build or an athletic body, between the ages

FD-302a (Rev. 11-15-83)

7-MW-26057

Continuation of FD-302 of ___JEFFREY L. DAHMER_____ , On __8/3/92___ , Page __3__

of 19 and 22. DAHMER stated that he never fantasied about children or young teenagers. DAHMER stated that his fantasies of a good looking well built young man having total control over him, being able to totally to dominate that person. DAHMER stated that he did not mean to kill, but wanted to create "love slaves" or zombies that would do everything DAHMER pleased.

DAHMER also tried to create a zombie by drilling holes into the frontal lobe of his victim's brains and pouring in muratic acid. DAHMER stated that this worked at first, but after a while the victims would die.

DAHMER further advised that he tried to freeze dry the perfect mate, so he could continually have sex with the body, and by freezing he felt that the body would not decompose. DAHMER stated that this did not work for very long.

DAHMER stated that he tried to control his obsession with heavy drinking, pornography, and masturbation. DAHMER stated that pornography and masturbation would not satisfy him, but would intensify the obsession and he absolutely had to get another body. DAHMER stated he sole purpose for living, the driving force behind his existence, was his need for pleasure. DAHMER stated that his fantasy and obsessions were all consuming, and took control of his whole life. DAHMER stated that he took some risks, but would never take unnecessary risks because he did not want to get caught. DAHMER stated that getting caught was his worst nightmare. DAHMER stated that some risks did add to the pleasure.

DAHMER stated that after taking a victim, this would satisfy him for a couple of months, then the fantasies and obsessions would start to increase and he needed more and more to get the same level of satisfaction, so he would have to get another victim. DAHMER stated that the intense desire was always present but he could get by with viewing photographs of his victims and some of his "mementos". DAHMER stated that he kept body parts of his victims as mementos to serve as arousal in place of new bodies, until he could get a new body.

DAHMER stated that he always kept the skulls, sometimes the genitals, hands, and some internal organs.

FD-302a (Rev. 11-15-83)

7-MW-26057

Continuation of FD-302 of ___JEFFREY L. DAHMER_____ , On __8/3/92___ , Page __4__

DAHMER stated that when he would turn to pornography to satisfy his obsessions, this would depress him and would make him want the real thing more and more.

DAHMER stated that once he stole a mannequin from a Boston Store (1986 or 1987) and he tried to satisfy his desires and compulsion with utilizing this mannequin but that did not work.

DAHMER stated that he tried to resist his temptation for killing, by looking in the newspaper in the obituary column and finding a death notice for any 19 or 20 year old male and he attended the funeral and when he saw the male in the casket, it was the perfect body so after the burial he went to the graveyard and tried to dig up the grave. DAHMER stated that he could not dig up the grave, because the ground was too hard, and while he was attempting to dig he was attacked by a graveyard dog.

DAHMER further advised that he would be sexually aroused by the different sounds that a body would make. DAHMER stated that he had a very extreme fascination with the human body. DAHMER stated that he liked to delicately slit the skin and peel it back and look at the capillaries and different blood vessels.

DAHMER stated that he found sexually arousing to look at the internal organs of the body or what DAHMER called the viscera, and the way that the internal organs would glisten. DAHMER stated that he had sexual thoughts and fantasies about the viscera (internal organs).

DAHMER was asked by the interviewing agents how he knew so much about the human anatomy, and DAHMER stated that he did some reading, along with calling some taxidermists. DAHMER also stated that he dissected by trial and error.

DAHMER advised that his normal routine was to go out on the prowl and find the perfect gymnastic type body or what DAHMER referred to as the "Chip and Dale" body, and entice them with offers of money for photographs and sex, and bring them back to his apartment and serve them drinks. DAHMER stated that he would then mix in sleeping pills, five to six halcium .125 milligrams and within a half an hour his victims would pass out, and then he would strangle them. DAHMER stated that he never wanted to cause

Continuation of FD-302 of ____JEFFREY L. DAHMER____ , On __8/3/92__ , Page __5__

any of his victims any pain. DAHMER stated that he just wanted total control over the body.

DAHMER stated that after having total control over the body he would have sex with the body. DAHMER was asked by the interviewing agents how he would perform his sex acts, and DAHMER stated that he would do penis to anus, penis to mouth, and he would make a slit in the body above the pubic line and have sexual intercourse then with the body.

DAHMER stated that he would also slit open the body and then masturbate.

DAHMER was asked what tools he would use for dismembering his victims, and DAHMER stated that he had a large hunting knife with rubber grips and a very sharp edge. DAHMER stated that it was not serrated, but had a large blade which was very sharp.

DAHMER stated that he would dismember his victims by slitting them from the sternum to the pubic area and then he would remove the internal organs and then would cut the flesh, starting from the calves, legs, then up the side. DAHMER stated that he would remove the head and put that in the freezer and then he would delicately take the flesh off and put that in a large 80 gallon cooking pot. DAHMER stated that he would then boil the skull and the bones, and have a clean skeleton.

DAHMER stated that he did this right in his own apartment, and he would dispose of the flesh, organs, and bones, by boiling them in hydrochloric muratic acid, until he could flush it down the toilet.

DAHMER was asked by the interviewing agents if he was concerned for security at his apartment, and DAHMER stated that he had installed a security system in his apartment, which cost $400. DAHMER stated that he had different locks on the bathroom, bedroom, and front door. DAHMER stated that he had a video camera set up for security.

DAHMER was asked by the interviewing agents if the cannibalism was sexually gratifying also. DAHMER stated that it was. DAHMER stated that the cannibalism started out as experimentation, but it made him feel that the victims were part

FD-302a (Rev. 11-15-83)

7-MW-26057

Continuation of FD-302 of     **JEFFREY L. DAHMER**     , On   8/3/92   , Page   6

of him. DAHMER stated that it gave him sexual arousal, total control over his victims, and when he would eat part of his victims, he felt at one with the victim.

DAHMER was asked by the interviewing agents what parts of the victims he ate, and DAHMER stated that he ate the hearts, liver, thigh meat and at one time he ate a bicep. DAHMER stated that he would prepare this feast by frying the organ in a skillet on the stove, the way you would prepare a regular piece of meat. DAHMER stated that he cut the pieces into small sizes that were small enough to eat. DAHMER stated that he found the meat to be very tasty and DAHMER described it as eating a filet mignon, which was very tender and juicy.

DAHMER was asked by the interviewing agents if he ever got out of jail, would it be possible for him to lead a normal life, and DAHMER stated that the best place for him is in prison because he knows if he ever gets out he would go right back to the same behavior, including killing.

DAHMER was asked by the interview agents if he had any fascination with fire, or if he was a bedwetter as a child, or any cruelty to animals. DAHMER stated that he has never had any fascination with fire, nor was he ever a bedwetter, and the only fascination he had with animals was the road kill that he brought home to dissect. DAHMER stated that he was never cruel to any animals.

DAHMER was asked by the interviewing agents if there was any clues in his life that his co-workers could have picked up on, or his neighbors could have seen that would have tipped off the fact that he was a serial killer. DAHMER stated that he kept his life very compartmentalized and their was a distinct split between his personal life, his work life, and his apartment life. DAHMER stated that there was never any clue to his dark side. DAHMER stated that people at work just thought he was a loner and kept to himself and did his job and did not bother anybody. DAHMER stated that his neighbors at the apartment complex thought him to be a nice young man who minded his own business, but was pleasant.

There was a split and his life was very compartmentalized, and that he would put up with his boss at work for eight hours telling him what to do, but he would not put up

FD-302a (Rev. 11-15-83)

7-MW-26057

with any other "shit" in other aspects of his life. DAHMER
stated that he did not like people telling him what to do.
DAHMER stated that as far as the probation and parole agent was
concerned, DAHMER was a model client. DAHMER stated that his
probation agent did not interfere with him at all and that he
just worked around the agent. DAHMER stated that as far as his
apartment was concerned, he maintained a very orderly and clean
apartment. DAHMER stated that anyone entering the apartment,
their first impression would be one of order and cleanliness.

DAHMER was asked by the interviewing agents if there
was anything law enforcement could have done to have stopped him
or catch him sooner, and DAHMER stated that he had had numerous
contacts with the police, but he is soft spoken and respectful to
the police and could usually talk his way out of problems.
DAHMER stated that there were many incidents which happened,
where he should have been caught, but he was not.

DAHMER advised that he should have been caught after
the first murder, STEVEN HICKS, but the police were not thorough.
DAHMER stated that he did not plan on picking up a hitchhiker and
killing him, it's just that everything fell into place on a
certain day. DAHMER stated that he had been fantasizing about
killing since he was about 16 years old, and when he was 18, he
was driving down the street and saw a young white male
hitchhiking. DAHMER knew that his parents and brother were gone
for the weekend, so it gave him the perfect opportunity to act
out his fantasies. DAHMER stated that he picked up STEVEN HICKS
and then brought him back to his parents' place and then killed
him. DAHMER stated that he had sex with the dead body. DAHMER
further advised that later that night, during the early morning
hours, he had the HICKS body cut up and placed in a trash bag and
was driving down the street when a patrol car stopped him.
DAHMER stated that two police officers then ordered him out of
the car, and they shined their flashlights in his car and saw the
garbage bag, and asked DAHMER what was in the bag and what the
terrible smell was, and DAHMER told them that he was just
bringing some old garbage to the city dump. DAHMER stated that
the officers never looked in the bag and just gave him a ticket
for driving left of center.

DAHMER stated that this incident frightened him and he
fully expected to have been caught. DAHMER stated that he did
not kill again for nearly 10 years.

FD-302a (Rev. 11-15-83)

7-MW-26057

Continuation of FD-302 of     **JEFFREY L. DAHMER**         , On   8/3/92   , Page   8

        DAHMER stated that his second murder was STEVEN TUOMI, and this murder took place at the AMBASSADOR HOTEL somewhere around 1986 or 1987. DAHMER stated that he did not intend to kill TUOMI, but he had a passed out and when he came to the next day he was laying on top of TUOMI, and TUOMI was dead. DAHMER realized that he had killed TUOMI. DAHMER then needed to dispose of the body, so he went out and purchased a large suitcase and came back to the AMBASSADOR HOTEL and then placed the body in the suitcase and called a cab. DAHMER stated that the cabbie then helped him carry the suitcase to the cab, and the cabbie asked DAHMER what was in the suitcase, because it smelled so bad and was very heavy. DAHMER did not respond to the cabbie, but had him drive DAHMER to his grandmother's house in West Allis, where DAHMER subsequently dissected and disposed of the body.

        DAHMER told of another incident where he feared apprehension. This took place in 1988 when he was arrested for taking photographs of an older SINTHASOMPHONE boy. DAHMER was arrested for lewd and lascivious behavior for taking nude photographs. DAHMER stated that the police then executed a search warrant at his apartment and when the police searched his bedroom drawers, DAHMER had a skull in one of the drawers, but the police missed it. DAHMER stated that he was experiencing extreme fear at being caught, but when the police officers searched the drawers, they evidently did not see the skull. DAHMER felt that they had tunnel vision and were looking for drugs and nude photographs and passed right over the skull, which he had covered with a towel. DAHMER stated that he sat in jail for 6 days waiting for the police to come back and confront him with this fact, but the police never did.

        DAHMER told about another incident when he had a mummified head in a small chest in a closet, which he subsequently took to work and kept in his locker. DAHMER stated that his locker was searched at one time, and the skull was found, but DAHMER had painted it with a gray paint, and the investigators thought that it was fake.

        DAHMER advised of another incident while he was at his apartment, the police were conducting a door-to-door investigation because someone had been killed on the 3rd floor. DAHMER stated that when the police came to his apartment to ask questions, he thought that he was going to get caught, because at the time that the police were there, he had a dead body on his

FD-302a (Rev. 11-15-83)

7-MW-26057

Continuation of FD-302 of     JEFFREY L. DAHMER                      , On   8/3/92   , Page   9

bed in his bedroom. DAHMER stated that the police entered his apartment and asked him if they could ask him some questions, and DAHMER agreed, and then the police asked him for permission to look around, and DAHMER did not know what to do so he told the police that they could look all they wanted to. The police then did not search his apartment or even look into the bedroom.

DAHMER talked about another incident where he had met a teenage boy working at a gay bar in Milwaukee, and brought this guy back to his apartment and did not have any sleeping pills remaining, so he tried to get the person drunk. DAHMER stated that it was not working to his satisfaction so he hit the guy in the head with a rubber mallet, and it dazed him, but did not knock him unconscious, so they got into a struggle and the person fled.

This guy then reported the incident to the police, but it sounded so bizarre that the police did not believe him.

DAHMER then spoke of another incident which happened with KONERAK SINTHASOMPHONE, when SINTHASOMPHONE ran out of DAHMER's apartment nude, and a neighbor called the police. The police then responded and brought SINTHASOMPHONE back to the apartment, and DAHMER stated that he (DAHMER) was totally terrified and was expecting to get caught and he attempted to stay calm and rational and told the police that he and SINTHASOMPHONE were lovers, and were having a lovers quarrel. DAHMER then showed the police some photographs that were taken of DAHMER and SINTHASOMPHONE that would depict them as being close lovers. DAHMER had told the police that SINTHASOMPHONE had too much to drink and was groggy. DAHMER stated that the police did not examine SINTHASOMPHONE completely, or take him to a hospital, if they had they would have easily seen a skull fracture where DAHMER had actually drilled some holes in the skull.

DAHMER advised that when he was caught, he had no secret subconscious wish to get caught, but the night that he was caught was different than any other night. DAHMER stated that he had met this ████████████ and they agreed to return to DAHMER's apartment, and they started drinking and DAHMER passed out and does not remember anything that happened. DAHMER stated that it was very rare for him to pass out, because he is a heavy drinker and can handle the alcohol and on evenings that he was on the "prowl", he did not drink to excess. DAHMER stated that the

b7C

FD-302a (Rev. 11-15-83)

7-MW-26057

Continuation of FD-302 of    JEFFREY L. DAHMER                        . On    8/3/92    . Page    10

ᑯ7c

evening of ▆▆▆▆▆ he does not know what happened, but when he
woke up there was some pounding on the door, and he answered the
door and there were police officers standing there with ▆▆▆▆▆
▆▆▆▆▆ and ▆▆▆▆▆ still had a handcuff cuffed to his arm.
DAHMER stated that he (DAHMER) panicked and did not have time to
think up a story, and opened the door and allowed the police to
enter.  DAHMER stated that the police then asked him for
permission to search his apartment, and when they did search the
apartment they found skulls, and then immediately arrested him.

DAHMER was asked if he was relieved that it was over
and that was finally arrested and DAHMER stated that he was not
glad that it was over.  DAHMER stated that he liked his lifestyle
and found it exciting and thrilling, and would have continued
forever.  DAHMER stated that the best place for him to be is in
prison, because if he was ever released he knows that he would go
right back to the same activities and behavior.  DAHMER was asked
if he had a premonition or a dream that he felt he was going to
be arrested, and DAHMER stated that he did have recurring
nightmares about a large tornado striking and him trying to hide
in the ditch and be saved.  DAHMER stated that he did feel things
were falling apart and he was starting to lose control in
February of 1991.  DAHMER explained that he had CURTIS STRAUGHTER
on his bed, and STRAUGHTER was drugged and was starting to pass
out, when STRAUGHTER rolled off the bed and knocked over a black
table which DAHMER had two griffins on.  DAHMER stated that these
griffins were part of the occult, and symbolized personal power
and made it that he did not have to answer to anyone.  DAHMER
stated that there were words written on each griffin, one had
leon and the other had apal.  DAHMER again stated that this
symbolized personal power, and he felt that this was a sign to
show that he was losing control.

DAHMER was asked if he was involved in the occult, and
DAHMER stated that he started dabbling in the occult and reading,
and his favorite movie was EXORCIST III, because it helped fit
into his fantasy.  DAHMER stated that in the movie EXORCIST III
the guy could create illusions, and DAHMER felt that he himself
could create illusions.

DAHMER was asked if he had any religious background and
DAHMER stated that he did not have the religious background
growing up, but after being discharged from the army he attempted
to turn to religion while living with his grandmother in West

FD-302a (Rev. 11-15-83)

7-MW-26057

Continuation of FD-302 of __JEFFREY L. DAHMER_____ , On __8/3/92__ , Page __11__

Allis. DAHMER had only committed one murder at this time, and he
had thought about going to the police, but decided against it.
DAHMER thought that turning to religion might help satisfy his
controlling urges and fantasies, but it did not work so he gave
up on religion.

DAHMER was asked that if there was a toll free 1/800
number that he could have called anonymously and talked to a
psychiatrist to try and get some help, would he in fact have made
that call. DAHMER stated emphatically that he would not have
made a call anonymously or otherwise to any toll free number.
DAHMER stated that he would not have trusted anyone, and he had
to keep his secret at all costs. DAHMER also felt that he could
not have been helped. DAHMER stated that his obsession was too
powerful and all consuming, and took over his life. DAHMER
stated that after his arrest he has had many, many hours with
psychiatrists, and he did not enjoy his sessions with the
different psychiatrists because all they could do is label him
such as a necrophilic (having sex with a dead body) or a
paraphiliac (sexual disorders), but the psychiatrists could not
say why it happened, or how it happened, or how to treat it.
DAHMER stated that it upset him that the psychiatrists would just
label him, but not be able to explain why or how to deal with it.

DAHMER was asked by the interviewing agents if he had
ever thought about suicide, and DAHMER stated that he had not and
that he enjoyed his lifestyle and that he was so much into his
obsession, that it was a primary motivator in his life, and he
did not want to end it. DAHMER stated that after his arrest he
thinks about suicide all the time and if he could do it he would
kill himself.

DAHMER was asked if he had any interest in other serial
killers and DAHMER stated that he never had an interest in any
other cases, or any interest to read or follow serial killing
cases. DAHMER stated that he was just caught up in his own
fantasies. DAHMER stated though that since he has been
incarcerated he has received letters from other killers who have
admitted killing and said that they know how he feels and what it
felt like to do it. DAHMER stated that he felt that these
letters were authentic and sincere, and DAHMER would be willing
to turn the letters over to the FBI.

FD-302a (Rev. 11-15-83)

7-MW-26057

Continuation of FD-302 of     JEFFREY L. DAHMER    , On   8/3/92  , Page   12

DAHMER was asked if he received more satisfaction out of the sex acts or the controlling of the individuals, and DAHMER stated that it was half and half. DAHMER stated that the total control of another individual was his fantasy and that would build the excitement that when he would ejaculate that it would be more pleasurable.

DAHMER stated that going out on the hunt was in itself a thrill, never knowing who he would meet or how nice looking they would be, or how much fun he would have with them. DAHMER stated that this in itself was part of the fantasy.

DAHMER stated that he had never tried a hetro-sexual relationship and never had any interest in doing so even on an experimental basis. DAHMER stated that his first homosexual encounter occurred when he was around 13 or 14, with a next door neighbor, and it was only kissing and heavy petting.

DAHMER again advised that he never hated any of his victims, nor was it ever a racial thing, in that many of his victims were white, black, Hispanic and even Jewish. DAHMER advised that what he was lusting for was the perfect "chip and dale" body and it did not matter to him who the individual was.

DAHMER stated that he was very insulted by the Milwaukee Journal trying to make his case look like a racially motivated or hate type of crime, and DAHMER stated that there was never any hate involved. DAHMER stated that the first two people he killed were white the third guy was an American Indian, the fourth victim was Hispanic, and then he killed some black males, then an Asian, a Jewish man a Puerto Rican, and another white male. DAHMER stated that his victims were chosen by appearance and body type, and availability to his proposals.

DAHMER was asked by the interviewing agents if he had any remorse for what he had done, and DAHMER stated that he did not. DAHMER stated that the only time he felt bad was after the first murder, STEVEN HICKS, and that had bothered him. DAHMER stated that after all of the other murders it never bothered him and he would not put on an act or fake crocodile tears to gain sympathy. DAHMER stated that it does bother him that he is not bothered by his actions. DAHMER stated though that if he had a conscience, he probably would not have killed anybody. DAHMER stated that while he was involved in his murders, he never

FD-302a (Rev. 11-15-83)

7-MW-26057

Continuation of FD-302 of ___JEFFREY L. DAHMER_____ , On __8/3/92__ , Page __13__

thought of the individuals as people, and having families that would grieve for the victims. DAHMER just viewed the victims as objects for his own personnel sexual gratification. DAHMER stated that he now looks back on it and feels bad for the families, and all the pain that he has caused them. DAHMER stated that he was very selfish and only cared about satisfying his own pleasures.

DAHMER advised that since his arrest he has turned to religion, and does believe in God and that there will be a final judgement, and he does not want any secrets any more. DAHMER stated that he does not believe in reincarnation.

DAHMER was asked by the interviewing agents if his compulsion to kill was so great that he could not control it under any circumstances and DAHMER stated that he would not kill a victim if there was a possibility of getting caught. DAHMER stated that he did not take unnecessary risks and was very cautious as to not be seen with the victims, i.e. cab drivers, bar patrons, etc. DAHMER stated that there was one individual by the name of ████████ who he had at his grandmother's house, and he fully intended on killing this individual, but his grandmother came in and saw the two of them together, so he did not kill this male, because he knew he would get caught.

DAHMER was asked by the interviewing agents what he felt was the reasons or the contributing factors to his serial killing, and if there was anything he could change. DAHMER stated that if he could eliminate his fantasies, the overwhelming fantasies that started when he was about age 15 and 16, when he was thinking and fantasizing about having sex with a dead body. DAHMER stated that if he could have short circuited those fantasies, then it may have stopped short of killings. DAHMER was asked if he felt that pornography and alcohol contributed to his problem and DAHMER stated that a lot of people drink and a lot of people use hardcore pornography, but they don't go out and kill. DAHMER stated that the alcohol would help overcome any inabitions or resistance that he may have had on his part and the hardcore pornography just led to more fantasies and masturbation. DAHMER was asked what came first the fantasies or the pornography and DAHMER said it was the fantasies. DAHMER stated that he then used the pornography to help satisfy his fantasies.

Continuation of FD-302 of ___JEFFREY L. DAHMER_____ , On _8/3/92_ , Page _14_

       DAHMER volunteered the fact that his fantasies always had the perfect "chip and dale" or gymnastic body of a 19-22 year old male. DAHMER stated that he never once had an interest in young children, and that he had nothing to do with the ADAM WALSH abduction and murder in Florida. DAHMER brought this up, because he knew that he was a suspect in that murder, but DAHMER stated that he had nothing to do with it, nor would it ever have crossed his mind. The interviewing agents asked DAHMER if he would confess to the ADAM WALSH murder if in fact he had committed it, and DAHMER stated that he absolutely would. DAHMER was asked why he would confess to that murder, and DAHMER stated that at this point he does not want any secrets, and he has already confessed to 17 murders, half of which the police would never have known about if he had not told them. DAHMER further advised that there comes a time when there will be a final judgement, and he knows that he has been judged now while he is on the earth, but he concerned about the final judgement and did not want any secrets.

       SA ▓▓▓▓ asked DAHMER from an interrogator's point of view, why did DAHMER confess to ▓▓▓▓▓▓▓▓▓▓▓▓▓▓▓ under interrogation. DAHMER stated that ▓▓▓▓▓ was not phony, and was very personable and easy to talk to. DAHMER stated that ▓▓▓▓ made him comfortable and made sure that his (DAHMER) needs were met. DAHMER stated that the second detective, ▓▓▓▓▓▓▓▓ was businesslike and hardnosed, and it was harder for DAHMER to open up to him.

       DAHMER stated that ▓▓▓▓ did not judge him (DAHMER), and did not play "hardass". DAHMER also felt that ▓▓▓▓ could tell if DAHMER was bluffing, and ▓▓▓▓ told DAHMER that he could not hide the truth forever. DAHMER stated that at this point he knew he was going to get caught because the police had already found all the skulls in his apartment, and he wanted to face the judgement now, as opposed to dying and facing a final judgement. DAHMER also advised that ▓▓▓▓ did not make DAHMER feel embarrassed over what he had done. ▓▓▓▓ said that it was okay, and that he ▓▓▓▓ has seen worse. DAHMER stated that he felt that ▓▓▓▓ was sincere, and very personable and seemed to care about him (DAHMER), as a person. DAHMER stated that it was very easy to talk to ▓▓▓▓ and that ▓▓▓▓ was honest with DAHMER, and did not play any games with him.

**INFORMATION COMMUNICATION**                                    Date:    11/18/92

TO:        MILWAUKEE

FROM:    MILWAUKEE   (C)
            MRA

POINT OF CONTACT:   SA ▮▮▮▮▮▮▮   b7c

TITLE:    DAHMER, JEFFREY;
            LACY, OLIVER - VICTIM (DECEASED);
            UNSUBS - VICTIMS (DECEASED);
            KIDNAPPING - HOMICIDE;
            OO:  MILWAUKEE

PURPOSE(S): For information of the file, the last remaining work
required in this matter was a detailed interview of JEFFREY
DAHMER in anticipation of contact with
 him at Columbia Correctional Institution in Portage, Wisconsin,
by the Behavioral Science Unit of Quantico, Virginia.  This has
been completed, the FD-302 dictated and forwarded to the
Behavioral Science Unit, and therefore, no further investigation
remains outstanding in the Milwaukee Division.

            In view of this fact, it is requested this matter be
administratively closed.

UCFN: 7-MW-26057 - 84

Q - File Copy
1 - Work Copy
NFP:kl▮▮ (2)

0002 MRI 00549

RR RUCNFB FBIMW FBISE

DE BON #0004 3281545

ZNR UUUUU

R 231435Z NOV 92

FM LEGAT BONN (7-MW-26057) (P)

TO DIRECTOR FBI/ROUTINE/

FBI MILWAUKEE/ROUTINE/

FBI SEATTLE/ROUTINE/

BT

UNCLAS CORRECTED COPY

CITE: //5300:BON710.328//

PASS: HQ CID, VCMOS, AND OLIA, FLU 1.


SUBJECT: JEFFREY L. DAHMER; OLIVER LACY - VICTIM (DECEASED);

KIDNAPING - HOMICIDE; OO: MW.

    RE MILWAUKEE AIRTEL TO FBIHQ AND BONN, AUG. 16, 1991;

BONN TELETYPE TO MILWAUKEE, NOV. 15, 1991; MILWAUKEE TELETYPE

TO BONN, JAN. 24, 1992.

    FOR THE INFO OF THE SEATTLE OFFICE, JEFFREY L. DAHMER, A

WHITE MALE, DOB MAY 21, 1960, HAS BEEN CONVICTED FOR NUMEROUS

PAGE TWO DE BUN 0004 UNCLAS

HOMICIDES IN MILWAUKEE, WISCONSIN. ALL OF HIS VICTIMS WERE
MALE AND MOSTLY HOMOSEXUAL.

DAHMER SERVED IN THE U.S. ARMY FROM DECEMBER 1978 TO
MARCH 26, 1981. HE WAS STATIONED IN GERMANY FROM JUNE 1979
UNTIL MARCH 1981 IN THE HEADQUARTERS COMPANY, 268TH ARMOR
DIVISION, 2ND BATTALION, 68TH ARMOR, BAUMHOLDER, GERMANY.

DAHMER HAS DENIED ANY HOMOSEXUAL ACTIVITIES WHILE IN
GERMANY.

ON AUG. 10, 1992, ███████████ ████████████████
████████ OLYMPIA, WASHINGTON, 98501, CONTACTED THE GERMAN
CONSULATE GENERAL, 1 UNION SQUARE, SUITE 2500, 600 UNIVERSITY  *b7C*
STREET, SEATTLE, WASHINGTON. ████████TOLD THE CONSULATE THAT
HE WAS IN THE SAME U.S. ARMY UNIT AS DAHMER AND SERVED WITH
HIM IN THE BAUMHOLDER, GERMANY AREA IN 1978. HE ALLEGEDLY
SHOWED THE CONSULATE AN ARTICLE PUBLISHED BY THE SEATTLE POST
INTELLIGENCER, WHICH STATED THAT DAHMER WAS GUILTY OF SEVERAL
MURDERS NEAR BAD KREUZNACH, GERMANY. ████████CLAIMED THAT HE
HAS EVIDENCE THAT WOULD LINK DAHMER TO FIVE MURDERS NEAR BAD
KREUZNACH. ████████STATED THAT HE NEVER FURNISHED ANY INFO  *b7C*
ABOUT THIS TO U.S. AUTHORITIES BECAUSE A HIGH RANKING U.S.
ARMY OFFICER WAS CONNECTED TO THESE HOMICIDES. THIS

PAGE THREE DE BON 0004 UNCLAS

INDIVIDUAL, WHO, ACCORDING TO ████ HAD A POSITION AS A
█████████████ SUPPRESSED ALL OF THE EVIDENCE ON THE FIVE
HOMICIDES.

_b7c_

U.S. ARMY CID, 2ND REGION, MANNHEIM, GERMANY, WAS UNABLE
TO LOCATE ANY RECORD FOR A ███████████ ANY FURTHER CHECK OF
ARMY PERSONNEL RECORDS WOULD REQUIRE A BIRTH DATE OF SOCIAL
SECURITY NUMBER.

████████████████████████████ HAS REQUESTED TO _b7D_
KNOW IF DAHMER, DURING THE SUMMER OF 1992, ADMITTED TO ANY
HOMICIDES IN GERMANY. (THIS AFTER THEY WERE INFORMED THAT HE
DID NOT ADMIT TO ANY HOMICIDES IN GERMANY IN MILWAUKEE LHM,
DATED AUG. 16, 1991.)

THEY ALSO REQUEST A COPY OF WHAT APPEARS TO BE AN AUGUST
1992 EDITION OF THE SEATTLE POST INTELLIGENCER IN WHICH DAHMER
ALLEGEDLY ADMITTED TO HOMICIDES IN GERMANY.

ALSO REQUESTED IS BACKGROUND ON, AND AN INTERVIEW OF,

████████ _b7c_

LEADS:

MILWAUKEE AT MILWAUKEE, WISCONSIN:

RECONTACT JEFFREY DAHMER AND AGAIN QUESTION HIM ABOUT HIS

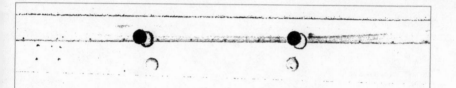

PAGE FOUR LE BON 0004 UNCLAS

ACTIVITIES IN GERMANY. ALSO DETERMINE IF THE COURT RECORDS IN

ANY OF DAHMER'S LEGAL PROCEEDINGS CONCERNS THEMSELVES WITH

HOMICIDES HE MAY HAVE COMMITTED IN GERMANY.

SEATTLE AT OLYMPIA, WASHINGTON:

CONTACT ██████ ████████ ████ b7C

OLYMPIA, WASHINGTON, AND INTERVIEW HIM REGARDING ANY INFO HE

MAY HAVE ABOUT DAHMER'S ACTIVITIES IN GERMANY. ALSO ATTEMPT

TO OBTAIN THE COPY OF THE SEATTLE POST INTELLIGENCER IN WHICH

HE CLAIMS HE READ ABOUT DAHMER'S CONFESSION TO FIVE HOMICIDES

IN GERMANY.

ALSO CONDUCT A CRIMINAL RECORD CHECK FOR ████ b7C

BT

#0004


NNNN

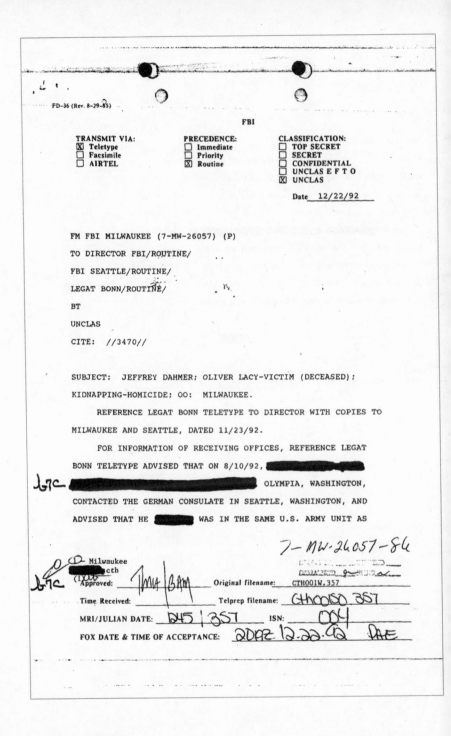

FD-36 (Rev. 8-29-85)

FBI

TRANSMIT VIA:
☒ Teletype
☐ Facsimile
☐ AIRTEL

PRECEDENCE:
☐ Immediate
☐ Priority
☒ Routine

CLASSIFICATION:
☐ TOP SECRET
☐ SECRET
☐ CONFIDENTIAL
☐ UNCLAS E F T O
☒ UNCLAS

Date 12/22/92

FM FBI MILWAUKEE (7-MW-26057) (P)

TO DIRECTOR FBI/ROUTINE/

FBI SEATTLE/ROUTINE/

LEGAT BONN/ROUTINE/

BT

UNCLAS

CITE: //3470//

SUBJECT: JEFFREY DAHMER; OLIVER LACY-VICTIM (DECEASED);

KIDNAPPING-HOMICIDE; OO: MILWAUKEE.

REFERENCE LEGAT BONN TELETYPE TO DIRECTOR WITH COPIES TO

MILWAUKEE AND SEATTLE, DATED 11/23/92.

FOR INFORMATION OF RECEIVING OFFICES, REFERENCE LEGAT

BONN TELETYPE ADVISED THAT ON 8/10/92, ███████████████

███████████████████████████ OLYMPIA, WASHINGTON,

CONTACTED THE GERMAN CONSULATE IN SEATTLE, WASHINGTON, AND

ADVISED THAT HE ███████ WAS IN THE SAME U.S. ARMY UNIT AS

7-MW-26057-84

Milwaukee
░░░░eth
Approved: _____ Original filename: CTH001W.357

Time Received: _____ Telprep filename: CTH00150 357

MRI/JULIAN DATE: 045 / 357 ISN: 004

FOX DATE & TIME OF ACCEPTANCE: 20AZ 12-22-92 PAE

JEFFREY L. DAHMER, AND SERVED WITH DAHMER IN BAUMHOLDER,

b7c GERMANY, IN 1978. ████████ CLAIMED TO HAVE EVIDENCE THAT WOULD

LINK DAHMER TO FIVE MURDERS NEAR BAD KREUZNACH.

DAHMER WAS INTERVIEWED BY MILWAUKEE AGENTS, AND DENIED

ANY KNOWLEDGE OR INVOLVEMENT IN ANY MURDERS IN GERMANY.

DAHMER STATED THAT HE DID NOT KNOW ANYONE BY THE NAME OF ████████

b7c ████████ DAHMER STATED THAT HE WAS NOT IN GERMANY IN 1978, AND

ENTERED THE ARMY ON 1/12/79, HAVING BASIC TRAINING AT FORT

MCCLELLAN, ALABAMA, AND ADVANCED INFANTRY TRAINING AT FORT SAM

HOUSTON, IN 1979.

DAHMER WAS STATIONED IN BAUMHOLDER, GERMANY, DURING 1980

TO 1981, AND SERVED IN THE 268 ARMOR DIVISION, SECOND

BATTALION. DAHMER'S RANK WAS E-2, AND HE WAS DISCHARGED FROM

THE ARMY ON 3/26/81. THIS INFORMATION IS VERIFIED BY DAHMER'S

MILITARY RECORDS, WHICH MILWAUKEE DIVISION HAS A COPY OF.

DAHMER ADVISED THAT WHILE IN GERMANY HE HAD NO VEHICLE,

AND THE ONLY CITY HE TRAVELED TO WAS IDAROBERSTEIN (PHONETIC).

DAHMER ADVISED THAT HE HAD ONLY ONE HOMOSEXUAL ENCOUNTER

WHILE HE WAS STATIONED IN GERMANY, AND THAT ENCOUNTER WAS A

MASTER SERGEANT WHOSE NAME DAHMER DOES NOT RECALL, BUT

DESCRIBES AS OLDER, WHITE MALE, WHO WAS SHORT AND HEAVY SET,
AND DAHMER MET AT THE LANDSTHEUL (PHONETIC) HOSPITAL.

DAHMER FURTHER ADVISED THAT WHILE HE WAS STATIONED IN
GERMANY, HE HEARD NEWS REPORTS PERTAINING TO THE HOMICIDES AND
SAW POSTERS, BUT DAHMER KNEW OF NO SPECIFICS CONCERNING THE
HOMICIDES.

DAHMER STATED THAT DURING HIS INTENSE QUESTIONING BY
MILWAUKEE POLICE DEPARTMENT - HOMICIDE DETECTIVES, DURING JULY
OF 1991, HE WAS REPEATEDLY ASKED ABOUT THE HOMICIDES WHICH
OCCURRED IN GERMANY.  DAHMER HAS CONSISTENTLY MAINTAINED THAT
HE WAS NOT INVOLVED IN ANY HOMICIDES IN GERMANY, OR ANYWHERE
ELSE, OTHER THAN WHAT HE HAS ALREADY ADMITTED TO.  DAHMER
STATED THAT IF, IN FACT, HE HAD COMMITTED ANY ADDITIONAL
HOMICIDES, HE WOULD ADMIT TO THEM.

MILWAUKEE LEAD AGENT CONTACTED███████████████████,
MILWAUKEE POLICE DEPARTMENT - HOMICIDE SQUAD, AND ███████

b7C ████████ VERIFIED THAT HE HAD EXTENSIVELY QUESTIONED DAHMER
REGARDING THE GERMANY HOMICIDES, DURING THEIR INTERROGATION OF
DAHMER IN JULY OF 1991. ███████████████ADVISED THAT DAHMER

^PAGE 4 7-MW-26057, UNCLAS

DENIED ANY KNOWLEDGE OR INVOLVEMENT IN ANY HOMICIDES IN
GERMANY.

AT THE CONCLUSION OF THE INTERVIEW WITH JEFFREY DAHMER,
DAHMER REITERATED THE FACT THAT HE DID NOT KNOW ANYONE BY THE
NAME OF ███████████ BUT STATED THAT IF A PHOTOGRAPH OF
███████ WAS AVAILABLE, THAT MAY REFRESH HIS MEMORY.

LEADS ARE BEING LEFT TO THE DISCRETION OF LEGAT BONN AS
TO WHETHER TO SHOW DAHMER A PHOTOGRAPH OF ███████████ IF
LEGAT BONN REQUESTS DAHMER BE SHOWN A PHOTOGRAPH OF ███████
THEN FBI SEATTLE WILL HAVE TO OBTAIN A PHOTOGRAPH OF ███████
AND FORWARD IT TO MILWAUKEE DIVISION.

BT

b7c

FD-36 (Rev. 11-17-88)

FBI

| TRANSMIT VIA: | PRECEDENCE: | CLASSIFICATION: |
|---|---|---|
| ☐ Teletype | ☐ Immediate | ☐ TOP SECRET |
| ☐ Facsimile | ☐ Priority | ☐ SECRET |
| ☒ AIRTEL | ☐ Routine | ☐ CONFIDENTIAL |
| | | ☐ UNCLAS E F T O |
| | | ☐ UNCLAS |

Date  2/5/93

TO      : SAC, MILWAUKEE (7-MW-26057)

FROM    : SAC, SEATTLE (7-MW-26057) (RUC) (OLYMPIA)

SUBJECT : JEFFREY L. DAHMER;
          OLIVER LACY - VICTIM (DECEASED);
          KIDNAPPING - HOMICIDE;
          OO: MILWAUKEE .

          RE: Milwaukee teletype to Seattle, dated November
23, 1992, and Seattle telcal to Milwaukee on November 25,
1992.

          Enclosed is one copy of the article requested by
Milwaukee, that appeared in the "SEATTLE TIMES", rather than
the "SEATTLE POST-INTELLIGENCER", dated July 26, 1991.

                              date of birth:
place of birth:      Washington, SSAN:          white
male, 6'1", 175 lbs., blond hair, blue eyes was located and
interviewed at MILLERSYLVANIA STATE PARK.          was located
through his

                    stated he served in Baumholder, Germany,
HHB, 5th BN, 6th Air Defense Artillery from September, 1976,
through May 24, 1978, when he was honorably discharged.
          re-enlisted in 1986 and was medically discharged in
December, 1990, for shoulder problems as well as suffering
from

                    told interviewing Agents that he never knew
DAHMER and was never in Germany at the same time as DAHMER.

(2)- Milwaukee (7-MW-26057) (Enc.          7-MW-26057-87
2 - Seattle (7-MW-26057)
   (1 - SA
JAS:lph
(4)

SEARCHED _____ INDEXED _____
SERIALIZED _____ FILED _____

FEB 11 1993

FBI — MILWAUKEE

Approved: _____ Transmitted _____
                          (Number)   (Time)  W/ ENCLOSURE

7-MW-26057

      While in Germany, ███████ was associated with the "Glub Club", a beer drinking group, and in this club were women who he became friends with. A German friend of ███████ told ███████ (sometime in 1984) that DAHMER was passing himself off as ███████ to get close to these women. ███████ only recalled two of the women's names, ███████ and ███████ and does not know if they were killed or not.

      The only higher up military official ███████ thought was involved, was ███████ whom he met at FORT LEWIS in April, 1975. ███████ could not make the connection of ███████ DAHMER or the five murdered women in Germany, he merely stated he felt ███████ had his own private agenda.

      Criminal records check on ███████ was negative.

      Insomuch as all investigation has been completed in the Seattle Division, pending further requests by the Office of Origin, this case is being placed in an RUC status.

2 *

0011 MRI 00995

RR RUCNFB FBIMW FBISE

DE BON #0002 0472149

ZNR UUUUU

R 162033Z FEB 93

FM LEGAT BONN (7-MW-26057) (P)

TO DIRECTOR FBI/ROUTINE/

FBI MILWAUKEE/ROUTINE/

FBI SEATTLE/ROUTINE/

BT

UNCLAS

CITE: //5300:BON108.043//

PASS: FBIHQ FOR CID, VCMOS; AND OLIA, FLU 1.


SUBJECT: JEFFREY DAHMER; OLIVER LACY - VICTIM (DECEASED):

KIDNAPPING-HOMICIDE; OO: MILWAUKEE.

    RE BONN TELETYPE TO DIRECTOR AND SEATTLE NOVEMBER 23,

1992.

    THE SEATTLE OFFICE IS REQUESTED TO PROVIDE BONN WITH

RESULTS OF REQUESTED INTERVIEW OF ▮▮▮▮▮▮ OLYMPIA,

WASHINGTON AS SOON AS POSSIBLE.

7-MW-26057-88

PAGE TWO DE BON 0002 UNCLAS

BONN WILL FORWARD SAME TO GERMAN AUTHORITIES, WHO

REQUESTED INTERVIEW.

BT

#0002

NNNN

OPCA-20 (12-3-96)

XXXXXX
XXXXXX
XXXXXX

### FEDERAL BUREAU OF INVESTIGATION
### FOIPA
### DELETED PAGE INFORMATION SHEET

__2__ Page(s) withheld entirely at this location in the file. One or more of the following statements, where indicated, explain this deletion.

☑ Deletions were made pursuant to the exemptions indicated below with no segregable material available for release to you.

| Section 552 | | Section 552a |
|---|---|---|
| ☐ (b)(1) | ☐ (b)(7)(A) | ☐ (d)(5) |
| ☐ (b)(2) | ☐ (b)(7)(B) | ☐ (j)(2) |
| ☐ (b)(3) | ☑ (b)(7)(C) | ☐ (k)(1) |
| _____ | ☑ (b)(7)(D) | ☐ (k)(2) |
| _____ | ☐ (b)(7)(E) | ☐ (k)(3) |
| _____ | ☐ (b)(7)(F) | ☐ (k)(4) |
| ☐ (b)(4) | ☐ (b)(8) | ☐ (k)(5) |
| ☐ (b)(5) | ☐ (b)(9) | ☐ (k)(6) |
| ☐ (b)(6) | | ☐ (k)(7) |

☐ Information pertained only to a third party with no reference to the subject of your request or the subject of your request is listed in the title only.

☐ Documents originated with another Government agency(ies). These documents were referred to that agency(ies) for review and direct response to you.

_____ Pages contain information furnished by another Government agency(ies). You will be advised by the FBI as to the releasability of this information following our consultation with the other agency(ies).

_____ Page(s) withheld inasmuch as a final release determination has not been made. You will be advised as to the disposition at a later date.

_____ Pages were not considered for release as they are duplicative of _____

_____ Page(s) withheld for the following reason(s): _____

☑ The following number is to be used for reference regarding these pages:
7-MW-26057-89 + 90.

XXXXXXXXXXXXXXXX
X   Deleted Page(s)   X
X   No Duplication Fee   X
X   for this page   X
XXXXXXXXXXXXXXXX

XXXXXX
XXXXXX
XXXXXX

FBI/DOJ

**INFORMATION COMMUNICATION**                           Date:    03/03/93

**TO:**      TRAINING DIVISION
             BEHAVIORAL SCIENCE UNIT (Encl. 3)

             MINNEAPOLIS (Encl. 3)

**FROM:**    MILWAUKEE  (P)
             SQUAD 6

**POINT OF CONTACT:**  SSA ███████████  b7c

**TITLE:**   DAHMER, JEFFREY, L.;
             KIDNAPPING - SERIAL MURDER;
             OO:  MILWAUKEE

             Caution Statement  ARMED AND DANGEROUS ;

             **Enclosures:**  Enclosed for Behavioral Science Unit and
             Minneapolis Division are one copy each of three letters
             received by JEFFREY L. DAHMER, while incarcerated at
             the Columbia Correctional Institution in Wisconsin.

**PURPOSE(S):**  Information.

**DETAILS:**  For the information of receiving offices, JEFFREY L.
DAHMER was convicted of 17 murders occurring in Milwaukee,
Wisconsin, and Ohio.  FBI Milwaukee has interviewed DAHMER on
several occasions, and maintains a favorable liaison with DAHMER.
DAHMER receives approximately 10 to 15 letters per day while
incarcerated in prison, and DAHMER has agreed to turn over to the
FBI any letters that he feels will be of value to the FBI.

SEE CAUTION STATEMENT

UCFN:  7A-MW-26057-91

SEARCHED_____ INDEXED_____
SERIALIZED ___ FILED ____

① - File Copy
1 - Work Copy
b7c ███████ cth  (6)

# FEDERAL BUREAU OF INVESTIGATION
## FOIPA
### DELETED PAGE INFORMATION SHEET

**8** Page(s) withheld entirely at this location in the file. One or more of the following statements, where indicated, explain this deletion.

☑ Deletions were made pursuant to the exemptions indicated below with no segregable material available for release to you.

| Section 552 | | Section 552a |
|---|---|---|
| ☐ (b)(1) | ☐ (b)(7)(A) | ☐ (d)(5) |
| ☐ (b)(2) | ☐ (b)(7)(B) | ☐ (j)(2) |
| ☐ (b)(3) | ☑ (b)(7)(C) | ☐ (k)(1) |
| _____ | ☐ (b)(7)(D) | ☐ (k)(2) |
| _____ | ☐ (b)(7)(E) | ☐ (k)(3) |
| _____ | ☐ (b)(7)(F) | ☐ (k)(4) |
| ☐ (b)(4) | ☐ (b)(8) | ☐ (k)(5) |
| ☐ (b)(5) | ☐ (b)(9) | ☐ (k)(6) |
| ☐ (b)(6) | | ☐ (k)(7) |

☐ Information pertained only to a third party with no reference to the subject of your request or the subject of your request is listed in the title only.

☐ Documents originated with another Government agency(ies). These documents were referred to that agency(ies) for review and direct response to you.

_____ Pages contain information furnished by another Government agency(ies). You will be advised by the FBI as to the releasability of this information following our consultation with the other agency(ies).

_____ Page(s) withheld inasmuch as a final release determination has not been made. You will be advised as to the disposition at a later date.

_____ Pages were not considered for release as they are duplicative of _____

_____ Page(s) withheld for the following reason(s): _____
_____

☑ The following number is to be used for reference regarding these pages:
7-MW-26057-91, pgs. 2-9.

XXXXXXXXXXXXXXXX
X   Deleted Page(s)    X
X   No Duplication Fee   X
X      for this page      X
XXXXXXXXXXXXXXXX

XXXXXX
XXXXXX
XXXXXX

FBI/DOJ

0004 MR1 00871

RR RUCNFB BON FBIMW

DE FBISE #0001 0741939

ZNR UUUUU

R 151740Z MAR 93

FM FBI SEATTLE (7-MW-26057) (RUC)

TO DIRECTOR FBI/ROUTINE/

LEGAT BONN/ROUTINE/

INFO FBI MILWAUKEE/ROUTINE/

BT

UNCLAS

CITE: //3840:5340//

SUBJECT: JEFFREY DAHMER; OLIVER LACY-VICTIM (DECEASED);

KIDNAPING-HOMICIDE; OO: MILWAUKEE.

ARMED AND DANGEROUS.

RE LEGAT BONN TELETYPE TO DIRECTOR DATED FEBRUARY 16,

1993.

AS PER REQUEST, THE FOLLOWING ARE THE RESULTS OF THE

INTERVIEW OF ███████████

███████████ DATE OF BIRTH: ███████████

PAGE TWO DE FBISE 0001 UNCLAS

PLACE OF BIRTH: ████████ WASHINGTON; SOCIAL SECURITY ACCOUNT

NUMBER: ████████ WHITE MALE; 6 FEET, 1 INCH; 175 POUNDS;

b7c

BLOND HAIR; BLUE EYES, WAS LOCATED AND INTERVIEWED AT NORTH

SKAMANIA STATE PARK. ████████ WAS LOCATED THROUGH HIS

████████████████████████████

████████ OLYMPIA, WASHINGTON, TELEPHONE ████████

████████ STATED HE SERVED IN BAUMHOLDER, GERMANY, HHD,

FIFTH BN, SIXTH AIR DEFENSE ARTILLERY, FROM SEPTEMBER, 1976,

THROUGH MAY 24, 1978, WHEN HE WAS HONORABLY DISCHARGED.

████████ REENLISTED IN 1986 AND WAS MEDICALLY DISCHARGED IN

DECEMBER, 1990, FOR SHOULDER PROBLEMS, AS WELL AS SUFFERING

b7c

FROM ████████

████████ TOLD INTERVIEWING AGENTS THAT HE NEVER KNEW

JEFFREY L. DAHMER AND WAS NEVER IN GERMANY AT THE SAME TIME AS

DAHMER.

WHILE IN GERMANY, ████████ WAS ASSOCIATED WITH THE "GLUB

CLUB," A BEER DRINKING GROUP, AND IN THIS CLUB WERE WOMEN WITH

WHOM HE BECAME FRIENDS. A GERMAN FRIEND OF ████████ TOLD

b7c

████████ (SOMETIME IN 1984) THAT DAHMER WAS PASSING HIMSELF OFF

AS ████████ TO GET CLOSE TO THESE WOMEN. ████████ ONLY RECALLED

TWO OF THE WOMEN'S NAMES, ████████████ AND ████████ AND

PAGE THREE DE FB1SE 0001 UNCLAS

DOES NOT KNOW WHETHER OR NOT THEY WERE KILLED.

THE ONLY HIGHER UP MILITARY OFFICIAL ███ THOUGHT WAS

INVOLVED WAS ███████████████████████ WHOM HE MET

AT FORT LEWIS IN APRIL, 1975. ████ COULD NOT MAKE THE

CONNECTION OF ████ DAHMER OR THE FIVE MURDERED WOMEN IN

GERMANY: HE MERELY STATED HE FELT ████ HAD HIS OWN PRIVATE

AGENDA.

CRIMINAL RECORDS CHECKS ON ████ WERE NEGATIVE.

INASMUCH AS ALL INVESTIGATION HAS BEEN COMPLETED IN THE

SEATTLE DIVISION, SEATTLE CONSIDERS THIS MATTER RUC.

ARMED AND DANGEROUS.

BT

#0001



NNNN

**INFORMATION COMMUNICATION**                              Date:    04/20/93

TO:        MILWAUKEE

FROM:      MILWAUKEE  (C)
           MRA

POINT OF CONTACT:  SA ⬛⬛⬛⬛⬛⬛⬛⬛  b7C

TITLE:     DAHMER, JEFFREY, L.;
           ET AL;
           KIDNAPPING - HOMICIDE;
           OO: MILWAUKEE

           **References:** Seattle airtel to Milwaukee, dated 2/5/93.

**PURPOSE(S):**  This matter was re-opened upon receipt information
from Legat Germany that German authorities had received
allegations from ⬛⬛⬛⬛⬛⬛⬛⬛ who reported that he was a
member of DAHMER's military unit while DAHMER was serving in
Germany, and that DAHMER was responsible for killing some women
while in Germany.

           In the course of this investigation, ⬛⬛⬛⬛ was
interviewed by Agents in Seattle on 11/23/92 and he recanted his
reported allegations.

           In view of the fact no further investigation remains in
this matter, this case should be administratively closed.

UCFN:  ⌐T-MW-26057 -93

1 - File Copy
1 - Work Copy
NFP:klh  (2)

**U.S. Department of Justice**

**Federal Bureau of Investigation**

In Reply, Please Refer to
File No.

330 East Kilbourn Avenue
Suite 600
Milwaukee, Wisconsin  53202-6627
April 21, 1993

████████              Department of Corrections
149 East Wilson Street
Post Office Box 7925
Madison, Wisconsin  53707-7925

                                    Re:   Inside Edition Interview
                                          of Jeffrey L. Dahmer

Dear ████████

        On Wednesday, March 24, 1993, Special Agent (SA) ████████
████████ of the Milwaukee Office of the Federal Bureau of
Investigation (FBI), met with yourself and ████████ of
your office to review the taped interview of Jeffrey L. Dahmer.

        Inside Edition publicly aired the interview of Jeffrey
L. Dahmer; however, the Department of Corrections has an uncut
and unedited video tape of the interview of Dahmer, including
several hours of preliminary discussions with Dahmer, his step
mother, Inside Edition personnel, and Department of Corrections
officials.

        The FBI has interviewed Jeffrey L. Dahmer in the past,
and has an investigative interest in Dahmer.  In the interview of
Dahmer, Dahmer has advised that he has received numerous letters
from other serial killers.  Dahmer has turned over to the FBI
several letters which he feels could be legitimate serial
killers.

        The FBI Behavioral Science Unit does extensive research
and training concerning serial killers and it would be extremely
beneficial to the FBI to obtain a copy of the unedited, uncut
video tape of interviews of Dahmer.

        In conversations between SA ████████ and
████████, ████████ advised that he does not have
the authority to release the tape to the FBI.

                                        7-MN-26057-94

1 - Addressee
1 - Milwaukee (7-26057)
DSC/11
(2)
                                        SEARCHED____ INDEXED____
                                        SERIALIZED__ FILED_____

In conclusion, the FBI would respectfully request copies of the video tape interview of Dahmer, to be used exclusively within the FBI Behavioral Science Unit for research and training.

Sincerely yours,

TOBY M. HARDING
Special Agent in Charge

By:

b7c

Supervisory Special Agent

cc: ████████████ Department of Corrections
149 East Wilson Street
Post Office Box 7925
Madison, Wisconsin 53707-7925

2

**INFORMATION COMMUNICATION**

Date:    06/23/93

**TO:**      TRAINING DIVISION
          BEHAVIORAL SCIENCE UNIT
              ATTN: ████████████ (Encl. 5)

          PACKAGE COPY

**FROM:**    MILWAUKEE (█)

**POINT OF CONTACT:**   SA ████████████

**TITLE:**   DAHMER, JEFFREY, L.;
          SERIAL KILLING;
          OO:  MILWAUKEE

          **References:**  Milwaukee Division telcall of SA ████
          ████████████ to the Behavioral Science Unit, ████
          ████████ on 6/14/93.

          **Enclosure:**  Four VCR tapes of a un-cut un-edited
          interview of JEFFREY L. DAHMER, and INSIDE EDITION.
          Also enclosure is a letter, dated 4/21/93 from FBI
          Milwaukee to ████████████████████████████
          Department of Corrections, Madison, Wisconsin,
          requesting the tapes to be used for FBI Behavioral
          Science Unit for research and training.

**PURPOSE(S):**  Information.

**DETAILS:**  For the information of the Bureau, Behavioral Science
Unit, liaison was established between FBI Milwaukee and ████
████████████████ Department of Corrections, Madison,
Wisconsin. ████████ turned over to FBI Milwaukee the un-cut and
un-edited video tapes of an interview of DAHMER by INSIDE
EDITION.  These tapes include several hours of preliminary
discussions with DAHMER, his step-mother, INSIDE EDITION
personnel, and Department of Corrections Officials.  INSIDE
EDITION publicly aired the interview of JEFFREY L. DAHMER,
however, the un-cut and un-edited tapes contain additional
information which may be of value to Behavioral Science Unit.

          The Department of Corrections Officials have agreed
that the FBI may use the tapes for research and training.

          The enclosed tapes may be retained by the Behavioral
Science Unit, and duplicated as they see fit.

UCFN: ✓-26057 -95

① - File Copy
1 - Work Copy
DSC:pae  (5)

U.S. Department of Justice

Federal Bureau of Investigation

In Reply, Please Refer to
File No. 7-MW-26057

330 East Kilbourn Avenue
Suite 600
Milwaukee, Wisconsin  53202-6627
August 27, 1993

b7c ▓▓▓▓▓▓▓▓▓

Division of Legal Counsel
Division of Corrections
State of Wisconsin
P.O. Box 7925
Madison, Wisconsin 53707

RE:  JEFFREY L. DAHMER;
     OLIVER LACY - VICTIM - HOMICIDE;
     UNSUBS - VICTIMS - HOMICIDES

Dear ▓▓▓▓▓▓▓

b7c

     This is confirm a discussion between yourself and
Special Agent (SA) ▓▓▓▓▓▓▓ regarding contacts with
subject Jeffrey L. Dahmer, who is currently an inmate at the
Columbia Correctional Institution, Portage, Wisconsin.  Dahmer is
currently serving several life sentences for a series of
homicides committed in the City of Milwaukee.

     In the course of the contacts the Federal Bureau of
Investigation (FBI) has had with Mr. Dahmer, as well as
statements made by Dahmer which were aired on National TV, it is
apparent that Mr. Dahmer has received communications in writing
from other individuals, identities unknown, who have told him
they had committed similar acts or identified themselves as
killers.

     With this in mind, it is requested the Bureau of
Prisons review the mail received by Mr. Dahmer for a period of at
least thirty days to determine if this type of communication to
Mr. Dahmer is continuing.

1 - Addressee
1 - Milwaukee (7-MW-26057)
NFP/emw
(2)

SEARCHED_____ INDEXED____
SERIALIZED___ FILED___

Your cooperation in this matter is appreciated and
contact will be maintained with you by Special Agent
of the Madison, Wisconsin Resident Agency

                    Yours Truly,

                    TOBY M. HARDING
                    Special Agent in Charge


                    By:
                    Supervisory Senior Resident
                    Agent

2*

OPCA-20 (12-3-96)

## FEDERAL BUREAU OF INVESTIGATION
### FOIPA
### DELETED PAGE INFORMATION SHEET

_____ Page(s) withheld entirely at this location in the file. One or more of the following statements, where indicated, explain this deletion.

☐ Deletions were made pursuant to the exemptions indicated below with no segregable material available for release to you.

| Section 552 | | Section 552a |
|---|---|---|
| ☐ (b)(1) | ☐ (b)(7)(A) | ☐ (d)(5) |
| ☐ (b)(2) | ☐ (b)(7)(B) | ☐ (j)(2) |
| ☐ (b)(3) | ☐ (b)(7)(C) | ☐ (k)(1) |
| _____ | ☐ (b)(7)(D) | ☐ (k)(2) |
| _____ | ☐ (b)(7)(E) | ☐ (k)(3) |
| _____ | ☐ (b)(7)(F) | ☐ (k)(4) |
| ☐ (b)(4) | ☐ (b)(8) | ☐ (k)(5) |
| ☐ (b)(5) | ☐ (b)(9) | ☐ (k)(6) |
| ☐ (b)(6) | | ☐ (k)(7) |

☐ Information pertained only to a third party with no reference to the subject of your request or the subject of your request is listed in the title only.

☐ Documents originated with another Government agency(ies). These documents were referred to that agency(ies) for review and direct response to you.

_____ Pages contain information furnished by another Government agency(ies). You will be advised by the FBI as to the releasability of this information following our consultation with the other agency(ies).

_____ Page(s) withheld inasmuch as a final release determination has not been made. You will be advised as to the disposition at a later date.

__/__ Pages were not considered for release as they are duplicative of 7-MW-26057-262.

_____ Page(s) withheld for the following reason(s): _____

☑ The following number is to be used for reference regarding these pages:
7-MW-26057-97.

FBI/DOJ

FD-491 (Rev. 4-21-80)

## Memorandum

TO : SAC, MILWAUKEE                                    DATE: 10-2-93

FROM : SAC, PITTSBURGH   (7-MW-26057) (RUC)

SUBJECT : JEFFREY L. DAHMER;
OLIVER LACY-VICTIM (DECEASED);            ☐ RUC
UNSUBS - VICTIMS (DECEASED)
KIDNAPPING-HOMICIDE;                      ☒ File Destruction Program
(OO: MILWAUKEE)

Enclosed are ___1___ items.

These items are forwarded your office since:

☐ All logical investigation completed in this Division

☒ You were OO at the time our case was RUC'd.

Enclosures are described as follows:

1   FD-340

7-mw-26057-98

SEARCHED _____
SERIALIZED _____

OCT 8   1993

FBI — MILWAUKEE

Enc. 1

NOTE: DO NOT BLOCK STAMP ORIGINAL ENCLOSURES.

FBI/DOJ

# FEDERAL BUREAU OF INVESTIGATION
## FOIPA
### DELETED PAGE INFORMATION SHEET

__2__ Page(s) withheld entirely at this location in the file. One or more of the following statements, where indicated, explain this deletion.

☒ Deletions were made pursuant to the exemptions indicated below with no segregable material available for release to you.

| Section 552 | | Section 552a |
|---|---|---|
| ☐ (b)(1) | ☐ (b)(7)(A) | ☐ (d)(5) |
| ☐ (b)(2) | ☐ (b)(7)(B) | ☐ (j)(2) |
| ☐ (b)(3) | ☒ (b)(7)(C) | ☐ (k)(1) |
| _____ | ☒ (b)(7)(D) | ☐ (k)(2) |
| _____ | ☐ (b)(7)(E) | ☐ (k)(3) |
| _____ | ☐ (b)(7)(F) | ☐ (k)(4) |
| ☐ (b)(4) | ☐ (b)(8) | ☐ (k)(5) |
| ☐ (b)(5) | ☐ (b)(9) | ☐ (k)(6) |
| ☐ (b)(6) | | ☐ (k)(7) |

☐ Information pertained only to a third party with no reference to the subject of your request or the subject of your request is listed in the title only.

☐ Documents originated with another Government agency(ies). These documents were referred to that agency(ies) for review and direct response to you.

_____ Pages contain information furnished by another Government agency(ies). You will be advised by the FBI as to the releasability of this information following our consultation with the other agency(ies).

_____ Page(s) withheld inasmuch as a final release determination has not been made. You will be advised as to the disposition at a later date.

_____ Pages were not considered for release as they are duplicative of _____

_____ Page(s) withheld for the following reason(s): _____
_____
_____

☒ The following number is to be used for reference regarding these pages:
7-mw-26057-99+100.

FD-302 (REV. 3-10-82)

- 1 -

## FEDERAL BUREAU OF INVESTIGATION

Date of transcription    5/4/94

b7C
b7D

On April 28, 1994, ▮▮▮▮▮▮ was received from ▮▮▮▮▮▮ Portage, Wisconsin. Enclosed in this communication was a reportedly received at ▮▮▮▮▮▮ from ▮▮▮▮▮▮ of ▮▮▮▮▮▮

Investigation on   4/28/94   at   Madison, Wisconsin    File #   7-MW-26057 -101

by   SA ▮▮▮▮▮▮ klj b7C    Date dictated   4/29/94

This document contains neither recommendations nor conclusions of the FBI. It is the property of the FBI and is loaned to your agency; it and its contents are not to be distributed outside your agency.

OPCA-20 (12-3-96)

XXXXXX
XXXXXX
XXXXXX

# FEDERAL BUREAU OF INVESTIGATION
## FOIPA
### DELETED PAGE INFORMATION SHEET

_____ Page(s) withheld entirely at this location in the file. One or more of the following statements, where indicated, explain this deletion.

☐ Deletions were made pursuant to the exemptions indicated below with no segregable material available for release to you.

| Section 552 | | Section 552a |
|---|---|---|
| ☐ (b)(1) | ☐ (b)(7)(A) | ☐ (d)(5) |
| ☐ (b)(2) | ☐ (b)(7)(B) | ☐ (j)(2) |
| ☐ (b)(3) | ☐ (b)(7)(C) | ☐ (k)(1) |
| | ☐ (b)(7)(D) | ☐ (k)(2) |
| _____ | ☐ (b)(7)(E) | ☐ (k)(3) |
| _____ | ☐ (b)(7)(F) | ☐ (k)(4) |
| _____ | | |
| ☐ (b)(4) | ☐ (b)(8) | ☐ (k)(5) |
| ☐ (b)(5) | ☐ (b)(9) | ☐ (k)(6) |
| ☐ (b)(6) | | ☐ (k)(7) |

☐ Information pertained only to a third party with no reference to the subject of your request or the subject of your request is listed in the title only.

☐ Documents originated with another Government agency(ies). These documents were referred to that agency(ies) for review and direct response to you.

_____ Pages contain information furnished by another Government agency(ies). You will be advised by the FBI as to the releasability of this information following our consultation with the other agency(ies).

_____ Page(s) withheld inasmuch as a final release determination has not been made. You will be advised as to the disposition at a later date.

__3__ Pages were not considered for release as they are duplicative of 7-MW-26057-1A8, pgs. 4-6.

_____ Page(s) withheld for the following reason(s): _____
_____
_____

☑ The following number is to be used for reference regarding these pages:
7-MW-26057-1D1, pgs. 2-4.

XXXXXXXXXXXXXXXX
X  Deleted Page(s)  X
X  No Duplication Fee  X
X   for this page   X
XXXXXXXXXXXXXXXX

XXXXXX
XXXXXX
XXXXXX

FBI/DOJ

OPCA-20 (12-3-96)

## FEDERAL BUREAU OF INVESTIGATION
### FOIPA
### DELETED PAGE INFORMATION SHEET

__5__ Page(s) withheld entirely at this location in the file. One or more of the following statements, where indicated, explain this deletion.

☑ Deletions were made pursuant to the exemptions indicated below with no segregable material available for release to you.

| Section 552 | | Section 552a |
|---|---|---|
| ☐ (b)(1) | ☐ (b)(7)(A) | ☐ (d)(5) |
| ☐ (b)(2) | ☐ (b)(7)(B) | ☐ (j)(2) |
| ☐ (b)(3) | ☑ (b)(7)(C) | ☐ (k)(1) |
| _____ | ☑ (b)(7)(D) | ☐ (k)(2) |
| _____ | ☐ (b)(7)(E) | ☐ (k)(3) |
| _____ | ☐ (b)(7)(F) | ☐ (k)(4) |
| ☐ (b)(4) | ☐ (b)(8) | ☐ (k)(5) |
| ☐ (b)(5) | ☐ (b)(9) | ☐ (k)(6) |
| ☐ (b)(6) | | ☐ (k)(7) |

☐ Information pertained only to a third party with no reference to the subject of your request or the subject of your request is listed in the title only.

☐ Documents originated with another Government agency(ies). These documents were referred to that agency(ies) for review and direct response to you.

_____ Pages contain information furnished by another Government agency(ies). You will be advised by the FBI as to the releasability of this information following our consultation with the other agency(ies).

_____ Page(s) withheld inasmuch as a final release determination has not been made. You will be advised as to the disposition at a later date.

_____ Pages were not considered for release as they are duplicative of _____

_____ Page(s) withheld for the following reason(s): _____
_____
_____

☑ The following number is to be used for reference regarding these pages:
7-MW-26057-102.

FBI/DOJ

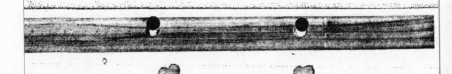

7-MW-26057
TPB:tam
1

The following investigation was conducted by SA ████████ at Wilmington, Delaware:

On 7/26/91, ████████████ Wilmington, Delaware Department of Police and ████████ Delaware State Police were contacted and were requested to review all missing persons, runaways, and unresolved kidnapping matters in an attempt to link these matters with the JEFFREY L. DAHMER investigation. On 7/26/91, a similar request was made of ████ ████████ New Castle County, Delaware Police.

On 7/29/91, ████████████ advised that he had no information linking any missing persons, runaways or unresolved kidnappings to the DAHMER matter.

On 8/27/91, ████████████, New Castle County, Delaware Police advised that information concerning missing person ████████████, a white male born ████ and who has been missing since 12/10/90, from New Castle County, Delaware had been provided to the Milwaukee Police Department at the inception of this investigation as a possible link to the DAHMER matter. The ████ investigation is being handled by New Castle County ████ and ████ case number is ████ ████ further advised that his department was in the process of obtaining missing person ████ dental records to submit to the Milwaukee Police Department for identification purposes.

On 8/28/91, ████████████ Wilmington, Delaware Department of Police advised that he had no information linking any missing persons, runaways or unresolved kidnapping matters to the DAHMER investigation.

b7c

7-MW-26057

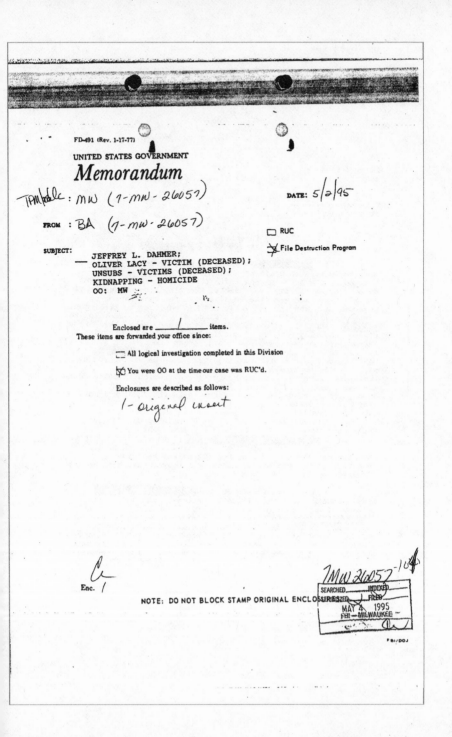

FD-491 (Rev. 1-17-77)

UNITED STATES GOVERNMENT

*Memorandum*

TPM/ddc : MW (1-MW-26057)                    DATE: 5/2/95

FROM: BA (1-mw-26057)

☐ RUC

☒ File Destruction Program

SUBJECT:
       JEFFREY L. DAHMER;
       OLIVER LACY - VICTIM (DECEASED);
       UNSUBS - VICTIMS (DECEASED);
       KIDNAPPING - HOMICIDE
       OO:  MW

      Enclosed are _____/_____ items.
These items are forwarded your office since:

      ☐ All logical investigation completed in this Division

      ☒ You were OO at the time our case was RUC'd.

      Enclosures are described as follows:

      1- original insert

Enc. /

NOTE: DO NOT BLOCK STAMP ORIGINAL ENCLOSURE(S)

MW 26057-104

SEARCHED _____ INDEXED _____
SERIALIZED _____ FILED _____
MAY 4 1995
FBI — MILWAUKEE

FBI/DOJ

CV 7-MW-26057
MLD:cd
1

CLEVELAND DIVISION
At Akron, Ohio

      The following investigation was conducted on July 24, 1991, by Special Agent (SA) ████████████████ at Akron, Ohio:

      SA ████████, Federal Bureau of Investigation (FBI), Madison, Wisconsin Resident Agency (RA), ████████, telephoned the Akron RA and indicated that JEFFREY L. DAHMER, date of birth May 21, 1960, Social Security Account Number 249-60-3333, had been arrested in Milwaukee for the slaying of numerous men, and through interview had admitted to killing his first victim in 1978 in or near Richfield, Ohio. According to ██████, DAHMER lived at 4480 West Bath Road, Bath, Ohio, at the time of the slaying. He also had identification indicating an address at 4485 West Grainger Road, Akron, Ohio, with a Driver's License that expired May 21, 1985. According to ████████ in DAHMER's confession, he indicated that when he was approximately 18, in 1978, he picked up a 19-year-old white male near his residence, took the male to his residence, which is believed to 4480 West Bath Road address, killed that individual at that house, dismembered his body and scattered the remains in a field near his residence.

      Contact was made with the Richfield, Ohio Police Department (Chief JOHN WALSH) and the Bath, Ohio Police Department ████████████, and the above information was related to them. According to both police departments, the Bath Police Department was handling the investigation of the matter since it appeared that this murder occurred in Bath.

      Contact was then made with ████████████████ of the Summit County Sheriff's Office to determine whether he had records of any missing persons in 1978 time frame. According to ████████ he had a report of a missing person by the name of STEVEN MARK HICKS, date of birth June 22, 1959, weight 150 pounds, height 5' 10", brown hair, brown eyes, with a scar on the right forearm, and a birthmark the size of a dime on his back. According to ████████████ dental records of HICKS are available with the Summit County Sheriff's Office. ████████████ indicated

*b7C*

7-MW-26051-8106

256 | APPENDIX 1

that HICKS was hitchhiking to the Chippewa Lake State Park at the time he was reported missing. HICKS was last seen on June 18, 1978. There was no indication in the Missing Persons file of any homosexuality on the part of HICKS.

An off-line search of the Missing Persons file for the State of Ohio was conducted by NCIC in Washington. The search parameters included white males with birthdates between January 1, 1958 and December 31, 1962. According to the person who made the search, 15 persons were identified to fall within those search parameters, but only one had a date of last contact in 1978. That person is STEVEN MARK HICKS, as described above. All of the individuals whose birthdays fall within that time frame have date of last contact in 1983 or later. That off-line search should have discovered all missing persons who were white males and approximately 19 years of age in 1978 who have been reported and included in the computer system for the State of Ohio.

Contact also was made with the FBI Military Records agents in the St. Louis Division. According to those records, JEFFREY L. DAHMER entered the United States Army on January 12, 1979, in Cleveland, Ohio. He was originally stationed at Fort McEllan in the Military Police School. DAHMER "washed out" of that school in approximately April of 1979 and was transferred to Fort San Houston for the Medical Specialist School. That school lasted approximately six weeks. Following that six-week school, DAHMER was transferred to Germany, but may have had leave just prior to leaving for Germany. DAHMER was apparently in Germany from 1979 through his release date of March 26, 1981. He was released from the army in Germany in 1981 for alcoholism. His address at the time of release from the military was 4480 West Bath Road, Bath, Ohio.

Photographs of STEVEN MARK HICKS have been sent to the FBI in Madison, Wisconsin (SA ███████████) and to the Milwaukee Police Department by the Bath Police Department. Additionally, aerial photographs of the area around DAHMER's house in Bath have also been submitted.

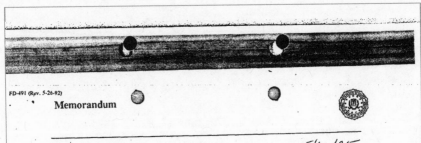

FD-491 (Rev. 5-26-92)

## Memorandum

To: SAC, MILWAUKEE (7-MW-26057)    Date 5/22/95

From: SAC, CLEVELAND (7-MW-26057) (ARA

Subject: JEFFREY L. DAHMER;
OLIVER LACY - VICTIM (DECEASED);
UNSUBS - VICTIMS (DECEASED);
KIDNAPPING - HOMICIDE;
OO: MW

☐ RUC
☑ File Destruction Program

Enclosed are _____1_____ items.

These items are forwarded to your office since file meets
criteria for destruction.

Enclosures are described as follows:

☐ Original Notes.

☑ Original FD-302's. *Insert*

☐ Laboratory and/or Technical Reports.

☐ Miscellaneous Documents.

7-mw-26057-107

SEARCHED____ INDEXED____
SERIALIZED____ FILED____
MAY 24 1995
FBI—MILWAUKEE

Enc.

NOTE:  DO NOT BLOCK STAMP ORIGINAL ENCLOSURES.

FD-491 (Rev. 5-26-92)

## Memorandum

To :     mw. 7-26051                    Date  6/3/86

From :   CC (7-mw-26051)

Subject:  Jeffrey L. Dahmer
          (Title)

☐ RUC
☒ File Destruction Program

Enclosed are ____¹/____ items.

These items are forwarded to your office since file meets
criteria for destruction.

    Enclosures are described as follows:

    ☐ Original Notes.

    ☐ Original FD-302's.

    ☐ Laboratory and/or Technical Support.

    ☒ Miscellaneous Documents.

        news art.

Enc. ( 1 )

NOTE:   DO NOT BLOCK STAMP ORIGINAL ENCLOSURES.

7-mw-26057
SEARCHED_____ INDEXED_____
SERIALIZED_____ FILED_____
JUN 5 1996
FBI - MILWAUKEE

Automated Serial Permanent Charge-Out
FD-5a (1-5-94)

Date: 10/03/97  Time: 09:50

Case ID: 7-MW-26057  Serial: 111

Description of Document:

    Type : NEWSPAPE
    Date : 09/27/97
    To   : MILWAUKEE
    From : MW JURNAL SENTINEL
    Topic: IDENTIFYING DAHMER VICTIMS POSED CHALLENGES

Reason for Permanent Charge-Out:

    ENTERED INTO WRONG FILE

Transferred to:

    Case ID: 7-MW-26057-A  Serial: 265.

Employee: ██████████████  b7C

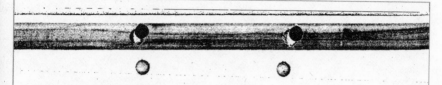

Automated Serial Permanent Charge-Out
FD-5a (1-5-94)

Date: 12/29/98  Time: 09:29

Case ID: 7-MW-26057  Serial: 112

Description of Document:

    Type  : NEWSPAPE
    Date  : 12/16/98
    To    : MILWAUKEE
    From  : MW JOURNAL SENTINEL
    Topic : PAIR OF DAHMER LAWSUITS DISMISSED

Reason for Permanent Charge-Out:

    SUB (A) IS NEWSPAPER FILE

Transferred to:

    Case ID: 7-MW-26057-A  Serial: 268

Employee: ████████████████ b7c

7-MW-26057-112

# APPENDIX 2:

# DEATH WARRANT
# FOR BOBBY JOE LONG

**RON DeSANTIS**
GOVERNOR

April 23, 2019

Warden Barry Reddish
Florida State Prison
7819 N.W. 228th Street
Raiford, Florida 32026-1000

Re: Execution Date for Robert Joseph Long, DC#494041

Dear Warden Reddish:

Enclosed is the death warrant to carry out the sentence of Robert Joseph Long, as well as a certified copy of his judgment and sentence. I have designated the week beginning at 12:00 noon on Monday, May 20, 2019, through 12:00 noon on Monday, May 27, 2019, for the execution. I have been advised that you have set the date and time of execution for Thursday, May 23, 2019, at 6:00 p.m.

This letter is incorporated into and made a part of the death warrant identified above.

Sincerely,

Ron DeSantis
Governor

Enclosures

THE CAPITOL
TALLAHASSEE, FLORIDA 32399 • (850) 717-9249

263

Warden Barry Reddish
April 23, 2019
Page 2


cc:

Honorable Charles Canady
Chief Justice
Supreme Court of Florida
500 South Duval Street
Tallahassee, Florida 32399

Honorable Ronald Ficarrotta
Chief Judge, Thirteenth Judicial Circuit
800 E. Twiggs St.
Tampa, Florida 33602

Secretary Mark Inch
Department of Corrections
501 South Calhoun Street
Tallahassee, Florida 32399-2500

Carolyn Snurkowski
Assistant Deputy Attorney General
Office of the Attorney General
The Capitol, PL-01
Tallahassee, Florida 32399-0001

Robert A. Norgard
310 East Main Street
Bartow, Florida 33830

Julia McCall, Coordinator
Office of Executive Clemency
4070 Esplanade Way
Tallahassee, Florida 32399-2450

Robert Joseph Long, DC#494041
Union Correctional Institution
7819 NW 228th Street
Raiford, Florida 32026-4400

# STATE OF FLORIDA

### ASHLEY MOODY
### ATTORNEY GENERAL

April 23, 2019

The Honorable Ron DeSantis
Governor
The Capitol
Tallahassee, Florida 32399—0001

RE: Robert Joe Long

Dear Governor DeSantis:

Robert Joe Long pleaded guilty to one count of first-degree murder on September 23, 1985, for the May 27, 1984, first-degree murder of a young woman he picked up on Kennedy Boulevard in Tampa, Florida. On September 23, 1985, he also pleaded guilty to seven additional first degree murder charges and numerous sexual batteries and kidnapping charges. He was sentenced to death on September 23, 1985, for the murder of the young woman he killed on May 27, 1984. The Florida Supreme Court, on direct appeal, affirmed Long's convictions and sentences on June 30, 1988, but as to the death penalty sentence, the court vacated the death sentence and remanded the case to the trial court for a new penalty phase. *Long v. State*, 529 So.2d 286 (Fla.1988).

On remand before a new jury, Long was again sentenced to death in Hillsborough County, Florida. After the jury returned its unanimous recommendation of a sentence of death, the trial court on July 21, 1989, followed that recommendation and sentenced Long to death. On appeal from resentencing, the Florida Supreme Court affirmed Long's new death sentence. *Long v. State*, 610 So.2d 1268 (Fla.1992). His convictions and other sentences and the death sentence became final when the United States Supreme Court denied his petition for writ of certiorari, October 4, 1993, in *Long v. Florida*, 510 U.S. 832 (1993).

Long filed his initial motion for post-conviction relief on December 29, 1994. That motion was denied August 1, 1995, and the appeal was dismissed in *Long v. State*, 672 So.2d 543 (Fla. 1996) (Table). A second motion for post-conviction relief was filed on October 4, 1995. The trial court, following a three day evidentiary hearing in May-June 2011, denied relief on November 29, 2011. Long filed his appeal of that decision to the Florida Supreme Court on December 12, 2011, and the court affirmed the denial of all post-conviction relief in *Long v. State*, 118 So.3d 798 (Fla. 2013).

*PL-01, The Capitol, Tallahassee, Florida 32399-1050, Telephone (850) 414-3300 Fax (850) 487-2564*

Long's litigation history reflects he then filed his initial federal petition for writ of habeas corpus in the U.S. District Court for the Middle District of Florida on August 12, 2013. The federal district court denied Long's habeas petition on August 30, 2016. Long filed an application for a certificate of appealability (COA). The Eleventh Circuit Court of Appeals denied the COA in *Long v. Secretary, Fla. Dept. of Corrections,* Case No. 16-16259-P (USDA Jan. 4, 2017).

During this same time-period, Long returned to the state trial court and filed a successive motion for post-conviction relief on September 9, 2014. On November 4, 2014, the trial court denied post-conviction relief. Long appealed to the Florida Supreme Court on November 26, 2014, and the court affirmed the denial of relief in *Long v. State,* 183 So.3d 342 (Fla. 2016).

Long then filed another successive post-conviction motion seeking *Hurst* relief on January 3, 2017. The trial court denied Long's *Hurst* claim on April 27, 2017, and the Florida Supreme Court affirmed the trial court's denial of relief on January 29, 2018, in *Long v. State,* 235 So.3d 293 (Fla. 2018). The United States Supreme Court denied Long's petition for writ of certiorari on October 1, 2018. *Long v. Florida,* 139 S.Ct. 162 (2018)(Mem).

The record has been reviewed and there are no stays of execution issued by any court of competent jurisdiction in this cause. Based upon the above-referenced summary of litigation affirming the judgment and sentence of death imposed for first-degree murder, the record is legally sufficient to support the issuance of a death warrant.

Sincerely,

*Ashley Moody*

Ashley Moody
Attorney General

# DEATH WARRANT
## STATE OF FLORIDA

WHEREAS, ROBERT JOSEPH LONG, on or about the 27th day of May, 1984, murdered Michelle Simms; and

WHEREAS, ROBERT JOSEPH LONG, on the 23rd day of September, 1985, pleaded guilty to the crimes of first degree murder, kidnapping, and sexual battery, and on the 21st day of July, 1989, was sentenced to death for the murder of Michelle Simms; and

WHEREAS, on the 26th day of January, 1992, the Supreme Court of Florida affirmed the death sentence of ROBERT JOSEPH LONG; and

WHEREAS, on the 11th day of July, 2013, the Supreme Court of Florida affirmed the trial court order denying ROBERT JOSEPH LONG's Motion for Postconviction Relief, and on the 21st day of January, 2016 and the 29th day of January, 2018, affirmed the trial court orders denying his Motions for Collateral Relief; and

WHEREAS, on the 30th day of August, 2016, the United States District Court for the Middle District of Florida denied ROBERT JOSEPH LONG's federal Petition for Writ of Habeas Corpus, and the United States Court of Appeals for the Eleventh Circuit denied his Application for Certificate of Appealability on the 4th day of January, 2017; and

WHEREAS, further postconviction motions and petitions filed by ROBERT JOSEPH LONG have been denied, and affirmed on appeal; and

WHEREAS, executive clemency for ROBERT JOSEPH LONG, as authorized by Article IV, Section 8(a), of the Florida Constitution, was considered pursuant to the Rules of Executive Clemency, and it has been determined that executive clemency is not appropriate; and

WHEREAS, attached hereto is a certified copy of the record of the conviction and sentence pursuant to section 922.052, Florida Statutes.

NOW, THEREFORE, I, RON DESANTIS, as Governor of the State of Florida and pursuant to the authority and responsibility vested in me by the Constitution and Laws of Florida, do hereby issue this warrant, directing the Warden of the Florida State Prison to

cause the sentence of death to be executed upon ROBERT JOSEPH LONG, in accord with the provisions of the Laws of the State of Florida.

IN TESTIMONY WHEREOF, I have hereunto set my hand and caused the Great Seal of the State of Florida to be affixed at Tallahassee, the Capital, this 23rd day of April, 2019.

GOVERNOR

ATTEST:

SECRETARY OF STATE

FILED

JUL 21 1989

RICHARD AKE, CLERK

RECORDED

JUL 21 1989

RICHARD AKE, CLERK

**1**

IN THE CIRCUIT COURT, THIRTEENTH
JUDICIAL CIRCUIT, IN AND FOR
HILLSBOROUGH COUNTY, FLORIDA

DIVISION _____ B _____

CASE NUMBER ___ 84-13346 ___

STATE OF FLORIDA

— vs —

ROBERT JOE LONG
_____
Defendant

# JUDGMENT

The Defendant, ___ ROBERT JOE LONG ___, being personally before this

Court represented by ___ ROBERT FRASER, ESQUIRE ___, his attorney of record, and having:

*(Check Applicable
Provision)*

☒ Been tried and found guilty of the following crime(s)
□ Entered a plea of guilty to the following crime(s)
□ Entered a plea of nolo contendere to the following crime(s)

| COUNT | CRIME | OFFENSE STATUTE NUMBER(S) | DEGREE OF CRIME | CASE NUMBER |
|-------|-------|---------------------------|-----------------|-------------|
| ONE | KIDNAPPING | 787.01(1)(a)(2) | 1F-PBL | |
| TWO | SEXUAL BATTERY | 794.011(3) | LF | |
| THREE | FIRST DEGREE MURDER | 782.04 | CF | |
| | | | | |
| | | | | |
| | | | | |
| | | | | |
| | | | | |
| | | | | |
| | | | | |

and no cause having been shown why the Defendant should not be adjudicated guilty, IT IS ORDERED THAT the Defendant
is hereby ADJUDICATED GUILTY of the above crime(s).

* * * * * * * * * * * * * * * * * *

The Defendant is hereby ordered to pay the sum of twenty dollars ($20.00) pursuant to F.S. 960.20 (Crimes
Compensation Trust Fund). The Defendant is further ordered to pay the sum of three dollars ($3.00) as a court cost pursuant
to F.S. 943.25(4).

### (Applicable if checked)

□ The Defendant is ordered to pay the sum of two dollars ($2.00) pursuant to F.S. 943.25(6). (Optional)

□ The Defendant is ordered to pay a fine in the sum of $_____ pursuant to F.S. 775.0835. (Optional)

□ The Defendant is ordered to pay the sum of two hundred dollars ($200.00) costs pursuant to F.S. 27.3455

□ The Defendant is ordered to pay additional costs in the sum of $ _____

Page 1 of ___6___  Order book _305_ page _346_

1322

LONG, BOBBY JO

(Applicable if checked)

☐ The Court hereby stays and withholds the imposition of sentence as to count(s) _____.

☐ The Court hereby defers imposition of sentence until _____.

☐ The Court places the Defendant on Probation for a period of _____ under the supervision of the Department of Corrections (conditions of probation set forth in separate order).

☐ The Court places the Defendant in Community Control for a period _____ under the supervision of the Department of Corrections (conditions of community control set forth in separate order).

The Defendant in Open Court was advised of his right to appeal from this Judgment by filing notice of appeal with the Clerk of Court within thirty days following the date sentence is imposed or probation/community control is ordered pursuant to this adjudication. The Defendant was also advised of his right to the assistance of counsel in taking said appeal at the expense of the State upon showing of indigency.

## FINGERPRINTS OF DEFENDANT

| 1.   R. Thumb | 2.   R. Index | 3.   R. Middle | 4.   R. Ring | 5.   R. Little |
|---|---|---|---|---|
| | | | | |
| 6.   L. Thumb | 7.   L. Index | 3.   L. Middle | 9.   L. Ring | 10.   L. Little |
| | | | | |

Fingerprints taken by:

B. Grapley   2015
Name and Title

DONE AND ORDERED in Open Court at Hillsborough County, Florida, this _____21st_____ day of _____JULY_____ A.D., 19__89__ . I HEREBY certify that the above and foregoing fingerprints are the fingerprints of the Defendant _____ROBERT JOE LONG_____ and that they were placed thereon by said Defendant in my presence in Open Court this date.

_____
JUDGE

Page __2__ of __6__   Order book 305 page 347

1323

FILED

JUL 21 1989

RICHARD AKE, CLERK

Defendant _____ROBERT JOE LONG_____

Case Number _____84-13346-B_____

# SENTENCE

(As to Count ____ONE____)

The Defendant, being personally before this Court, accompanied by his attorney, _____ROBERT FRASER, ESQUIRE_____

_____, and having been adjudicated guilty herein, and the Court having given the Defendant an opportunity to be heard and to offer matters in mitigation of sentence, and to show cause why he should not be sentenced as provided by law, and no cause being shown.

*(Check either provision if applicable)*

☐ and the Court having on _____ deferred imposition of sentence until this date. (date)

☐ and the Court having placed the Defendant on probation and having subsequently revoked the Defendant's probation by separate order entered herein.

☐ and the Court having placed the Defendant in community control and having subsequently revoked the Defendant's community control by separate order entered herein.

IT IS THE SENTENCE OF THE LAW that:

☐ The Defendant pay a fine of $_____, plus $_____ as the 5% surcharge required by F.S. 960.25

☒ The Defendant is hereby committed to the custody of the Department of Corrections

☐ The Defendant is hereby committed to the custody of the Sheriff* of Hillsborough County, Florida
*(Name of local corrections authority to be inserted at printing, if other than Sheriff)*
To be imprisoned (check one; unmarked sections are inapplicable)

☒ For a term of Natural Life    WITH CREDIT TIME

☐ For a term of _____

☐ For an indeterminate period of 6 months to _____ years.

*If "split" sentence complete either of these two paragraphs*

☐ Followed by a period of_____ on probation under the supervision of the Department of Corrections according to the terms and conditions of probation set forth in a separate order entered herein.

☐ However, after serving a period of _____ imprisonment in _____ the balance of such sentence shall be suspended and the Defendant shall be placed on probation for a period of _____ under supervision of the Department of Corrections according to the terms and conditions of probation set forth in a separate order entered herein.

## SPECIAL PROVISIONS

By appropriate notation, the following provisions apply to the sentence imposed in this action.

*Firearm – 3 year mandatory minimum* ☐ It is further ordered that the 3 year minimum provisions of F.S. 775.087(2) are hereby imposed for the sentence specified in this count, as the Defendant possessed a firearm.

*Drug Trafficking – mandatory minimum* ☐ It is further ordered that the _____ year minimum provisions of F.S. 893.135(1)( )( ) are hereby imposed for the sentence specified in this count.

*Retention of Jurisdiction* ☐ The Court pursuant to F.S. 947.16(3) retains jurisdiction over the defendant for review of any Parole Commission release order for the period of _____. The requisite findings by the Court are set forth in a separate order or stated on the record in open court.

*Habitual Offender* ☐ The Defendant is adjudged a habitual offender and has been sentenced to an extended term in this sentence in accordance with the provisions of F.S. 775.084(4)(a). The requisite findings by the court are set forth in a separate order or stated on the record in open court.

*Jail Credit* ☒ It is further ordered that the Defendant shall be allowed a total of ____SINCE 11-10-84____ credit for such time as he has been incarcerated prior to imposition of this sentence. Such credit reflects the following periods of incarceration (optional):

*Consecutive/ Concurrent* It is further ordered that the sentence imposed for this count shall run ☐ consecutive to ☒ concurrent with (check one) the sentence set forth in count____TWO____ * ____ above.

* AND CONCURRENT WITH COUNT THREE (3).

Page____3____ of ____6____

1324

Defendant __ROBERT JOE LONG__

Case Number __84-13346-B__

*Consecutive/*
*Concurrent*
*(As to other*
*convictions)*

It is further ordered that the composite term of all sentences imposed for the counts specified in this order shall run ☐ consecutive to ☒ concurrent with (check one) the following:

☐ Any active sentence being served.
COUNTS 1 & 2 CONC.W/
☒ Specific sentences: 84-13343, 84-13344, 84-13345, 84-13347, 84-13348,

84-13349, 84-13350, 84-13310 & 84-4213

In the event the above sentence is to the Department of Corrections, the Sheriff of Hillsborough County, Florida is hereby ordered and directed to deliver the Defendant to the Department of Corrections together with a copy of this Judgment and Sentence.

The Defendant in Open Court was advised of his right to appeal from this Sentence by filing notice of appeal within thirty days from this date with the Clerk of this Court, and the Defendant's right to the assistance of counsel in taking said appeal at the expense of the State upon showing of indigency.

In imposing the above sentence, the Court further recommends _____

_____

_____

_____

_____

\* SENTENCING GUIDELINES FILED.

DONE AND ORDERED in Open Court at Hillsborough County, Florida, this _____21st_____ day of _____JULY_____ A.D., 19⁸⁹.

_____
JUDGE

Page ___4___ of ___6___

1325

Defendant _____ ROBERT JOE LONG _____

Case Number _____ 84-13346-B _____

# SENTENCE

(As to Count _____ TWO _____)

The Defendant, being personally before this Court, accompanied by his attorney, _____ ROBERT FRASER, ESQUIRE _____

_____, and having been adjudicated guilty herein, and the Court having given the Defendant an opportunity to be heard and to offer matters in mitigation of sentence, and to show cause why he should not be sentenced as provided by law, and no cause being shown.

☐ and the Court having on _____ deferred imposition of sentence until this date.                (date)

(Check either provision if applicable)

☐ and the Court having placed the Defendant on probation and having subsequently revoked the Defendant's probation by separate order entered herein.

☐ and the Court having placed the Defendant in community control and having subsequently revoked the Defendant's community control by separate order entered herein.

IT IS THE SENTENCE OF THE LAW that:

☐ The Defendant pay a fine of $_____, plus $_____ as the 5% surcharge required by F.S. 960.25

XXX The Defendant is hereby committed to the custody of the Department of Corrections

☐ The Defendant is hereby committed to the custody of the Sheriff of Hillsborough County, Florida

(Name of local corrections authority to be inserted at printing, if other than Sheriff)

To be imprisoned (check one; unmarked sections are inapplicable)

XXX For a term of Natural Life   WITH CREDIT TIME

☐ For a term of _____

☐ For an indeterminate period of 6 months to _____ years.

☐ Followed by a period of _____ on probation under the supervision of the Department of Corrections according to the terms and conditions of probation set forth in a separate order entered herein.

If "split" sentence complete either of these two paragraphs

☐ However, after serving a period of _____ imprisonment in _____ the balance of such sentence shall be suspended and the Defendant shall be placed on probation for a period of _____ under supervision of the Department of Corrections according to the terms and conditions of probation set forth in a separate order entered herein.

## SPECIAL PROVISIONS

By appropriate notation, the following provisions apply to the sentence imposed in this action.

Firearm – 3 year mandatory minimum   ☐ It is further ordered that the 3 year minimum provisions of F.S. 775.087(2) are hereby imposed for the sentence specified in this count, as the Defendant possessed a firearm.

Drug Trafficking – mandatory minimum   ☐ It is further ordered that the _____ year minimum provisions of F.S. 893.135(1)( )( ) are hereby imposed for the sentence specified in this count.

Retention of Jurisdiction   ☐ The Court pursuant to F.S. 947.16(3) retains jurisdiction over the defendant for review of any Parole Commission release order for the period of _____. The requisite findings by the Court are set forth in a separate order or stated on the record in open court.

Habitual Offender   ☐ The Defendant is adjudged a habitual offender and has been sentenced to an extended term in this sentence in accordance with the provisions of F.S. 775.084(4)(a). The requisite findings by the court are set forth in a separate order or stated on the record in open court.

Jail Credit   XX It is further ordered that the Defendant shall be allowed a total of _____ SINCE 11-10-84 _____ credit for such time as he has been incarcerated prior to imposition of this sentence. Such credit reflects the following periods of incarceration (optional):

Consecutive/ Concurrent   It is further ordered that the sentence imposed for this count shall run ☐ consecutive to XXX concurrent with (check one) the sentence set forth in count _____ ONE * _____ above.

* AND CONCURRENT WITH COUNT THREE (3).

Defendant _____ ROBERT JOE LONG _____

Case Number _____ 84-13346-B _____

# SENTENCE

(As to Count _____ THREE _____ )

The Defendant, being personally before this Court, accompanied by his attorney, ROBERT FRASER, ESQUIRE

_____, and having been adjudicated guilty herein, and the Court having given the Defendant an opportunity to be heard and to offer matters in mitigation of sentence, and to show cause why he should not be sentenced as provided by law, and no cause being shown.

□ and the Court having on _____ deferred imposition of sentence
until this date.                                    (date)

(Check either provision if applicable)

□ and the Court having placed the Defendant on probation and having subsequently revoked the Defendant's probation by separate order entered herein.

□ and the Court having placed the Defendant in community control and having subsequently revoked the Defendant's community control by separate order entered herein.

IT IS THE SENTENCE OF THE LAW that:

□ The Defendant pay a fine of $_____, plus $_____ as the 5% surcharge required by F.S. 960.25
☒ The Defendant is hereby committed to the custody of the Department of Corrections
□ The Defendant is hereby committed to the custody of the Sheriff* of Hillsborough County, Florida
(Name of local corrections authority to be inserted at printing, if other than Sheriff)
To be imprisoned (check one; unmarked sections are inapplicable)

□ For a term of Natural Life
☒ For a term of _____ DEATH BY ELECTROCUTION _____
□ For an indeterminate period of 6 months to _____ years.

□ Followed by a period of _____ on probation under the supervision of the Department of
Corrections according to the terms and conditions of probation set forth in a separate order entered
herein.

If "split" sentence complete either of these two paragraphs

□ However, after serving a period of _____ imprisonment in _____
the balance of such sentence shall be suspended and the Defendant shall be placed on probation
for a period of _____ under supervision of the Department of Corrections
according to the terms and conditions of probation set forth in a separate order entered herein.

## SPECIAL PROVISIONS

By appropriate notation, the following provisions apply to the sentence imposed in this action.

Firearm – 3 year mandatory minimum
□ It is further ordered that the 3 year minimum provisions of F.S. 775.087(2) are hereby imposed for the sentence specified in this count, as the Defendant possessed a firearm.

Drug Trafficking – mandatory minimum
□ It is further ordered that the _____ year minimum provisions of F.S. 893.135(1)( )( ) are hereby imposed for the sentence specified in this count.

Retention of Jurisdiction
□ The Court pursuant to F.S. 947.16(3) retains jurisdiction over the defendant for review of any Parole Commission release order for the period of _____. The requisite findings by the Court are set forth in a separate order or stated on the record in open court.

Habitual Offender
□ The Defendant is adjudged a habitual offender and has been sentenced to an extended term in this sentence in accordance with the provisions of F.S. 775.084(4)(a). The requisite findings by the court are set forth in a separate order or stated on the record in open court.

Jail Credit
☒ It is further ordered that the Defendant shall be allowed a total of _____ SINCE 11-10-84 _____ credit for such time as he has been incarcerated prior to imposition of this sentence. Such credit reflects the following periods of incarceration (optional):

Consecutive/ Concurrent
It is further ordered that the sentence imposed for this count shall run □ consecutive to □ concurrent with (check one) the sentence set forth in count _____ above.

23rd        March      18

Page ___ 6 ___ of ___ 6 ___

1327

Eileen Salas-Acevedo

# APPENDIX 3

## SAMUEL LITTLE'S DRAWINGS OF HIS UNIDENTIFIED VICTIMS

**MONROE, LOUISIANA**
UNMATCHED CONFESSION: BLACK FEMALE BETWEEN 30–40 YEARS OLD
KILLED IN 1982

**CHARLESTON, SOUTH CAROLINA**
UNMATCHED CONFESSION: BLACK FEMALE, AGE 28, KILLED BETWEEN 1977 AND 1982

**UNMATCHED CONFESSION:** WHITE FEMALE KILLED IN 1984. MET VICTIM IN COLUMBUS, OHIO. BODY DISPOSED OF SOMEWHERE IN NORTHERN KENTUCKY (CITY UNSPECIFIED).

**TAMPA BAY, FLORIDA**
**UNMATCHED CONFESSION:** BLACK FEMALE KILLED IN 1984

**ATLANTA, GEORGIA**
**UNMATCHED CONFESSION:** BLACK FEMALE BETWEEN 35–40 YEARS OLD KILLED IN 1981

**ATLANTA, GEORGIA**
**UNMATCHED CONFESSION:** BLACK FEMALE BETWEEN 23–25 YEARS OLD KILLED IN 1984.
VICTIM POSSIBLY A COLLEGE STUDENT.

**MONROE, LOUISIANA**
UNMATCHED CONFESSION: BLACK FEMALE, AGE 24, KILLED BETWEEN 1987 AND THE
EARLY 1990S

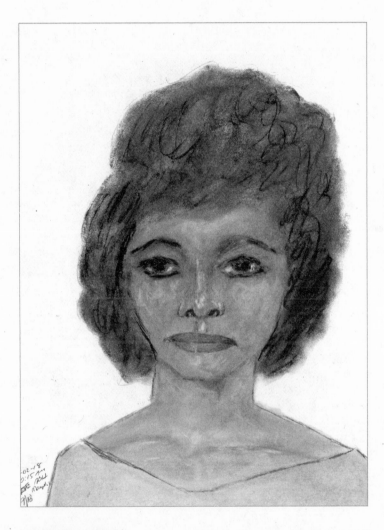

**WEST MEMPHIS, ARKANSAS**
**CONFESSION MATCHED TO A JANE DOE:** BLACK FEMALE BETWEEN 28–29 YEARS OLD
KILLED IN 1984. VICTIM PICKED UP IN MEMPHIS, TENNESSEE.

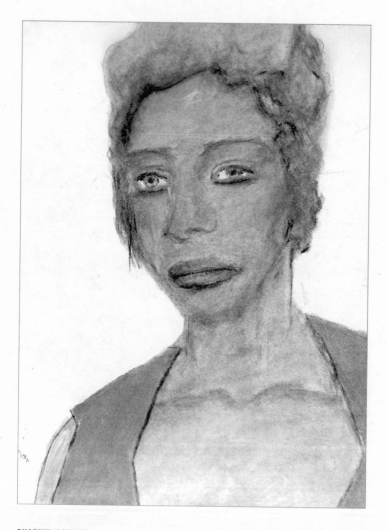

**PHOENIX, ARIZONA**
UNMATCHED CONFESSION: HISPANIC FEMALE IN HER 40S. KILLED IN 1988 OR 1996. VICTIM
POSSIBLY FROM PHOENIX.

**NEW ORLEANS, LOUISIANA**
**CONFESSION MATCHED TO A JANE DOE:** WHITE FEMALE BETWEEN 33–44 YEARS OLD.
KILLED IN 1982.

**SAVANNAH, GEORGIA**
UNMATCHED CONFESSION: BLACK FEMALE AGE 23 KILLED IN 1984

# INDEX

Pages in *italics* indicate photos

# IMAGE CREDITS

**Alamy:** ARCHIVO GBB: 75; ©The Sacramento Bee/SUMA Wire: 20; ©Skip Shuman/Sacramento Bee/ZUMA Wire: 15; ZUMA Press Inc.: 45

**AP Images:** 61 left, 113; Alaska Daily News: 29; Rachel D'Oro: 40; Damian Dovarganes: 169; Brendan Farrington: 56; FBI: 86; Florida Department of Corrections: 95; Cheryl Hatch: 157; Travis Heying: 121; Lennox McLendon: 78; Rich Pedroncelli: 3; Paul Sakuma: 1

**Courtesy of the FBI:** 153, 173, 275–285

**Getty Images:** 85, 99; Bettmann: 61 right, 115; Curt Borgwardt/Sygma: 137; Ralf-Finn Hestoft/Corbis: 145; *iStock/Getty Images Plus:* asmakar: cover; Marek Trawczynski: ii

# ABOUT THE AUTHOR

**JANE FRITSCH** is a journalist who was a co-finalist for the Pulitzer Prize and a reporter for *The New York Times*, *Los Angeles Times*, *Newsday*, and *Chicago Tribune*, where she covered the trial of the serial killer John Wayne Gacy. She served as a consultant on the Hulu series on West Coast serial murderers, *City of Angels, City of Death*, and is the author of *Serial Killers of the '70s*. She lives in Arizona.